Finally—a coherent statement of current dispensational thi~' leaves the zealous mistakes of Scofield and the All'~ ' far behind. It presents hermeneutics grour than naive literalism, unity as well as divei Davidic as well as new covenants inaugurat based framework for understanding progre: a thoughtful presentation of a truly biblical-t mark for future discussions.

    *Gerry Breshears*, Professor of The   ~.ern Seminary

This excellent work by Blaising and Bock presents a strong case for the significant refinements within progressive dispensationalism. It also provides a splendid sequel to *Dispensationalism, Israel and the Church*, edited by the same authors. I highly recommend it.

    *Kenneth J. Barker*, Executive Director, NIV Translation Center

With their latest work . . . Blaising and Bock have produced a tour de force, a clear and unambiguous statement of the thought of an increasingly large segment of contemporary dispensationalism. Regardless of whether Christians of other traditions (or even fellow dispensationalists) accept their premises and theological conclusions in every respect, there can no longer be any doubt as to what "progressive dispensationalism" means and how two of its leading proponents argue its case.

    *Eugene H. Merrill*, Professor of Old Testament Studies,
    Dallas Theological Studies

Anyone who learned dispensationalism in the 50s or 60s and thinks that it has not changed should read a book like this. Blaising and Bock give a fine overview of what is called progressive dispensationalism. . . .

    *Paul D. Feinberg*, Professor of Biblical and Systematic Theology,
    Trinity Evangelical Divinity School

This is the most scholarly and insightful work yet in print on dispensational theology. Hopefully, those who embrace this system. . . . will themselves be able to change, grow, and progress in their thinking about dispensationalism.

    *James C. McHann*, President, William Tyndale College

Blaising and Bock have thoughtfully and biblically given the Christian community a long overdue work. Their presentation of Christ's rule over God's kingdom in this age and the age to come, plus their skillful unfolding of the connection between covenants make it a must in prophetic reading.

    *James O. Rose, Jr.*, Senior Pastor,
    Calvary Baptist Church (New York City)

A
BRIDGEPOINT
BOOK

BridgePoint,
an imprint of
Baker Books,
is your connection
for the best in
serious reading
that integrates
the passion of
the heart with
the scholarship
of the mind.

# PROGRESSIVE DISPENSATIONALISM

## Craig A. Blaising & Darrell L. Bock

*A BridgePoint Book*

BakerBooks

A Division of Baker Book House Co
Grand Rapids, Michigan 49516

Published by Bridgepoint Books
an imprint of Baker Books
a division of Baker Book House Company
P.O. Box 6287, Grand Rapids, MI 49516-6287

Paperback edition published August 2000

First published by Victor Books, a division of Scripture Press Publications, Inc. Wheaton, Illinois

Printed in the United States of America

**Library of Congress Cataloging-in-Publication Data**

Blaising, Craig A.
    Progressive dispensationalism / Craig A. Blaising & Darrell L. Bock.
—1st pbk. ed.
      p.     cm.
    Originally published: Wheaton, Ill. : BridgePoint, c1993.
    Includes bibliographical references and index.
    ISBN 0-8010-2243-6 (pbk.)
    1. Dispensationalism. I. Bock, Darrell L. II. Title
BT157 .B53   2000
230′.0463—dc21                                 00-033684

For information about academic books, resources for Christian leaders, and all new releases available from Baker Book House, visit our web site:
http://www.bakerbooks.com

# Contents

# Preface
## to the Paperback Edition

Seven years have passed since the initial publication of *Progressive Dispensationalism,* and a new millennium is beginning! The convergence of these two events is purely coincidental, but the coincidence furnishes the occasion to ask what contribution this book makes to advance the church's understanding of the plan of God and what purpose there might be for the book's continued publication. Over the past seven years, reader interest has remained steady. If simply for that reason alone, the authors are grateful that Baker Books has chosen to make it available in a paperback edition.

We have found that many use the work as a textbook, focusing especially on part 3. Of the book's four parts (three parts in the previous printing), part 3, the longest section, offers an exposition of the biblical covenants and the kingdom of God in relation to the Pauline structure of *oikonomia* (dispensation). However, interest in the other essays also remains high. Readers have commented that each part of the book is valuable as much for its unique contribution to an individual subject as to the overall development of the book. Readers interested in hermeneutical method continue to regard part 2 as a readable essay relating the key issues in canonical hermeneutics. Others are interested in part 1 for its helpful definition of dispensationalism and its overview of the movement's history and development. In this printing, chapter 9 has been designated as part 4, Theology and Ministry, in order to call attention to its content, which goes beyond the purpose of the chapters in part 3. When taken together, the different parts of the book still provide a complete survey of the issues and concerns that characterize what has become known as progressive dispensationalism.

Books and articles have been written responding to *Progressive Dispensationalism.* Regrettably, many of these have not helped to advance a true understanding of the continuities and differences between progressive and traditional dispensationalists. A notable exception, however, is the recently published *Three Central Issues in Contemporary Dispensationalism: A Comparison of Traditional and Progressive Views,* edited by Herbert W. Bateman IV. The reader who wishes to pursue the dispensational discussion of issues raised in *Progressive Dispensationalism* would do well to consult that work. In addition, one should note the following articles written by Darrell Bock that further the discussion beyond what has been written here: "The Son of David and the Saints' Task: The Hermeneutics of Initial Fulfillment," *Bibliotheca Sacra* 150 (1993): 440–57; "Current Messianic Activity and Old Testament Promise: Dispensationalism, Hermeneutics, and New Testament Fulfillment," *Trinity Journal* 15 n.s. (1994): 55–87; and "Why I Am a Dispensationalist with a Small 'd,' " *Journal of the Evangelical Theological Society* 41 (1998): 383–96.

Darrell Bock and I wish to express our appreciation to the publishers for making this book available and to you the reader for choosing it. We pray that it will bring honor to the Lord Jesus Christ and serve in some way to advance the knowledge of his word.

Craig A. Blaising

## Chapter One
# The Extent and Varieties of Dispensationalism

**D**ispensationalism may not be a household term, but it designates one of the most widespread and influential traditions in evangelical theology today. If you are an evangelical Christian, it is most likely that you know of some who call themselves dispensationalists. And it is just as likely that you have certain beliefs and interpretations of Scripture that have been shaped in some way by dispensationalism.

This book explains a significant change presently taking place in dispensational interpretations of Scripture. This change affects the way dispensationalists understand key biblical themes such as the kingdom of God, the church in God's redemptive program, the interrelationship of the biblical covenants, the historical and prophetic fulfillment of those covenants, and the role of Christ in that fulfillment.

Changes of this sort are not entirely new to dispensationalism, as we will see. And yet certain beliefs and emphases have remained much the same or have varied only slightly through the history of these changes. Such beliefs constitute the abiding identity of dispensationalism, while the process of rethinking and reinterpretation reveals its vitality.

Where did dispensationalism come from? How widespread is

it? What are its common features, and what changes have taken place? This chapter seeks to answer these questions. The significance of the present form of dispensationalism can best be understood in this light, for it's only as we know where we've come from and how we got here that we have a better appreciation for where we are.

## The Rise and Spread of Dispensationalism

Dispensationalism first took shape in the Brethren Movement in early nineteenth century Britain. The Brethren Movement emphasized the unity of all believers in Christ and the freedom of Christians to gather in His name without regard for sectarian or denominational divisions. They rejected the special role of an ordained clergy, which perpetuated such ecclesiastical divisions, and stressed instead the spiritual giftedness of ordinary believers and their freedom, under the Spirit's guidance, to teach and admonish each other from the Scripture.

By enhancing the integrity and responsibility of the laity, Brethrenism witnessed a surge of interest in Bible study and private devotions. The movement generated a large volume of expositional and devotional literature, some authors of which became well known, including John Nelson Darby, Benjamin Wills Newton, George Müller, Samuel P. Tregelles, William Kelly, William Trotter, and Charles Henry Mackintosh.

The writings of the Brethren had a broad impact on evangelical Protestantism. This is especially true in the United States, where they influenced prominent ministers such as D.L. Moody, James Inglis, James Hall Brookes, A.J. Gordon, J.R. Graves, and C.I. Scofield. While not following the Brethren in a radical rejection of clergy and denominational ministry, they founded a new forum *alongside* established ministries which promoted the Brethren experience of freely gathering in Christ to worship and study the Scripture: the Bible Conference. Beginning with the popular Niagara Bible Conference in the 1870s, Bible conferences began to spring up in various parts of the country, becoming what has been called the Bible Conference Movement by the early twentieth century.

C.I. Scofield, a participant in this movement, formed a board of Bible conference teachers and in 1909 produced through Oxford Press a reference Bible (second edition in 1917) which became famous throughout the United States and around the world. The *Scofield Reference Bible* was filled with expositional and theological annotations which put a "Bible Conference" into the hands of thousands of evangelical Christians. The interpretations presented in the notes formed a recognizable system of biblical interpretation. That system was soon tagged "dispensationalism," a label which has come to mark the tradition which both led to and developed from the *Scofield Reference Bible.*

The term *dispensationalism* comes from the word *dispensation* which refers to a distinctive way in which God manages or arranges the relationship of human beings to Himself. Recognizing different dispensations in Scripture, such as the dispensation of Israel with its distinctive regulations and ceremonies and the dispensation of the church today, has been quite common in the history of biblical interpretation. Distinguishing between these different dispensations can be helpful in understanding the complexity and diversity of the Bible. *Dispensationalists,* however, had some distinctive views about these dispensations which differed from most other interpreters of Scripture. Because of this, they were especially tagged with the label *dispensationalism* whereas others who referred to different dispensations in Scripture were not. We will refer to some of these distinctives in the next sections of this chapter.

Through the Bible conferences and the *Scofield Reference Bible,* dispensationalism came to characterize the views and beliefs of a large constituency of American evangelicalism scattered throughout mainstream Protestantism. But it was especially concentrated in Presbyterian, Baptist, and Congregationalist circles. When the struggle between fundamentalism and modernism broke into the open, dispensationalists were found on the fundamentalist side, their ecumenical emphases contributing to the cohesion of the fundamentalist movement.

As fundamentalists proceeded to establish new churches and new denominations in reaction to the modernist control of traditional churches, dispensationalism came to characterize some of these resulting groups almost completely. These include, for example, The General Association of Regular Baptist Churches, The Conservative Baptist Association, The Fellowship of Grace Brethren Churches, and the Independent Fundamentalist Churches of America.

Some of the schools associated with these churches have become well known for teaching dispensationalism. They include Grace College and Grace Theological Seminary, Northwestern College, Grand Rapids Baptist Seminary, Western Conservative Baptist Seminary (now Western Seminary). Dispensationalism has also been taught (though not exclusively) at Denver Seminary (formerly Denver Conservative Baptist Seminary). Over the years, some of these schools have become more self-consciously "evangelical" than fundamentalist, and the dispensationalism which they teach has undergone changes as well.

Dispensationalism has also been well represented in other denominations such as the Evangelical Free Church of America, and dispensational theologians have taught at Trinity College and Trinity Evangelical Divinity School. The Christian and Missionary Alliance, of the holiness tradition, has advocated dispensational views. And dispensationalism has also impacted Pentecostal and charismatic churches as well.

A number of Bible schools, institutes, colleges, and seminaries have taught dispensationalism. Moody Bible Institute, founded through the revivalist ministry of D.L. Moody is a well known example. The Bible Institute of Los Angeles, founded on the model of Moody, is now Biola University and includes the Talbot School of Theology. Philadelphia College of Bible and Dallas Theological Seminary were direct products of the Bible Conference Movement. Graduates of Dallas Seminary have staffed many of the aforementioned dispensational schools and founded others, including, for example, Multnomah Bible College/Biblical Seminary and William Tyndale College (formerly Detroit Bible College).

Not only do graduates of these schools minister in the associations and denominations we have noted (including some mainline churches), but they have established and pastored a number of independent Bible churches so that the Bible Church Movement mostly reflects a dispensational exposition of Scripture.

In this century, the broadcast media has helped to highlight the ministries of prominent pastors, some of whom teach dispensational views. These would include, to name only a few, the late Donald Grey Barnhouse (Presbyterian), W.A. Criswell, Adrian Rogers, and Charles Stanley (Southern Baptist), and Chuck Swindoll (Evangelical Free Church). Popular radio ministries featuring a dispensational view of Scripture have included the late Charles Fuller and the "Old Fashioned Gospel Hour" (which led to the founding of Fuller Theological Seminary— though broadly evangelical today, Fuller's early faculty included the well-known dispensationalists Wilber Smith and Everett Harrison), the late M.R. DeHaan and Richard DeHaan on the "Radio Bible Class," the late Theodore Epp and Warren Wiersbe on the "Back to the Bible," the late J. Vernon McGee's "Through the Bible," Jerry Falwell's "Old Time Gospel Hour," and Chuck Swindoll's "Insight for Living."

Dispensationalists have participated in and encouraged the founding of faith missions (such as Central American Mission, founded by C.I. Scofield) and parachurch ministries (such as Young Life, founded by Jim Rayburn). Dispensationalists have ministered with Campus Crusade for Christ, the Navigators, Youth For Christ, and InterVarsity Christian Fellowship. Dispensational themes appear in some of the teaching materials of these ministries. In addition, some of the most famous evangelists including Billy Graham have affirmed and taught dispensational views.[1]

In summary, clergy and laity alike who share dispensational views of Scripture can be found in most Protestant denominations, mission agencies, and parachurch ministries to varying degrees. From its introduction in the Bible conferences to the present day, dispensationalism has expanded to become one of the most common expressions of evangelical Christianity.

Dispensationalism is not a monolithic movement; diversity exists today on a number of matters of interpretation. However, there are some broad features which unite these diverse elements into a common tradition. Together, these features provide a descriptive definition of dispensationalism.

## Common Features of the Dispensational Tradition

*Authority of Scripture*. From the early Brethren Movement, through the American Bible conferences, the *Scofield Bible,* Bible institutes, colleges and seminaries, to popular expositional ministries in churches and parachurch movements, dispensationalism has been known as a Bible exposition movement. It has produced a number of popular expositors of Scripture who not only helped spread dispensationalism but have impacted large portions of evangelicalism.

Dispensationalists have upheld the belief that the Bible is the sole inerrant verbal revelation of God available to the church today and that it provides a sure foundation for Christian life and faith. They believe that dispensational ideas and interpretations help people understand the Bible and help make the Scripture more intelligible to them, allowing them to more knowledgeably appropriate it in their everyday lives. Furthermore, the dispensational system of relating the various parts of Scripture together has helped to give people a sense of having an answer to attacks upon Scripture's integrity by theological liberalism.

The Bible Conference Movement was an attempt to make the Bible a sure basis for evangelical ecumenicity—an ecumenicity that was not seen as structural, administrative, or denominational, but an ecumenicity of faith, hope, and love. Interdenominational schools and ministries have attempted to carry on that vision to varying degrees, a vision which has helped contribute to the sense of evangelical identity in some quarters of evangelicalism.

Dispensationalists, of course, were not the only evangelicals to emphasize the authority of the Bible. But their transdenominational vision and their practical orientation to expositional ministry made an emphasis on Scripture a hallmark of the movement, one that continues today as well.

***Dispensations***. The word *dispensation* refers to a particular arrangement by which God regulates the way human beings relate to Him.[2] Dispensationalism believes that God has planned a succession of different dispensations throughout history, both past, present, and future. Furthermore, dispensationalists believe that these dispensations are revealed in Scripture, in both biblical history and prophecy. Understanding these dispensations, these different relationships God has had and will have with humanity, is crucial for comprehending the teaching and message of the Bible.

Of course, a primary concern for us today is our own relationship with God. As a result, a dispensational exposition of Scripture will focus especially on the present dispensation and the Scripture dealing explicitly with it. We then seek to interpret other portions of Scripture in light of the dispensations to

14

which they belong or of which they speak. We have a better understanding of how those Scripture texts relate to us when we know how their dispensation relates to or differs from our own. Consequently, understanding the dispensations is crucial to understanding how the whole of Scripture relates to Christian faith and practice.[3]

For example, suppose we speak of the old dispensation which covered Israel's relationship to God under the Mosaic covenant. Then we speak of the present dispensation which refers to the church, the body of Christ, first constituted as such by Christ Himself on the Day of Pentecost just after His ascension to heaven. We then speak of the future dispensation as the arrangement of God's relationship to humankind after Christ's return to earth. Practically all of the Old Testament was written under — and most of it refers to — the old dispensation, as we have just defined it. Much of the New Testament refers to the present dispensation. But we find prophecies in the Old Testament and in the New Testament that speak of the future dispensation.

| PAST DISPENSATION(S) | PRESENT DISPENSATION | FUTURE DISPENSATION |
|---|---|---|
| | | |

Also, when a Christian today reads the Old Testament, it helps to know that he or she is reading literature which speaks directly about Israel and her relationship to God under the old dispensation. God commanded certain forms of worship. He specifically instructed Israel on national policy as it related to events in the first and second millennia B.C.

God, of course, is the everlasting God. We are dealing today with the same God. So, there are a lot of lessons to learn from the way God related to people in the old dispensation. The New Testament guides us here. It also reveals the fact that God's relationship to the church differs in some significant ways from the dispensation with Israel. In the present dispensation, God is blessing Jews and Gentiles equally with certain

15

blessings of the Holy Spirit to a degree which he had only promised in the old dispensation. This includes, for example, the permanent indwelling of the Holy Spirit. There are also new forms of worship (as Jesus revealed to the Samaritan woman in John 4:21, 23). Consequently, although there are similarities, there are also important differences between the church and Old Testament Israel. Understanding the different dispensations helps a reader of Scripture know how to relate to what he or she reads in the Old Testament.

The dispensations are structured by various covenants God has made or promised. Since the Bible has much to say about these covenants, a dispensational understanding of Scripture will place special emphasis upon them. In this book, we will examine both dispensations and covenants in chapters 4–6.

***Uniqueness of the Church.*** Traditionally, dispensationalism has always viewed the church as a distinctively *new* dispensation in biblical history. The church finds its historical origin in the "Christ event"—that is the death, resurrection, and ascension of Jesus Christ—and particularly in the "baptism of the Spirit" which Christ has bestowed equally upon believing Jews and Gentiles since that feast Day of Pentecost following His ascension.

What makes the church a new dispensation are these *blessings of the Holy Spirit* which are qualitatively different from the blessings of the Holy Spirit in the Old Testament. Also, contributing to the uniqueness of the church is the fact that these blessings are given *equally* to Jews and Gentiles. Furthermore, in this dispensation, God has not been granting certain political and material blessings to the degree that He promised by covenant to Israel (with implications for nations). Biblical prophecy predicts these blessings for a future dispensation to be established when Christ returns to earth.

Understanding the uniqueness of the church helps Christians interpret both Old and New Testaments intelligibly. Knowing, for example, that believers in Christ have been sealed with the Holy Spirit assures them of His permanent indwelling and helps them not to be alarmed by David's prayer (Ps. 51:11) that the Holy Spirit not be taken from him. They can understand David's prayer historically in the context of the dispensation in which David related to God.

At the same time, Scripture speaks of the Holy Spirit's bless-

16

ing in this dispensation as a deposit, a down payment, *toward* our full redemption in the future (Eph. 1:13-14). This qualitative progression from David's experience of the Holy Spirit to that of our own and then to that of the future dispensation shows how the dispensations do not simply follow or replace one another but actually progress forward to a future eschatological goal.

***Practical Significance of the Universal Church.*** Dispensationalists have always supported the belief that the reality of the church is to be found in Christ, and that reality transcends the denominational divisions which separate Christians from one another.

The Brethren Movement began as open assemblies of Christians having communion with one another in Christ's name alone, without reference to denominational authorities or memberships. However, a part of the movement, known as Exclusive Brethren, soon viewed their local assemblies as true Christianity *over against* other churches and denominations. This exclusivity extended even to the point of excommunicating other Brethren assemblies over trifling issues. As a result, the early ecumenicity of the movement was greatly diminished or lost entirely for some.

What was lost in Brethrenism was pursued anew in the American Bible Conference Movement. But it required a different vision of the church. While the Brethren had focused their attention on the local church, the leaders of the Bible conferences sought to draw out the practical significance of the universal church, that one body of Christ which transcended local churches and denominations. The Bible conference was a visible, tangible Christian communion based solely on the reality of the universal church. It could not and did not try to replace local church communion and ministry.

American dispensationalism has been a strong force seeking and encouraging other such ministries which bring out the practical significance of the universal church and thus give tangible expression to the true Christian unity which transcends denominational and local church ministries. These include many faith missions and parachurch evangelistic and discipling ministries. Also included are interdenominational Bible institutes, colleges, and seminaries which carry on the Bible conference ideal in lay and ministerial training.

The true spirit of American dispensationalism would view these ministries as neither in competition with nor as a part of local church ministry but as complementary to local church ministry. Admittedly, practice sometimes falls short of the ideal, but the ideal remains a goal, the vision of which needs to be renewed.

Early fundamentalism also affirmed an ecumenical evangelical identity, although it affirmed that identity in conscious opposition to modernism. However, eventually fundamentalism turned in upon itself, practicing degrees of separation, fracturing and splintering the earlier unity. Dispensationalism suffered some of the same effects; some dispensationalists lost sight of the practical value of an intra-evangelical biblical dialogue. Like some other evangelicals, they resorted to isolation and separation, betraying an earlier confidence in the Spirit of Christ guiding the body of Christ in the knowledge of the Scripture.

In recent years, however, there have been positive signs within evangelicalism of mutual appreciation and affirmation contributing to the healing of some old wounds and divisions stemming from the fundamentalist and post-fundamentalist eras. There are signs that dispensationalists today are also beginning to reaffirm the positive value of mutual evangelical biblical dialogue.

***Significance of Biblical Prophecy.*** Dispensationalism finds the historical meaning of biblical prophecy relevant for understanding God's purpose for the earth and for its human inhabitants. There are other theological traditions which interpret Bible prophecy almost exclusively in relation to the present ministry of Christ in the church or to a believer's personal experience of salvation. Dispensationalism, however, interpreting these prophecies in a more "literal" manner, has always expected God's future blessings to include earthly, national, and political aspects of life. Many of these blessings belong to a future dispensation which will be marked by the return of Christ to earth.

As a result, the dispensational tradition has offered a broader concept of redemption than found in some other theologies. Redemption extends to political and national levels as well as to spiritual renewal. However, at the same time, early dispensationalism also embraced a strong dualism which *disassociated* these broader prophetic features of redemption *from* the blessings of *the church*. Consequently, the broader aspects of redemption were effectively irrelevant to the church. As a result, for some dispensationalists, much of Bible prophecy has tended to be more of a curiosity feature than a vital aspect of Christian hope. This kind of dispensationalism has offered little restraint to (and even contributed to) the sensational tendencies of popular apocalypticism.

There has been a gradual revision of early dispensationalism's dualism, as we will see in the next section. There has also been reaction to the excesses of apocalyptic sensationalism. This does not mean that prophecy possesses less significance. Rather, it has become much more relevant for the actual faith and hope of the church.

***Futurist Premillennialism.*** Dispensationalism is a form of premillennialism. That is, it holds to the belief that Christ will return to this earth and rule over it for 1,000 years. Like most premillennialists, dispensationalists interpret biblical prophecy to teach that Christ will return during a time of trouble traditionally called "the Tribulation." However, unlike most premillennialists, most dispensationalists have advocated the doctrine of the pretribulational Rapture—the doctrine that Christ will come *for the church* prior to the Tribulation, resurrecting the dead in Christ, translating living believers into immortal life, and then taking the church with Him to heaven prior to His millennial return in which He will visibly rule the nations on earth.

Because they have believed that the church will not be on earth during the Tribulation, dispensationalists have traditionally rejected attempts to identify present events as the fulfillments of Tribulation prophecies. As a result, dispensationalism should be classified as a form of "futurist" premillennialism. They believe that Tribulation events will be fulfilled at some time in the future (that is, after the Rapture) as opposed to the "historicist" view which believes that such events are being fulfilled today.

At the same time, however, some dispensationalists have been drawn into and have actually carried forward historicist interpretations of popular religious apocalypticism. Events in

the post-war world seemed to follow some dispensational interpretations of political and military movements envisioned in
Daniel and Revelation. As a result, in the latter twentieth century, the lines between futurism and historicism have weakened.
The writings of Hal Lindsay (*Late Great Planet Earth* [1970],
*There's a New World Coming* [1973], and *The 1980's: Count-
down to Armageddon* [1980]) are typical of dispensational
forms of historicism. But even more respected theologians have
ventured in this direction, such as John Walvoord (*Armageddon, Oil and the Middle East Crisis*; [1974, rev. ed. 1990]) and
Charles Ryrie (*The Living End*, [1976]).

One of the results of *futurist* premillennialism is the eschew-
ing of setting dates for the second coming of Christ. A major
factor in the spread of dispensationalism in the United States in
the late nineteenth century was the fact that it offered a premillennialism which avoided the date-setting hermeneutic of the
Millerite Adventist movement. William Miller distinguished himself by claiming to have discerned the date of Christ's return.
When Christ failed to appear by Miller's calculations, premillennialism generally suffered disgrace. Dispensationalism saved
face by rejecting the Millerite hermeneutic. However, the blur-
ring of lines between historicism and futurism within some
quarters of late twentieth century dispensationalism has led
some perilously close to the same mistake.[4]

***The Imminent Return of Christ.*** In the Bible and prophecy
conferences of the late nineteenth century, the imminent return of Christ meant belief in premillennialism. Postmillennial-
ism taught that Christ's return was at least 1,000 years away,
after the church had finished the task of Christianizing the
world. Premillennialists believed that Christ would return before the millennium, they believed that He would return in a
time of trouble, and that the present time evidenced sufficient
trouble for Him to return at any time.

Historicist and dispensational premillennialism both also
took great interest in the apocalyptic descriptions of a Tribulation prior to Christ's descent to earth. Dispensationalists interpreted apocalyptic chronologies in Daniel and Revelation to
mean that Christ will return to the earth to rule the nations
after a Tribulation of seven years.[5]

Since dispensationalists were futurists, believing that the

Tribulation lay completely in the future, they consequently believed that the Lord's descent to the earth was at least seven years away. But dispensationalists also believed that Christ would come for the church before the Tribulation. That coming could take place literally at any moment. Consequently, when dispensationalists spoke of imminency, they spoke primarily of the pretribulational Rapture. By the insistence of Arno Gaebelein, C.I. Scofield, and others at the turn of the century, imminency came to be defined exclusively by the doctrine of the pretribulational Rapture.

Most dispensationalists to the present day have held to a pretribulational Rapture. In his 1976 book, *The Blessed Hope and the Tribulation,* John Walvoord recognized the existence of dispensational posttribulationalism. Although not a doctrine of imminency by later standards, it nevertheless held to the *nearness* of Christ's coming, and was recognized as a variant within the dispensational tradition.

*A National Future for Israel.* One of the most well-known features of the dispensational tradition is the belief in a future for national Israel. That future includes at least the millennial reign of Christ and for some dispensationalists, extends into the eternal state as well. Because of this strong belief, some early dispensationalists, such as W.E. Blackstone, played a key role in garnering support for the Zionist movement. That has carried forward to present times in the pro-Israeli political activities of Jerry Falwell and Pat Robertson.

While not all dispensationalists have strongly supported the modern Zionist movement, still they have traditionally held that prophecies regarding the political, national restoration, and blessing of Israel will be fulfilled in the next dispensation. And while other theologies have also come to the point of according the future of Israel serious consideration, it has often been due to the insistence of dispensationalists who have always made national Israel a prominent feature of their biblical interpretation.

## Forms of Dispensationalism

The preceding eight features constitute the abiding concerns and emphases that characterize the dispensational tradition. However, dispensationalism has not been a static tradition.

There has been no standard creed freezing its theological development at some arbitrary point in history.[6] As dispensationalism has developed, the characteristics noted above have been reconfirmed through the dynamics of renewed biblical interpretation. The evidence of this continuity testifies to the strength of the dispensational tradition.

However, the same dynamics of continued biblical study have modified the ways in which some of the above features have been understood. While it is not easy to classify all the differences between various dispensational theologians, three broad forms of dispensational thought can be identified. These need to be understood in order to grasp the history of the tradition.[7]

We will use the designation *classical dispensationalism* to refer generally to the views of British and American dispensationalists from the writings of John Nelson Darby, the foremost theologian of the early Brethren Movement, to the eight volume *Systematic Theology* of Lewis Sperry Chafer, the founder and first president of Dallas Theological Seminary. The interpretive notes of the *Scofield Reference Bible* might be considered a key representative of classical dispensationalism, although there are various points at which different dispensationalists of that period would differ with it. The designation *dispensationalism* was first applied to the interpretations offered in the *Scofield Reference Bible*. And it has functioned as a reference point for the future development of the tradition.

*Revised dispensationalism* designates the views of dispensational theologians writing primarily between the late 1950s and the late 1970s, although it also applies to some publications in the 1990s as well. The designation *revised* is taken from the *revision* of the *Scofield Bible,* completed in 1967 and offering views much more compatible to writers of this second period. Some of the more well-known *revised dispensationalists* include Alva J. McClain, John Walvoord, Charles Ryrie, J. Dwight Pentecost, and Stanley Toussaint.

*Progressive dispensationalism,* the subject of this book, is a more contemporary form of dispensational thought which has developed through continued biblical study of the concerns and emphases of the dispensational tradition. Progressive dispensationalism offers a number of modifications to classical and revised dispensationalism which brings dispensationalism closer to contemporary evangelical biblical interpretation. Although the name is relatively recent, the particular interpretations that make up this form of dispensationalism have been developing over the past fifteen years. Sufficient revisions had taken place by 1991 to introduce the name *progressive dispensationalism* at the national meeting of the Evangelical Theological Society that year. This present book along with the publications: *Dispensationalism, Israel and the Church: The Search for Definition* and *The Case for Progressive Dispensationalism* are key representatives of this viewpoint.[8]

As we evaluate the different forms of dispensationalism, we will see that some of the issues distinguishing them from one another are of a technical nature. These issues can only be mentioned briefly here. But the reader will find a more extended discussion of biblical interpretation, the different dispensations, the biblical covenants, and the kingdom of God in the following chapters. The following pages should be read in conjunction with those chapters.

## Classical Dispensationalism

***The Central Dualism.*** Perhaps the most important feature of classical dispensationalism is its dualistic idea of redemption. In order to understand the Bible, one needed to recognize that God was pursuing *two different purposes,* one related to *heaven* and one related to the *earth.* These two purposes affected God's dealings with humanity. In fact, they resulted in an anthropological dualism: a heavenly humanity and an earthly humanity.

To put it another way, one of God's purposes in redemption was to release the earth from the curse of corruption and decay, and to restore upon it a humanity free from death and sin. This was the earthly purpose of God. God will restore permanently the paradise lost in the Fall, granting immortality to earthly humanity. Some writers envisioned these blessings in quite physical terms, including human reproduction to increase the plenitude of the human race.

It is important to understand that in classical dispensationalism this earthly humanity is eternal. It first appears in the Millennium (the future 1,000-year reign of Christ), but it will not have reached its eternal glory until the end of that time. It will then continue onto the new earth populating it forever.

But God has a second purpose, a heavenly purpose which envisions a heavenly humanity. This heavenly humanity was to be made up of all the redeemed from all dispensations who would be resurrected from the dead. Whereas the earthly humanity concerned people who had not died but who were preserved by God from death, the heavenly humanity was made up of all the saved who had died, whom God would resurrect from the dead.

By the nature of the case, the heavenly humanity would be a "transdispensational" community. All the saved of previous dispensations are dead, and all those of the present dispensation prior to this generation are likewise dead. They are, of course, with the Lord now. But their future hope lies in the resurrection, by which they will fully receive their heavenly salvation in a heavenly inheritance.

The earthly humanity will begin with that generation of the saved who are present on earth at the Lord's return. They will be preserved from death, as will all their descendants who are of faith. They will not be resurrected from the dead, for they would never have been dead nor will they be transformed into a resurrection mode of life. They are *earthly* people and they experience the earthly salvation which God has designed according to His purpose for the earth.

In summary, the central dualism of classical dispensationalism asserts that God is pursuing two purposes in redemption, one relating to heaven and a heavenly people and one relating to the earth concerning an earthly people. Both purposes will be accomplished and confirmed forever.

***The Dispensations.*** Classical dispensationalism saw the dispensations as different arrangements under which human beings are tested. God arranged the relationship of humankind to Himself to test their obedience to Him. In the earlier dispensations, God gave promises regarding earthly life, but humans repeatedly sinned and failed to obtain the promises in any *lasting* sense. The present dispensation of the church is the first dispensation which clearly presents God's *heavenly* purpose. When Christ is revealed at the end of this dispensation, He will confirm the two purposes, first in a millennium, which tests humanity one last time before the judgment, and then in eternity.

24

One of the differences between the church in this dispensation and the people of God in past dispensations is that the church is supposed to know that it is a heavenly people destined for an eternal inheritance in heaven. People of past dispensations sought to obtain the earthly promises. They died however, without obtaining them. They either did not know of a heavenly destiny or were dimly aware of it. Although they failed to attain the earthly promises, God in His grace will include those who trusted in Him (that is, the elect) in the heavenly salvation.

But the church is supposed to know that she has a heavenly future and is called to a heavenly way of life. The failure of this dispensation comes when the church thinks that it has an earthly purpose, when it begins to think of itself as an earthly people and becomes preoccupied with earthly things. Such preoccupation has brought about what is called "Christendom" — that political cultural phenomena of the Western "Christian" nations. Classical dispensationalism viewed Christendom as a perversion of sinful humanity which tries to substi-

### THE DISPENSATIONS AND THE PURPOSES OF GOD IN CLASSICAL DISPENSATIONALISM

| PAST DISPENSATIONS | PRESENT DISPENSATION | FUTURE DISPENSATION | ETERNITY |
|---|---|---|---|
| | HEAVENLY PURPOSE HEAVENLY PEOPLE (Church) | HEAVENLY PURPOSE/PEOPLE FULFILLED IN HEAVEN FOREVER (Resurrected Church/O.T. Saints)[1] | |
| EARTHLY PURPOSE EARTHLY PEOPLE (Israel/Gentiles) | | EARTHLY PURPOSE EARTHLY PEOPLE RESUMED (Israel/Gentiles) | EARTHLY PURPOSE /PEOPLE FULFILLED ON THE NEW EARTH FOREVER[2] (Israel/Gentiles) |

1. The earthly people of past dispensations failed to realize God's earthly purpose. Instead, the saved will be included in God's heavenly purpose when that purpose is fulfilled.
2. Many classical dispensationalists (such as Scofield) did not regard the eternal state as a dispensation.

tute itself for the real church of God. Christendom, the human failure of this dispensation, will be judged at the return of Christ.[9]

With this central dualism in mind, we could visualize the dispensations of classical dispensationalism in the manner illustrated on page 25.[10]

***The Nature of the Church.*** The heavenly nature of the church's salvation was interpreted by classical dispensationalists in an individualistic manner. Political and social issues were *earthly* matters which did not concern the church. The church was a spiritual unity found in Christ. This unity manifested itself not only in the oneness of Christ but in the oneness of personal salvation—the individual nature of salvation. Issues in the church were individual, private, spiritual matters, not social, political, earthly matters.[11]

We could illustrate this in the following manner.

## THE CHURCH AS A PARENTHESIS
## IN CLASSICAL DISPENSATIONALISM

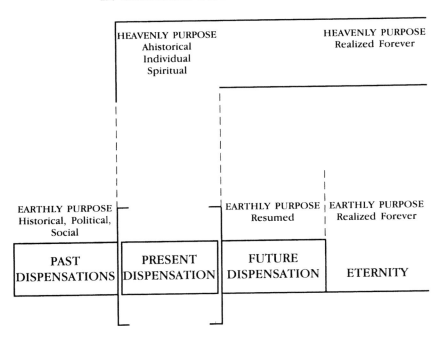

The heavenly, individualistic, and spiritual nature of the church could not be more distinct from the earthly, social, and political nature of Israel and the Gentile nations. The difference helped underscore the well-known classical dispensational belief that the church is a *parenthesis* in the history of redemption, the history of *earthly* redemption, that is. The church is not related to that earthly purpose and so is like a parenthesis inserted into history. Lewis Sperry Chafer felt that parenthesis did not go far enough, so he called the church an *intercalation.*

In fact, the new, hitherto unrevealed purpose of God in the out calling of a heavenly people from Jews and Gentiles is so divergent with respect to the divine purpose toward Israel, which purpose preceded it and will yet follow it, that the term parenthetical, commonly employed to describe the new age-purpose, is inaccurate. A parenthetical portion sustains some direct or indirect relation to that which goes before or that which follows; but the present age-purpose is not thus related and therefore is more properly termed an *intercalation.* The appropriateness of this word will be seen in the fact that, as an interpolation is formed by inserting a word or phrase into a context, so an intercalation is formed by introducing a day or a period of time into the calendar. The present age of the Church is an intercalation into the revealed calendar or program of God as that program was foreseen by the prophets of old. Such, indeed, is the precise character of the present age.[12]

**Biblical Interpretation.** Classical dispensationalists interpreted the Bible in accordance with their central dualism. They believed that if the Old Testament were interpreted literally, then it would reveal God's earthly purpose for the earthly people. However, if it were interpreted spiritually (which they usually termed "typologically"), then it would reveal God's spiritual purpose for a spiritual people. The spiritual purpose and spiritual people were found literally revealed in the New Testament.

As for the meaning of "literal" interpretation, classical dispensationalists sometimes spoke of grammatical and historical interpretation. Some classical dispensationalists were especially skilled in grammar and offered helpful commentaries on the grammatical sense of Scripture. By historical interpretation, they meant the historical references in a text (i.e., to rulers, geographical areas, chronology, etc.) or the text's dispensational setting.

In the American Bible conferences, classical dispensationalists promoted what was called "Bible Readings," which was a practice of stringing texts together dealing with a common word, phrase, or theme. These texts were then read one after the other, sometimes without much regard for context. Implications were then drawn from the exercise.

***The Biblical Covenants.*** Classical dispensationalists saw God's covenant with Abraham (in Gen. 12 and following) as the foundational covenant in Scripture. One of the promises God made to Abraham was, "I will make your descendants as the dust of the earth" (Gen. 13:16). Classical dispensationalists believed that this promise revealed God's earthly purpose for earthly peoples. It first of all promised physical descendants to Abraham who would become a great nation in a territory which God specified. They would be blessed above all peoples and would mediate God's blessing and curse to the Gentile peoples on earth.

This covenant could also be interpreted spiritually, however, to reveal the heavenly purpose and heavenly people of God. God promised Abraham, "I will greatly multiply your seed as the stars of the heavens" (Gen. 22:17). Interpreting this promise spiritually would lead to the spiritual descendants of Abraham, the heavenly people. It was believed that the New Testament follows this spiritual interpretation when it interprets the church as descendants of Abraham.

The Mosaic, Palestinian, and Davidic covenants[13] were all interpreted as earthly covenants. They dealt with God's earthly purpose, not with the heavenly/spiritual purpose.

The new covenant (a covenant prophesied in Isaiah, Jeremiah, and Ezekiel) was interpreted primarily or solely as an earthly covenant, even though it promised that God would put His Spirit in His people. Darby believed that when it appeared in the Bible, the new covenant always referred to Israel and consequently had nothing to do with God's heavenly people. Chafer followed Darby as closely as possible, but had to recognize that the New Testament did speak of a "new covenant" which was in force for the church in this dispensation. He argued that this was a completely different "new covenant" than that which will be made with Israel. (In the same manner, he argued that the spiritual blessings which would be given to Israel under the new covenant of Jeremiah and Ezekiel, would be distinctly different from those given to the church today.) Scofield, on the other hand, interpreted the New Covenant in the same manner as he did the Abrahamic covenant: literally it had to do with God's earthly plan for Israel; spiritually it revealed God's spiritual plan for the church (the blessing of the Spirit for Israel in Ezekiel 36 *typified* the church's blessing of the Spirit). So, even though there was general agreement about the covenants in classical dispensationalism, there were always differences in how the details worked together to support the overall position.

Classical dispensationalists believed that the biblical cove-

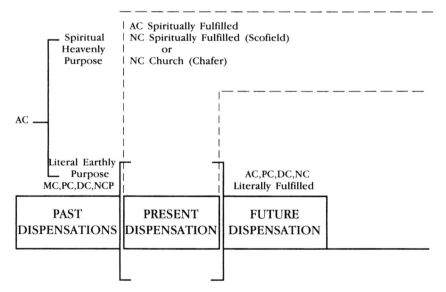

**CLASSICAL DISPENSATIONALISM AND THE BIBLICAL COVENANTS IN LITERAL AND SPIRITUAL FULFILLMENT**

KEY:

| | | |
|---|---|---|
| AC | Abrahamic Covenant |
| MC | Mosaic Covenant |
| PC | Palestinian Covenant |
| DC | Davidic Covenant |
| NC | New Covenant |
| NCP | New Covenant Predicted |

29

nants would be fulfilled for earthly people in the Millennium and eternal state. Since the covenants did not concern heavenly people (except in a typological or spiritual sense) it was not proper to say that they were being fulfilled in the present dispensation (except in a spiritual or typological manner).

***The Kingdom of God and the Kingdom of Heaven.*** The kingdom of God is one of the most important themes in the Bible and an important concern for dispensational interpretation. The most well known classical dispensational view of the kingdom is that of C.I. Scofield. His view depends on a substantive distinction between the terms *kingdom of God* and *kingdom of heaven.* He believed that the term *kingdom of God,* found in all four Gospels, referred to the moral rule of God in the hearts of those subject to Him. It is everlasting in extent. The *kingdom of heaven,* found in the New Testament only in Matthew, was thought to be the fulfillment of the covenant made to David, in which God promised to establish the kingdom of His Son. The kingdom of heaven begins to appear with Jesus Christ, a descendant of David, culminates in the Millennium, and merges with the kingdom of God in the eternal state. (Prior to the kingdom of heaven, we find the Davidic kingdom which had been interrupted by the times of the Gentiles—the kingdom of heaven is the eschatological [that is, "last days"] fulfillment of the Davidic kingdom.)

Scofield taught that the kingdom of heaven had three forms. The first was in the preaching of Jesus. The kingdom of heaven was present, or "at hand" in Jesus' preaching. He offered the kingdom to Israel. But Israel rejected it, so it was postponed to a future time.

The kingdom of heaven is now present in *mystery form.* That mystery form is Christendom, the earthly, political, liturgical reality which names Christ as its king. Two things should be noted here: for Scofield, the mystery form of the kingdom is not the church, it is Christendom. Also when Scofield speaks of the mystery form of the kingdom, he means a mystery form *of the kingdom,* that is of the kingdom of heaven, the kingdom of the Davidic covenant.[14] Accordingly, the Davidic covenant finds a form of fulfillment today. But, it is not the church. On the other hand, the presence of the church gives Christendom whatever legitimacy it has. Consequently, the church has *some connection to* the present reality of the kingdom of heaven.

The kingdom of heaven will be fulfilled in the Millennium. One recalls that for Scofield, like other classical dispensationalists, the Davidic covenant is merely a political covenant. It will be fulfilled according to its earthly purpose for the earthly people of the Millennium, that is, Israel. Of course, as the promises are eternal, the fulfillment continues forever, but the glorifying and preserving grace of God will eliminate the possibility of sin and rebellion in eternity. Since God will rule morally in every heart in the eternal kingdom (the unsaved having been consigned to hell), the kingdom of heaven is said to merge with the kingdom of God.

### THE KINGDOM IN
### CLASSICAL DISPENSATIONALISM (Scofield)

| | | | | |
|---|---|---|---|---|
| THE KINGDOM OF GOD (In Heaven) | | | | KINGDOM OF GOD IN HEAVEN |
| Davidic Kingdom | THE KINGDOM OF HEAVEN (On Earth) | | | KINGDOM OF GOD ON THE NEW EARTH |
| | 1. "At Hand" | 2. Mystery Form (Christendom) | 3. Prophetic (Millennial) | |
| PAST DISPENSATIONS | Jesus Christ | PRESENT DISPENSATION | FUTURE DISPENSATION | |

### Revised Dispensationalism

***Revision of the Central Dualism.*** The most important revision introduced by the dispensationalists of the '50s and '60s was their abandonment of the *eternal* dualism of heavenly and earthly peoples. They did not believe that there would be an eternal distinction between one humanity in heaven and another on the new earth. Consequently, they mostly dropped the terms *heavenly* and *earthly* peoples. Instead, they reworked the dualism in more of an organizational sense (closer to the meaning of the term dispensation). There were simply two groups of people. Not heavenly versus earthly, but those repre-sented by Israel and the church. These two groups contain different people (a person could only be in one group or the other, not in both at the same time). They are structured differ-ently, with different dispensational prerogatives and responsi-bilities. But the salvation which they receive — the eternal life — is the same for both, with the one exception that some belong to one group and others belong to another. There will be an eternal distinction between Israel and the church, not in meta-physically distinctive kinds of salvation, but in name — the church is always church, Israel is always Israel.[15]

***The Eternal State.*** In the eternal state, all will be resurrected from the dead or transformed into a resurrection mode of life. There will be *no difference in the kind of eternal life* experi-enced by saved humanity, whether they be Israel or the church. Revised dispensationalists differed among themselves, however, on the nature and sphere of that eternal life. Whereas classical dispensationalists placed the heavenly people in heaven and the earthly people on the new earth, revised dispensationalists either placed all the redeemed in "heaven" or they placed them all on the new earth.

As a result there are two different conceptions of eternity in revised dispensationalism. McClain, Pentecost, and Hoyt envi-sion eternity as resurrection life on the new earth where the city of God is located. For them the promises of an everlasting kingdom on earth are literally fulfilled on the renewed earth.

Walvoord and Ryrie, although using the terminology of "new earth," actually work with a more platonic conception of "heaven" which bears closer relationship to the "heaven" of classical dispensationalists. They claim that promises about an earthly kingdom forever do not really mean *forever.* Or, they say that they only apply to time and history such that when time and history have come to an end and give way to a time-less eternity, then the *everlasting* promises, which only apply to time and history, will be considered as having been fulfilled. The key in their mind is that the promises must be in a state of fulfillment *at the moment that* time and history end. This leads to the curious view that a slightly more than 1,000-year possession of some of the land, plus a 2,000-year dispossession, plus a future 1,000-year possession of all the land just before time and history end equals an everlasting possession of the land!

Ryrie speaks of Israel being taken up into heaven at the end of the Millennium in the same book in which he claimed to interpret Scripture in a consistently literal manner. Classical dispensationalists, however, argued that only a *spiritual* interpretation would place Israel's eternal future in heaven.

**The Dispensations.** Revised dispensationalists were able to retain much of classical dispensationalism's structure on this side of eternity. They usually retained the Scofield division of dispensations. They distinguished between God's purposes in the dispensations prior to Grace (the dispensations prior to the church), His purpose in the dispensation of Grace (the church), and His purpose in the Kingdom dispensation (the Millennium). Prior to the present dispensation, God was pursuing His purpose for Israel and the nations. This purpose is political, national, and territorial. But it was also spiritual. God granted eternal life to those who were of faith. In the present dispensation, God is pursuing an individual, spiritual purpose only. The spiritual purpose is the same as that given to Israel past and future *except* for certain ministries of the Spirit such as baptism, sealing, and permanent indwelling. Also, the structure of the church is unique in this dispensation (e.g., offices and ministries), and she has a unique dispensational relationship to Christ. She relates to the Christ who is in heaven, not the Christ to come or the Christ on earth. He is her Head, not her king since the church is not a political, national entity.

Putting the above features together, we might visualize the revised views of dispensationalism as indicated in the charts on page 34.

**The Nature of the Church.** Like classical dispensationalists, revised dispensationalists saw the church as a spiritual entity. Salvation and sanctification were viewed primarily in an individualistic manner. Little thought was given to the social nature of the church. However, in the early '70s the Body Life movement began with strong leadership from dispensationalist Ray Stedman.[16] Dispensationalists began to consider the community nature of the church. Gene Getz also contributed to this change

**THE DISPENSATIONS AND THE PURPOSES OF GOD
IN REVISED DISPENSATIONALISM**

**1. HEAVENLY FULFILLMENT VIEW**

| | Purpose for the Church | Purpose for Church Fulfilled | Purpose for Church/Israel Fulfilled in Heaven Forever |
|---|---|---|---|
| Purpose for Israel | | Purpose for Israel Resumed and Fulfilled | |
| PAST DISPENSATIONS | PRESENT DISPENSATION | FUTURE DISPENSATION | |

**THE DISPENSATIONS AND THE PURPOSES OF GOD
IN REVISED DISPENSATIONALISM**

**2. NEW EARTH FULFILLMENT VIEW**

| | Purpose for the Church | Purpose for Church Fulfilled | |
|---|---|---|---|
| Purpose for Israel | | Purpose for Israel Resumed | Purpose for Church/Israel Fulfilled on New Earth Forever |
| PAST DISPENSATIONS | PRESENT DISPENSATION | FUTURE DISPENSATION | NEW EARTH |

of view by stressing the "one another" commands of the New Testament.[17] The result has been a gradual modification of the highly privatized view of Christianity in early dispensationalism.[18]

***Biblical Interpretation.*** Revised dispensationalists continued classical dispensationalism's emphasis on the literal interpretation of prophecy. They spoke of the grammatical and historical interpretation of Scripture, and they continued the "Bible Reading" hermeneutic in the way they taught and presented theological themes.

However, they differed from classical dispensationalists in their gradual withdrawal from "typology," the spiritual hermeneutic of the earlier dispensationalists. Revised dispensationalists claimed to follow *only* a literal interpretation of Scripture, and they claimed that the results of such an interpretation would yield dispensationalism (that is, *revised* dispensationalism). In *Dispensationalism Today,* Charles Ryrie insisted that *consistent* literal interpretation belonged to the essence of dispensationalism.[19] Only dispensationalists, he claimed, were consistently literal in their interpretation. While, as we have noted, this was not true for classical dispensationalism, nevertheless, revised dispensationalists came to understand themselves in this way.

In the 1950s and '60s, other evangelicals were also shying away from "spiritual hermeneutics" in favor of grammatical-historical interpretation. However, evangelical grammatical-historical interpretation was also broadening in the mid-twentieth century to include the developing field of biblical theology. Grammatical analysis expanded to include developments in literary study, particularly in the study of genre, or literary form, and rhetorical structure. Historical interpretation came to include a reference to the historical and cultural context of individual literary pieces for their overall interpretation. And by the late 1980s, evangelicals became more aware of the problem of the interpreter's historical context and traditional preunderstanding of the text being interpreted. These developments are now shared by evangelical biblical scholars of different traditions, including many dispensationalists. They have opened up new vistas for discussion which were not considered by earlier interpreters, including classical and many revised dispensationalists. These are the developments which have led to what is now called "progressive dispensationalism."

Hermeneutics has become much more complex today than when Charles Ryrie affirmed literal interpretation as the "clear, plain, normal" method of interpretation. Perhaps we can explain it this way: Ryrie set up an equation: dispensationalism = literal interpretation = clear-plain-normal hermeneutics = grammatical-historical interpretation. Then he claimed that only dispensationalists practiced consistently literal interpretation. If a person practiced consistently literal interpretation (as defined by the equation) then he or she would be a dispensationalist.

Now, even at the time this was published, evangelical biblical scholars were beginning to move toward a more consistent grammatical-historical interpretation, but it was a grammatical-historical interpretation which was developing in sophistication beyond that which was practiced by classical dispensationalists or even early revised dispensationalists. Over the past three decades, the practice of consistently grammatical-historical interpretation (where "grammatical-historical" has developed to a more advanced form of literary study) has not led evangelicals to become classical or revised dispensationalists. Furthermore, a number of dispensationalists who today practice consistent grammatical-historical interpretation (in its more developed sense) have revised some of the distinctive interpretations of earlier dispensationalism. Literary interpretation has developed so that some things which earlier interpreters thought they "clearly" saw in Scripture, are not "clearly" seen today at all.

This raises a question both about the meaning of "literal" interpretation and the claim that its consistent practice is the essence of dispensationalism. It seems that "literal" is often used to mean the system and tradition of revised dispensationalism. But traditional interpretation must always be tested by ongoing historical-literary interpretation as that interpretation develops in its understanding, methods, and procedures. It must, that is, if one remains committed to Scripture as the primary authority in theology.

When we read Ryrie's claim that consistently "clear, plain, normal" hermeneutics is the essence of dispensationalism, we have to interpret the remark historically. It may have been true as an ideal or goal for revised dispensationalism, but the statement is not true as a comprehensive principle inclusive of classical dispensationalism. When we substitute the phrase *grammatical-historical* for *literal* or *clear-plain-normal*, then we have these observations: (1) once again, the remark is not true of classical dispensationalism since they did not seek to practice such a hermeneutic *consistently* or exclusively. Consequently, if the word "dispensationalism" in the phrase "essence of dispensationalism" is meant to identify the dispensational tradition, then the remark is at best oversimplified, at worst false. (2) The remark is not true of revised dispensationalism's actual practice (as we saw with the "everlasting" promises of Israel and as we will see with the biblical covenants), although it did function as a stated goal. (3) The remark is not true if one reads back into the term "grammatical-historical" what that phrase has come to mean hermeneutically today. This risks the error of anachronism. Finally, (4) as a goal, consistently grammatical-historical interpretation, in the sense in which grammatical-historical is meant today, is much closer to being realized in the hermeneutics of progressive dispensationalism.

Consequently, Ryrie's remark, even though it failed as a description of dispensationalism's unchanging essence, nevertheless pointed a direction in which dispensational hermeneutics was to develop. The old principle of spiritualization has been left behind, and dispensationalists, first revised and then progressive, have pursued the goal of consistent historical-grammatical hermeneutics even as they developed it in meaning and method and in consultation with other evangelicals.

***The Biblical Covenants.*** Revised dispensationalists generally accepted the way in which classical dispensationalists viewed the covenants. The Abrahamic covenant was seen as fundamental. The Mosaic, Palestinian, and Davidic covenants were seen as earthly, political, and national. In spite of revised dispensationalism's insistence on consistent literal interpretation, they believed that the church was the "spiritual" seed of Abraham, that is, the Abrahamic covenant was fulfilled "spiritually" in the church. Literally, however, they believed that it would be fulfilled in national, political terms for Israel in the future.

Revised dispensationalists who were disciples of Lewis Chafer, notably Ryrie and Walvoord, originally defended Chafer's opinion that the new covenant which the New Testament saw fulfilled in the church, was not the new covenant predicted by Jeremiah and Ezekiel. Charles Ryrie wrote in 1953 that if the doctrine of two new covenants were given up, dispensationalism would be weakened.[20] Soon after that, however, both he and Walvoord abandoned the view, for the simple reason that it was not biblically defensible. Moreover, the opposite view, that the same new covenant predicted by the Old Testament prophets was in fact regulating God's relationship to the church today, was undeniably taught in Scripture! This was argued convincingly by John F. McGahey in 1957 in a doctoral dissertation at Dallas Theological Seminary. (McGahey became a long-term faculty member and chairman of the Bible and Theology department at Philadelphia College of Bible until his death in 1986.)

To acknowledge that the New Testament "literally" taught that spiritual blessings of Israel's new covenant were being fulfilled by the church today required explanation. What about the "literal" interpretation of the Old Testament? Generally, revised dispensationalists fell back on classical dispensationalism's *spiritual* hermeneutic to interpret the Old Testament's relationship to the church: the new covenant was being fulfilled *spiritually* in the church today, but Israel would experience the national and political aspects (the earthly features) of the covenant in the future. This was also the way the Abrahamic covenant was handled and the way Scofield had treated the new covenant as well. Nevertheless, they had to acknowledge a covenantal link between Israel and the church in the "literal" teaching of the New Testament.

Once again we can see the tension between revised dispensationalism's hermeneutical method and their actual hermeneutical practice. Nevertheless, the acknowledgment that the New Testament actually taught a covenantal link between Israel and the church was important especially in light of how vigorously the opposite viewpoint (two new covenants) had been defended as *systematically* important for dispensationalism. However, the linkage could not for long be explained by a "spiritual" interpretation since dispensationalists had been set on a course of following the literary-historical meaning of Scripture wherever that might lead. Eventually, the church would have to be seen as standing in the line of a *historical* fulfillment of the new covenant promise to Israel. It would be a dispensation in the historical progress of redemption, not a parenthesis (or intercalation) unrelated to it. Consequently, the revised view of the new covenant proved a significant breakthrough for rethinking the relationship of Israel and the church in Scripture, leading to further developments in dispensationalism.

*The Kingdom.* The kingdom of God versus the kingdom of heaven distinction in classical dispensationalism was important for expressing the central dispensational dualism. The spiritual (kingdom of God) was seen to be distinct from the earthly (kingdom of heaven) even as the heavenly and earthly purposes were kept distinct.

In 1952, George E. Ladd, working with the methods of biblical theology, strongly criticized the classical dispensational distinction of these terms.[21] Two criticisms are particularly important: (1) a substantive (or metaphysical) distinction of these terms is exegetically indefensible, and (2) the separation of earthly and spiritual kingdom characteristics into two separate kingdoms is inaccurate. Revised dispensationalists strongly criticized Ladd for failing to adequately account for the political and national aspects of Jesus' teaching on the kingdom. Mostly, however, he was critiqued for advocating a view which "might lead to" amillennialism (even though Ladd himself was one of the foremost defenders of premillennialism).[22] Nevertheless, although they refused to acknowledge him, revised dispensationalists appear to have taken part of Ladd's criticism to heart. They dropped the classical distinction between the terms kingdom of heaven and kingdom of God. Furthermore, many revised dispensationalists began to find a way to speak of a spiritual kingdom in the present dispensation. A number of alternative kingdom views were proposed.

In the following paragraphs we will survey four representative kingdom theologies fielded by revised dispensationalists. The main point in this survey is to demonstrate that there is no *one* revised dispensational view of the kingdom. Several alternate views have been proposed. However, for the reader who has some awareness of revised dispensationalism, we believe that a survey of the differences might be helpful, since such differences have rarely been set out side by side.

*Alva J. McClain:* McClain introduced the terminology *univer-*

*sal kingdom* and *mediatorial kingdom* in his book *The Greatness of the Kingdom.*[23] The universal kingdom was defined as God's sovereignty over all things. The universal kingdom has been constant through all dispensations. The mediatorial kingdom referred to God's rule over the earth through a divinely chosen mediator. McClain believed that Abraham was the first such mediator. A succession of mediators followed through the kings of Israel. Jesus Christ is the rightful Davidic heir and the mediator of the messianic mediatorial kingdom. However, since Jesus is not presently on earth, McClain believed that there is no mediatorial kingdom present on the earth during this dispensation. Consequently, he titled the present dispensation the *Interregnum,* the period between the reigns. The mediatorial kingdom will appear again at the return of Christ. At the end of the Millennium, the mediatorial kingdom will merge with and become simply the universal kingdom of God.

Stanley Toussaint agreed with McClain that there is no mediatorial kingdom present today. He argued that all passages in the New Testament that speak of the presence of the kingdom should be understood proleptically. They refer to the *future* kingdom.[24]

## THE KINGDOM THEOLOGY
## OF ALVA J. McCLAIN

| UNIVERSAL KINGDOM OF GOD | | | |
|---|---|---|---|
| MEDIATORIAL KINGDOM | INTERREGNUM No Mediatorial Kingdom | MEDIATORIAL KINGDOM | |
| Present in History / Present in Prophecy | | | ETERNITY: |
| PAST DISPENSATIONS | PRESENT DISPENSATION | FUTURE DISPENSATION | A New Earth |

*Charles Ryrie:* Ryrie agreed with McClain on the idea and terminology of the *universal kingdom*. One should recognize

40

that God is, always has been, and always will be sovereign over all things. Some of what the Bible has to say about God's kingdom refers to this attribute of divine sovereignty. With regard to a political kingdom on earth, he preferred to follow the substance of Scofield's doctrine of the kingdom of heaven, but without Scofield's terminology. Instead, he simply spoke of the Davidic kingdom. The Davidic kingdom had appeared in the old dispensation, but it had been put on hold in the Exile and had not been restored even to the coming of Jesus. With Jesus, a threefold kingdom program begins. First is the Davidic kingdom offered by Jesus to Israel, but rejected by them (this is essentially the same as Scofield's kingdom of heaven in the preaching of Jesus). Next is the mystery form of the kingdom which Ryrie defines as Christendom (identical to Scofield's kingdom of heaven in mystery form). Next is the Davidic, millennial kingdom which is the final fulfillment of the Davidic kingdom (again equal to Scofield). At the end of the Millennium, however, Israel and the church will both be in heaven under the universal kingdom of God.[25]

Ryrie also supplements Scofield's scheme by adding *another* kingdom in the present dispensation: *the spiritual kingdom.* This spiritual kingdom is the rule of Christ over believers today. It is precisely equal to "the true church, the body of Christ." This is an important revision for it defines Christ's relation to the church as a kingdom. His rule is spiritual, the power of regeneration.[26]

Ryrie's spiritual kingdom appears to be equivalent to Scofield's kingdom of God, however Ryrie limits it to this dispensation only. In that regard, his view is similar to Ladd, except that Ryrie completely distinguishes it from the fulfillment of the Davidic kingdom.

The dispensational uniqueness and isolation of the spiritual kingdom produces a number of inconsistencies in Ryrie's theology. On the one hand, he says that the spiritual kingdom is the sphere of new birth. Since the spiritual kingdom is limited to this dispensation, logically it would seem that regeneration is likewise so limited. However, elsewhere Ryrie teaches that regeneration is transdispensational. Also, the existence of a spiritual kingdom which is the church would indicate that Christ relates to the church *as a King.* On the one hand, Ryrie acknowledges that Christ rules the church as His kingdom and

41

that He is a King today. However, in the same work he contradicts himself by denying that Christ is the King of the church or by asserting that even if He is king, He does not rule![27] What we have here is an example of a tradition trying to deal with biblical criticisms brought against it. Nevertheless, problems remain.

## THE KINGDOM THEOLOGY
## OF CHARLES RYRIE

| UNIVERSAL KINGDOM OF GOD | | | |
|---|---|---|---|
| DAVIDIC KINGDOM | SPIRITUAL KINGDOM (Church) MYSTERY FORM OF THE KINGDOM (Christendom) | DAVIDIC/ MESSIANIC KINGDOM | ETERNITY IN HEAVEN |
| PAST DISPENSATIONS | PRESENT DISPENSATION | FUTURE DISPENSATION | |

*John Walvoord:* Walvoord distinguishes between a universal kingdom and a spiritual kingdom. The universal kingdom is God's sovereignty over all He has made. This concept is essentially the same as McClain's doctrine of universal kingdom. The spiritual kingdom is God's rule over the saved of all ages including the present dispensation. He also defines it as the sphere of voluntary submission to God, which is essentially the same concept as Scofield's kingdom of God. A third kingdom, the Davidic kingdom is defined as a subdivision of the universal kingdom. He understands the Davidic kingdom merely as a political kingdom. It is God's theocratic rule through David or a Davidic descendant acting as God's mediator. Hence, Walvoord's Davidic kingdom is practically the same as McClain's mediatorial kingdom except that for Walvoord, such a kingdom begins with David, whereas for McClain it began with Abraham.

Walvoord then introduces two terms related to the Davidic kingdom: the postponed kingdom, which is the Davidic kingdom that Jesus offered to Israel but was postponed when they rejected Him; and the millennial kingdom, which is the fulfillment of the postponed kingdom, that Davidic kingdom which is realized in Christ's 1,000-year rule on earth.

Walvoord gives us yet another category of kingdom in the mystery form of the kingdom. This is the spiritual rule of Christ in the church today. In his scheme, this is really the spiritual kingdom. Yet he believes that the parables of Matthew 13 predict this kingdom in a special sense for this dispensation when they speak of mysteries of the kingdom of heaven. He also connects the mystery form of the kingdom to the New Testament's teaching on the kingdom's presence for the church. He believes it is a mystery because the Old Testament had not anticipated the presence of the spiritual kingdom apart from the Davidic, the purely (according to him) political kingdom. Note that Walvoord uses Scofield's language (also used by Ryrie): the mystery form of the kingdom. But he defines it in a way that is completely different from Scofield (and from Ryrie). Whereas Scofield saw today's mystery form of the kingdom (predicted in Matthew 13) as Christendom, an aspect of the Davidic kingdom, and stressed that it was *not* the church, Walvoord argues (from the same passage) that it has nothing to do with the Davidic kingdom, but is precisely *the church.*

Walvoord still defends a distinction between the kingdom of heaven and the kingdom of God. As noted above, his category spiritual kingdom is essentially the same as Scofield's category kingdom of God. Like Scofield, he believed the kingdom of heaven is a sphere of profession different from, but inclusive of, the kingdom of God (or spiritual kingdom). And he continues to believe that the usage of the terms in Matthew's Gospel supports the distinction.[28]

At the end of the Millennium, Walvoord sees the earthly (Davidic) kingdom coming to an end. The universal and spiritual kingdoms will be united forever. Although he sometimes uses the new earth language of Revelation 21, Walvoord makes a radical distinction between the millennial and eternal states. He does not relate the everlasting promises of Old Testament hope to this eternal state, but sees them fulfilled in the Millennium. In fact, Walvoord is insistent that they *cannot* be fulfilled on the new earth. This is due to the *radical difference* between the two states, such that the latter does not possess the conditions for the fulfillment of these promises. It would seem that Walvoord is working with a view of the new earth that differs little from a classical non-earthly, nontemporal view of heaven.[29]

## THE KINGDOM THEOLOGY
## OF JOHN WALVOORD

| UNIVERSAL KINGDOM OF GOD | | | |
|---|---|---|---|
| SPIRITUAL KINGDOM OF GOD | | | |
| DAVIDIC KINGDOM | MYSTERY FORM OF THE KINGDOM (Church) | MILLENNIAL KINGDOM | ETERNITY IN HEAVEN |
| PAST DISPENSATIONS | PRESENT DISPENSATION | FUTURE DISPENSATION | |

Walvoord's doctrine of the kingdom illustrates a persistent problem for revised dispensationalism. Whereas Jesus preached the coming kingdom of God, Walvoord transforms that message into the proclamation of several kingdoms. He is not able to see how these different "kingdoms" are actually different aspects of *one* eschatological kingdom. Jesus announced this kingdom, revealed some of its aspects in Himself, and began to bring it into progressive fulfillment, inaugurating some aspects today while promising to fulfill all aspects completely in the future.

*J. Dwight Pentecost:* Like other revised dispensationalists, Pentecost uses kingdom terminology to distinguish between God's absolute and relative attributes. He uses the term *eternal kingdom* to refer to God's omnipotence over all He has made. Eternal is taken in the sense of timelessness. He even postulates the order of the Trinity itself as the divine kingdom. Like McClain, he sees this eternal kingdom mediated in a temporal, contingent manner through a divinely chosen mediator. McClain called this the mediatorial kingdom; Pentecost terms it the theocratic kingdom. Unlike McClain, however, Pentecost sees this mediated kingdom revealed in ten successive stages running from the Creation to the Millennium. The first four and last two stages are equivalent to six of Scofield's seven dispensations. Pentecost divides Scofield's dispensation of Law into four successive theocratic kingdoms: Judges, Kings, Prophets, and Christ.[30]

It is important to note that Pentecost believes the theocratic kingdom is present today in this dispensation. Furthermore, he believes that the church itself is an aspect of that theocratic kingdom. In this belief, he is noticeably different from McClain and Toussaint. His view is similar to Walvoord's except that he uses terminology which connects the kingdom in this dispensation to earthly manifestations of the kingdom in past and future dispensations. This *connection* points the direction in which dispensationalism has modified and developed its understanding of the kingdom.

Pentecost also sees the kingdom continuing in an earthly form in the eternal state. He believes that both Israel and the church will be together with Christ on the new earth after the Millennium. Pentecost also envisions national identities continuing into the eternal state, with distinctions drawn between Israel and Gentile nations. Here the promises of Christ's everlasting kingdom will be fulfilled on a new earth forever.[31]

## THE KINGDOM THEOLOGY
## OF J. DWIGHT PENTECOST

| ETERNAL KINGDOM OF GOD | | | |
|---|---|---|---|
| PAST THEOCRATIC KINGDOMS<br><br>Successive Rulers | PRESENT THEOCRATIC KINGDOM<br><br>Civil Government, Home, Employers, the Church | FUTURE THEOCRATIC KINGDOM<br><br>Davidic/Messianic Kingdom | |
| PAST DISPENSATIONS | PRESENT DISPENSATION | FUTURE DISPENSATION | ETERNITY ON THE NEW EARTH |

It seems that Pentecost sees a closer interrelationship between his categories eternal and theocratic than Walvoord saw between his different forms of kingdom. But that relationship appears to be confined within each stage of the theocratic kingdom. Although the terminology is the same, the various theocratic kingdoms seem relatively independent of each other, like the dispensations of classical dispensationalism. What is lacking is a real sense of historical continuity and progression linking them together. To put it another way, the unity of the theocratic kingdoms is found vertically in the timeless eternal kingdom. It is not found in an eschatologically converging work of God in history.

As an example of this, while Pentecost recognizes a manifestation of spiritual blessings in the present theocratic kingdom, as well as a manifestation of spiritual blessings in the future theocratic kingdom of Christ's return, he does not see these as connected in an unfolding revelation of the kingdom of *Jesus, Son of David.* He does not see them as part of a progressive revelation united in the person of Christ Himself.

***Conclusion.*** In the late '50s and '60s, some dispensationalists introduced important revisions to classical dispensationalism. Those revisions became widely accepted such that many graduates of dispensational schools in the '60s and '70s hardly knew what classical dispensationalism was. Many have not even been aware of the variety of views within revised dispensationalism. Nevertheless, revised dispensationalism is a distinctive form of the dispensational tradition, which through its modifications and the problems it was dealing with prepared the way for the eventual development of progressive dispensationalism.[32]

## Progressive Dispensationalism

***Holistic Redemption in Progressive Revelation.*** Dispensationalism is known for its recognition of multiple purposes in divine redemption. These include earthly, national, political, social, and spiritual purposes. Dispensationalists generally have recognized that these purposes will be fulfilled in eternal salvation (except for some revised dispensationalists who believed that earthly and political purposes would be terminated in the Millennium). Dispensationalists have also recognized that some of these purposes have been emphasized more strongly in some dispensations than others. However, understanding the relationship between these different purposes has always been a problem.

Classical dispensationalism advocated an eternal heavenly/ earthly dualism in order to explain the different purposes of redemption. Revised dispensationalism rejected this eternal dualism, which forced them to choose between a more heavenly or a more earthly view of eternity. Some chose one, some chose the other. The collapse of the heavenly/earthly dualism brought believing Israel from the Old Testament and Millennial Israel together. Believing Gentiles were also brought together in one eternal redemption. However, Jews and Gentiles of the church dispensation were thought to be an entirely separate group of people.[33] Many revised dispensationalists could not comprehend how the church could be related to the plan of redemption without sacrificing the future fulfillment of ethnic, national, and political promises which distinguish between Jews and Gentiles. Many of their opponents interpreted those promises as having been "transformed" into the church, leaving no "literal" fulfillment of national promises to Israel in the future.

Progressive dispensationalists agree with revised (and classical) dispensationalists that God's work with Israel and Gentile nations in the past dispensation looks forward to the redemption of humanity in its political and cultural aspects. Consequently, there is a place for Israel and for other nations in the eternal plan of God.

On the other hand, progressive dispensationalists believe that the church is a vital part of *this very same plan of redemption.* The appearance of the church does not signal a secondary redemption plan, either to be fulfilled in heaven apart from the new earth or in an elite class of Jews and Gentiles who are forever distinguished from the rest of redeemed humanity. Instead, the church today is a revelation of spiritual blessings which *all the redeemed* will share in spite of their ethnic and national differences.

Consequently, progressive dispensationalism advocates a *holistic and unified* view of eternal salvation. God will save humankind in its ethnic and national plurality. But, He will bless it with the same salvation given to all without distinction; the same, not only in justification and regeneration, but also in sanctification by the indwelling Holy Spirit. These blessings will come to all without distinction through Jesus Christ, the King of Israel and of all the nations of redeemed humanity.

***The Dispensations.*** Progressive dispensationalists understand the dispensations not simply as *different* arrangements between God and humankind, but as *successive* arrangements in the *progressive* revelation and accomplishment of redemption. The plan of redemption has different aspects to it. One dispensation may emphasize one aspect more than another, for example the emphasis on divinely directed political affairs in the past dispensation and the emphasis on multiethnic spiritual identity in Christ in the present dispensation. But all these dispensations point to a future culmination in which God will *both* politically administer Israel and Gentile nations *and* indwell all of them equally (without ethnic distinctions) by the Holy Spirit. Consequently, the dispensations *progress* by revealing different aspects of the final unified redemption.

The dispensations also reveal a qualitative progression in the manifestation of grace. For example, there were manifestations of grace in the dispensation of Old Testament Israel which were qualitatively better than that which was revealed to the patriarchs prior to the Exodus. Likewise, the Scripture teaches that there are manifestations of grace in the present dispensation that are qualitatively greater than what was revealed to Jews and Gentiles in the past dispensation. And there will be a qualitative advancement of grace in the future dispensation as well (our future glorification). Consequently, the dispensations are not simply different historical expressions of the *same* experience of redemption (as in some forms of covenantalism), although they do lead to and culminate in one redemption plan.

In progressive dispensationalism, the political-social and spiritual purposes of God complement one another. The spiritual does not replace the political nor do the two run independent of each other. They are related aspects in a holistic plan of redemption. The final dispensation will reveal all these aspects in complementary relationship to each other. Prior to that, different dispensations may reveal more of one aspect or more of another, but each dispensation is related to the final dispensation in which the plan culminates. Because they all have the same goal, there is a real, progressive relationship between them. As each leads to the goal of final redemption, Scripture draws various connections between them which relate them together in a truly progressive fashion. It is from this progressive relationship of the dispensations to one another that the name *progressive dispensationalism* is taken.

***The Nature of the Church.*** Like earlier dispensationalists, progressive dispensationalists view the church as a *new manifestation of grace,* a new dispensation in the history of redemption. Earlier dispensationalists viewed the church as a completely different kind of redemption from that which had been revealed before or would be revealed in the future. The church then had its own future separate from the redemption promised to Jews and Gentiles in the past and future dispensations. Progressive dispensationalists, however, while seeing the church as a new manifestation of grace, believe that this grace is precisely *in keeping with* the promises of the Old Testament, particularly the promises of the new covenant in Isaiah, Jeremiah, and Ezekiel. The fact that these blessings have been inaugurated in the church distinguishes the church from Jews and Gentiles of the past dispensation. But, only *some* of those blessings have been inaugurated. Consequently, the church should be distinguished from the next dispensation in which *all* of the blessings will not just be inaugurated, but completely fulfilled (which fulfillment will be granted to the saints of all dispensations through the resurrection of the dead).

One of the striking differences between progressive and earlier dispensationalists, is that progressives do not view the church as an anthropological category in the same class as terms like Israel, Gentile Nations, Jews, and Gentile people. The church is neither a separate race of humanity (in contrast to Jews and Gentiles) nor a competing nation (alongside Israel and Gentile nations), nor is it a group of angelic-like humans destined for the heavens in contrast to the rest of redeemed humanity on the earth. The church is precisely redeemed humanity itself (both Jews and Gentiles) as it exists *in this dispensation* prior to the coming of Christ. When Paul speaks of the church as "one new man" in Christ (Eph. 2:15), he means precisely redeemed humanity as opposed to the unsaved. Jews and Gentiles outside of Christ are "the world," the "old man." When Paul speaks of there being neither Jew nor Greek in Christ, he is not speaking of some kind of ethnic homogenization any more than he is of some kind of gender androgyny when he says that there is neither male nor female in the church. Ethnic, political, national, and cultural differences *remain* in the church. But Paul's point is that the blessings of the Spirit which constitute the church as the new dispensation are given equally without ethnic, gender, or class distinction.

The prophetic promises envision Christ ruling forever over the nations of the redeemed. The church is not another "people-group" in that picture. Those Jews and Gentiles who compose the church prior to Christ's coming join the redeemed Jews and Gentiles of earlier dispensations to share equally in resurrection glory. Those who during their dispensation had certain blessings only in promise or in an inaugurated form will all be brought to the same level of complete fulfillment when they are raised together from the dead. Redeemed Jews and Gentiles will share equally in the completed blessings of the Spirit. The church in this dispensation testifies to this aspect of redemption. The same redeemed Jews and Gentiles will be directed and governed by Jesus Christ according to their different nationalities. The national identities and political promises of Israel and the Gentiles in the last dispensation testifies in turn to this aspect of redemption.

We can illustrate this progressive dispensational view of the church in the case of Jewish Christians. A Jew who becomes a Christian today does not lose his or her relationship to Israel's future promises. Jewish Christians will join the Old Testament remnant of faith in the inheritance of Israel. Gentile Christians will be joined by saved Gentiles of earlier dispensations. All together, Jews and Gentiles, will share the same blessings of the Spirit, as testified to by the relationship of Jew and Gentile in the church of this dispensation. The result will be that all peoples will be reconciled in peace, their ethnic and national differences being no cause for hostility. Earlier forms of dispensationalism, for all their emphasis on a future for Israel, excluded Jewish Christians from that future, postulating the church as a different people-group from Israel and Gentiles.

By thinking of the church as a different people group, a race of humanity different from Jews and Gentiles, some earlier dispensationalists have not been as sensitive as they should have been to actually existing ethnic and cultural differences within the body of Christ today. Lack of sensitivity here leads to the cultural domination of one group over another within the church (such as the Gentilization of Jewish Christians, or the Anglicization or Americanization of third-world Christians). This in turn becomes a hindrance to the unity of the body. The problem, not unique to dispensationalists, manifests itself especially in missions as the problem of contextualization. The work of the Spirit is not cultural domination but reconciliation, not the elimination of human, ethnic, cultural, and national differences, but the redemption of them from enmity against the true God to holiness and from a state of hostility against one another to one of peace.

## THE DISPENSATIONS AND THE PURPOSES OF GOD IN PROGRESSIVE DISPENSATIONALISM

| | CHRIST ASCENDED | CHRIST DESCENDED | |
|---|---|---|---|
| Political — Theocratic Israel, Gentile Nations | Political — Theocratic | Political — Theocratic Israel, Gentile Nations | |
| | | Personal, Social | |
| Personal, Social, Prophetic Remnant of Faith[1] | Personal, Social, Evangelistic The Church[2] | Evangelistic The Redeemed[3] | Fulfillment The Redeemed[4] |
| PAST DISPENSATIONS | PRESENT DISPENSATION | (Millennial) (Eternal) FUTURE DISPENSATION | |

1. Remnant of Faith = Believing Jews and Gentiles (a remnant of Israel and the Gentile Nations)
2. The Church = Believing Jews and Gentiles (a remnant of Israel and the Gentile Nations)
3. The Redeemed = Believing Jews and Gentiles (a remnant of Israel and the Gentile Nations), including the church of the present dispensation and the believing remnant of past dispensations, joined together in resurrection life.
4. The Redeemed = Believing Jews and Gentiles of all previous dispensations raised from the dead.

***Biblical Interpretation.*** We have already noted in our discussion of revised dispensationalism how biblical interpretation developed from the middle to the latter part of the twentieth century. Dispensationalists changed from advocating a dual hermeneutic of spiritual and literal interpretation to an emphasis on consistently literal interpretation. This "literal" interpretation then developed from the "clear, plain" method of attaching to words whatever meaning "seemed clear" to the interpreter to a more critical awareness of how bias (or pre-understanding) conditions our intuitions, our impressions of certainty, and clarity of interpretation. Literal interpretation also developed as grammatical-historical interpretation. From an early emphasis on the grammatical analysis of words, interpretation broadened to include syntactical, rhetorical, and literary study. Historical interpretation expanded beyond dates and chronologies to include the historical setting and development of themes, words, and ideas. It also came to bear on the history of interpretation, the matter of tradition, and the historical context of the interpreter.

These developments in biblical interpretation have been a major factor in the rise of progressive dispensationalism. Progressive dispensationalists are themselves revised dispensationalists who through more developed historical-literary interpretation have come to what they believe is a more accurate understanding of certain biblical issues.

It should be noted that progressive dispensationalism is not an abandonment of "literal" interpretation for "spiritual" interpretation. Progressive dispensationalism is a development of "literal" interpretation into a more consistent historical-literary interpretation.

This is the way in which progressive dispensationalism's interest in typology should be understood. Progressive dispensationalists view typology as an aspect of historical-literary interpretation. This is not the same kind of typology as practiced in classical dispensationalism. The latter was oftentimes a form of "spiritual" interpretation in which material objects, persons, or other phenomena represented something in the spiritual world. For example, oil was thought to be a "type" of the Holy Spirit, and leaven was considered a "type" of evil.

In contrast to this, typology in historical-literary hermeneutics refers to patterns of resemblance between persons and events in earlier history to persons and events in later history. For example, the Davidic-Solomonic kingdom is a type of the eschatological kingdom, the Day of the Lord judgment in the sixth century B.C. is a type of a future, eschatological Day of the Lord. Consequently, typology for progressive dispensationalism is primarily a "horizontal" (historical) relationship rather than a "vertical" (spiritual) one.[34]

A more extensive discussion of these hermeneutical issues follows in chapters 2 and 3 of this book.

*The Biblical Covenants.* Progressive dispensationalism offers a more unified view of the biblical covenants than earlier dispensationalism. The Abrahamic covenant is seen as the foundation for all other covenants. The blessings of later covenants explicate the promise given to Abraham: "I will bless you." The new covenant is *the form* in which the Abrahamic covenant has been inaugurated in this dispensation and will be fulfilled in full in the future. The Davidic covenant is both an aspect of Abrahamic blessing and *the means* by which the blessings are now inaugurated and will be bestowed in full.

Progressive dispensationalists do not believe that the Abrahamic, Davidic, and new covenants are being fulfilled today "in a spiritual sense." The spiritual blessings being given today are blessings actually predicted by the new covenant. These blessings are given in a partial and inaugurated form, which looks forward to complete fulfillment at the return of Christ.

The fact that new covenant blessings are being given to Gentiles as well as Jews today is consistent with the Abrahamic promise to bless not only the Jews but also the Gentiles. The humanity-wide scope of Abrahamic blessing directs the way the new covenant is being fulfilled today.

The present inauguration and future fullness of new covenant fulfillment reveals another aspect in which the Abrahamic and Davidic covenants are being fulfilled today. All of these covenants will be fulfilled in a future dispensation consistent with the historical-grammatical sense of their promises. However, the progressive nature of the dispensations and the interconnection between the covenants is such that present blessings are a *partial,* not "allegorical," fulfillment of those promises. They look forward to complete fulfillment at the return of Christ.

A fuller presentation of a progressive dispensational view of the covenants can be found in chapters 5 and 6.

***The Kingdom of God.*** The theme of the kingdom of God is much more unified and more central to progressive dispensationalism than it is to revised dispensationalism. Instead of dividing up the different features of redemption into self-contained "kingdoms," progressive dispensationalists see one promised eschatological kingdom which has both spiritual and political dimensions. That kingdom is always centered in Christ. The progressive revelation of one or another aspect of the eschatological kingdom (whether spiritual or political) prior to the eternal reign of Christ, follows the history of Jesus Christ and is dependent on Him as He acts according to the will of the Father. Whether or not certain features of the eschatological kingdom (whether spiritual or political) will be enacted or revealed prior to the full establishment of that kingdom is not to be determined by reasoning from full-orbed descriptions of Old Testament prophets alone. Rather, it is a matter of the Father's will for this and any intervening dispensation, a matter which is discerned through New Testament revelation. The New Testament clarifies how the kingdom predicted by the Old Testament prophets is being revealed today, how it will in fact appear in a millennial form, and how these contribute to that everlasting kingdom in which all prophecies will be fulfilled.

Progressive dispensationalists put primary emphasis on the eternal kingdom for understanding all previous forms of the kingdom including the Millennium. They make no substantive distinction between the terms kingdom of heaven and kingdom of God. And they see Christ's present relationship to the church today as a form of the eschatological kingdom which affirms and guarantees the future revelation of the kingdom in all its fullness. See the chart on page 55 for a visualization of this view.

Chapter 7 will offer a fuller discussion of the kingdom of God in progressive dispensationalism.

## Conclusion

In this chapter we have seen that dispensationalism has been a significant and widespread tradition of American evangelical thought. But dispensationalism has not been static. Besides the dynamics of nuance and inflection by individual teachers and theologians, the dispensational tradition underwent a signifi-

**THE KINGDOM OF GOD IN PROGRESSIVE DISPENSATIONALISM**

**DIVINE PRESENCE AND POWER REVEALED
IN PROGRESS OF REDEMPTION**

THE ESCHATOLOGICAL KINGDOM OF GOD

CHRIST ASCENDED

CHRIST DESCENDED

THE KINGDOM OF GOD

THE KINGLY ACTS OF GOD

IN THE PERSON OF CHRIST — JESUS CHRIST

IN THE COMMUNITY OF CHRIST (The Church) — PRESENT DISPENSATION

IN THE MILLENNIAL EMPIRE OF CHRIST — (Millennial) FUTURE DISPENSATION

IN ETERNAL FULFILLMENT — (Eternal)

PAST DISPENSATIONS

cant modification in the third quarter of this century. This did not mean that all classical dispensationalists became revised dispensationalists at once. In fact, some more classical dispensationalists can be found even today. But a change did occur and became so established that revised dispensationalism has become the dispensationalism that most people know.

There is a significant change taking place in dispensationalism today, which further modifies the views of revised dispensationalism. This is what we have called progressive dispensationalism. In this chapter, we have attempted to outline both its continuity with earlier dispensational emphases and briefly explain its differences. Its major distinctive is found in its conception of the progressive accomplishment and revelation of a holistic and unified redemption. That redemption covers personal, communal, social, political, and national aspects of human life. It is revealed in a succession of dispensations which vary in how they stress the aspects of redemption, but all point to a final culmination in which all aspects are redeemed together.

The following chapters discuss in more detail some of the distinctives raised here. These are presented in two parts: (1) principles for interpreting the Bible and (2) an exposition of biblical structures which support progressive dispensationalism. In the latter part we will seek to interpret the Bible's teaching on dispensations, covenants, and the kingdom of God. The last chapter will list some ministerial and theological implications for further reflection.

Progressive dispensationalism is a phenomena of change and continuity within the dispensational tradition. Progressive dispensationalists will differ with each other on various points. There are undoubtedly interpretations and viewpoints offered here which will be corrected by the insights and contributions of others. However, we believe that what is presented here is sufficient to reveal the overall direction as well as some of the issues and problems in which a broad number of dispensationalist theologians and biblical scholars are working today.

## Chapter Two
# Interpreting the Bible — How We Read Texts

P ractice without theory is blind, but theory without practice is dumb," observes noted New Testament scholar
N.T. Wright in *The New Testament and the People of
God.*[1] This citation cautions us in our approach to interpreting
the Bible. It warns us that interpretation must wed theory and
practice. We can create expectations about how we wish interpretation of the Bible to work or what it means, but in the end
we must test those theories within the text. As interpreters, we
must ask why we see the text as we do. This is especially important in a world where many competing views exist about what
the Bible says. What creates such diversity, and how do we
engage in discussion about such differences? How does one
sort out the options? It is through the discipline known as
*hermeneutics,* or the study of "how we determine what a passage means."

For some, interpretation is like the popular Nike™ television
commercial: just as one merely laces up new basketball shoes
and hits the floor to "just do it," so the interpreter should
merely open up the text and "just read it." Unfortunately, it
isn't quite that simple. Theologians and students of literature
have debated over how to read texts for a long time, and in the

twentieth century discussions have taken many fresh twists and turns. The debate has focused on four interacting elements that influence our understanding of texts: (1) the author(s), (2) the text, (3) ourselves as reader(s), and (4) the worldviews we and the text bring to the reading. Different hermeneutical approaches argue for a differing range of priority and relationship between these four elements, but all agree that each has an impact on how we perceive texts. In biblical interpretation, we work with all four elements. We seek to understand the perspective of the author and the manner in which he expressed his ideas in the text. At the same time, we must also be aware of the fact that our understanding may be insightful or it may be limited or colored by our own perspectives as readers. In fact what emerges is that everyone has a "hermeneutic" (a grid of understanding with which one approaches a text) that impacts one's "hermeneutics" (the interpretive principles one uses to find meaning in the text). These two closely related terms summarize two intricately bound up sides of the one coin of interpretation. Failure to pay attention to either side of the coin results in confusion about how one understands the text of the Bible.

In this chapter we will discuss the dynamic interplay between author(s), text, readers, and worldviews by focusing on them in pairs. That focus may seem somewhat mechanical and tedious, like a jump shot being analyzed by a computer, but it is our hope that the analysis will enable the reader to not "just do it," but do it well. As interpreters, we must be sensitive to (1) how we approach texts (or speak to them) and (2) how we let the text speak. We will work backward from how a text is read, rather than how it is created.

## How We Approach the Text:
## Looking through a Prism

***Readers and Worldviews, Part 1.*** According to Charles Ryrie, "Hermeneutics is that science which furnishes the principles of interpretation. These principles guide and govern anybody's system of theology. They ought to be determined *before* one's theology is systematized, but in practice the reverse is usually true."[2]

Recognizing that there are different ways by which we all

read texts, Ryrie warns us that we ought to know how we are coming to the text before we construct a theology about it. Skeptics often say, "The Bible can be made to say anything." That isn't accurate, but it is true that we can read our own ideas into the text or misunderstand it due to our own limitations of knowledge and understanding. In fact, each of us has our own way of seeing, a grid for understanding, that impacts what we expect to see in the text, the questions we ask of it, and thus the answers we get.

Both our limitations and our grid combine to form a prism through which we interpret reality and through which we read texts. This is our worldview. As good as the text is that we read, it always comes to us through the prism we construct of reality.

Now many people would say that this prism is merely a matter of "presuppositions." If one has good presuppositions, they will stand nearer to truth than one who has bad presuppositions. But worldviews are not so simple. They are the result of both presuppositions and what we might call "preunderstandings."

Any *presupposition* is an element in one's thinking that is not up for negotiation, unless it comes under extreme duress. It is a very fixed conviction on which perceptions or views are built and may be conscious or unconscious. Imagine yourself a medieval reader of the Bible and you come upon the lines in Psalm 19:4b-6, "In the heavens He has pitched a tent for the sun, which is like a bridegroom coming forth from his pavilion, like a champion rejoicing to run his course. It rises at one end of the heavens and makes its circuit to the other; nothing is hidden from its heat" (NIV). Now the medieval reader would have told you that this describes how the sun moves around the earth. His presupposition about the universe, shared uniformly with others in his time, was that the earth is at its center and everything revolves around this center of God's creation. This was the prism through which the world was understood. As long as that supposition was held, this would be an aspect of the verse's interpretation. The issue we are concerned about here is not whether the presupposition was right or wrong, but that it existed and influenced the way the text was understood.

A few centuries later, astronomers, using telescopes, began to argue that the earth is not at the center of the universe. Those with the original presupposition of the earth at the center, and who did not consider their presupposition negotiable, came to regard this suggestion quite negatively, probably because it was a direct challenge on how they viewed reality and God's portrayal of it. They could not see reality any differently. The lens was fixed at this point, because of a key presupposition.

On the other hand, *preunderstandings* are beliefs or perceptions that are fluid in that they are open to adjustment, refinement, or development by further interaction and reflection. Someone with a presupposition about the earth at the center of the universe could look at the astronomers' evidence and say as a result, "This is a new consideration; I will look closer at that question." The moment that approach is adopted, a presupposition within the prism has become preunderstanding instead. Investigation then continues on a different level from those who maintain the presupposition that the earth is at the center. Next someone else made a suggestion that such language in the psalm is "phenomenological," that is, it describes reality as we perceive it as phenomena and not how it is scientifically. If the one with a preunderstanding about the earth at the center embraces this literary suggestion about the text's interpretation and comes to believe the earth is no longer at the universe's center, then both preunderstanding at this point and worldview, to a degree, have changed. The view of the details of cosmology and the Bible shifts, though that person remains a theist at the most basic level.

This is but one example of a crucial area that impacts our perception at many levels, though we often do not examine it carefully. So what difference does understanding worldview, presupposition, and preunderstanding make?

*First,* we all view the world with presuppositions; that is a given we cannot deny. One major issue is which presuppositions do we have that are helpful and which are not. One may contend that those that are helpful are those of the Bible, but we have already seen the potential to read something as "biblical" that may not be. So we must carefully assess what makes for biblical perspective.

*Second,* we all also possess preunderstandings, though we may not be conscious of them all. As we examine an issue or the text, it is helpful to consider how we are approaching the question and why. Sometimes it is dialogue with someone who thinks differently that helps us see why we see things the way we do.

*Third*, some changes in preunderstanding do not alter worldview. They simply open one up to examining alternatives or create the possibility of new categories for understanding by looking at the question in a fresh way. But other changes in preunderstanding do impact worldview. Being open to the question of what is at the center of the universe opened up the possibility of a literary answer to the dilemma, even though one never answered the original question of where the center of the universe is! In fact, it became a less important theological question as a result of the shift in worldview.

*Fourth*, not every presupposition or preunderstanding is a good one, just as not every presupposition or preunderstanding is a bad one. In fact, some presuppositions should operate more like preunderstandings. On the other hand, some presuppositions and preunderstandings are the product of reflection already and can be held with good reason. Not every shift in understanding is good, since we make good and bad decisions, but we can never learn without being open to change in our thinking.

*Fifth*, some presuppositions and preunderstandings are the product of the time or culture in which one lives. The medievalist's view of reality was defined by the limits of the worldview of that era. Only as new data opened up fresh possibilities could the textual data be considered from new angles.

Most importantly, worldview is a combination of presuppositions and preunderstandings that exist in differing combinations in different people. They influence perspective and impact interpretation; they also can create differences in reading. But if their role is appreciated, they can become the subject of fruitful discussion, even where disagreement exists. Still, impasse does exist where presuppositions differ. Those who have a worldview that allows for miracles will read the Bible differently from those who insist they do not occur. It is impossible for them to agree on the role of miracles in the Bible. But misunderstanding can also exist where preunderstandings differ. Knowing the difference is important, because it is possible to discuss preunderstandings where they are known. Many too quickly confine all disagreement to the level of presupposition and thus say, in effect, we cannot discuss our differences. But there may be opportunity to engage in mutually fruitful discussion about the text, if one can distinguish between presupposition and preunderstanding.

So then we recognize that we as readers contribute (rightly or wrongly) to our interpretation of the text. We turn now to two other elements involved in approaching the interpretive process, the author(s) and the text itself.

**Author(s) and Text.** The emergence of the Bible started with communicators whose message eventually wound up in texts. That is a roundabout way to say the Bible has authors, but it is important to recognize that often the Bible contains a mediated message. That mediation occurs in various forms: authorship, message, and history.

*Mediation of authorship* means the communication of divine will through human authors. *Mediation of message* concerns the question of the speaker of the message, as well as the author of the text. These are not always the same. For example, Jesus, the central figure of the New Testament, did not write a single book in it. Rather, He is present through the eyes and words of the four evangelists. This first type of message mediation is obvious in the way the Gospels often tell the same story about Jesus in different words. Secondly, some individual psalms are attributed to the "sons of Korah" (Pss. 84–85), making them the product of multiple human authorship. The production of other texts, like the epistles, is simpler, since one human author produces his message. What is more, the Bible is not about mere abstract ideas, but about events, experiences, and ideas that relate to God's activity or presence among people. This record of divinely directed events presents God's mediation in history. In addition, it is important to realize that this record itself is an inseparable part of the third type of mediation, the *mediation of history*. In other words, there is God's activity in history and then there is the presentation of that history through human authors. These multiple levels of mediation make discussion about meaning complex, because the various considerations described above are themselves complex and interrelated.

Such complexity should not be disturbing for it serves as the basis for the depth, beauty, and intricacy of the biblical message. The Bible becomes a beautiful tapestry with various strands of concerns woven through it. Part of that diversity emerges in the various literary means or genres the authors use to convey their message, a point to be examined later.

In addition to the complexities of a mediated message, there is the theological concept of inspiration to consider. The reality of inspiration requires that any discussion of the meaning of the biblical text brings into view multiple authors (the human and the divine), as well as the speaker or historical event associated with their message. Whose intent is to be pursued? Are they always the same?

A debate rages. Some argue that we cannot gain access to the human author, so we are left with the text God gave us. It is Scripture which is God-breathed and it is Scripture that we study, so it is Scripture's meaning that we must pursue. But those who object reply: Can a text by itself—loosed from its social, historical, and literary context—generate meaning? Does not the meaning of a text, if it is not tied to the original communication of an author, float to an audience of readers?

These deep questions have produced much discussion and cannot be reduced to an either-or choice. Author(s) and text go together. This link is important, because it asserts that we are interested not in the author's state of mind during the text's production—nor in an intention that can be reduced to a singular purpose—but in the message he sought to present in the text. It is that message the people of God ultimately received and passed on to subsequent generations. Even in a book like Hebrews or certain psalms, cases where authorship is uncertain, we have access to the author and his message in the text that was left to us. It was the desire to communicate that produced these texts, and so the starting point for interpretation is the pursuit of that message.

To deal adequately with interpretation of a mediated corpus involving multiple human authors and one divine author, three issues need attention: (1) inspired authorship, (2) the text and meaning, and (3) the reuse of texts by later human authors.

In one sense, this entire chapter and the next deal with the issue of inspired authorship, that is, God's choice to speak truthfully and authoritatively at various times within history through human agents. But it is important to consider what inspiration means practically. This can be summarized in three points.

(1) As the Word of God, the biblical text functions in a unique, privileged position. It addresses us as an exclusively authoritative text. God speaks truthfully in its message.

(2) There is design and unity in the whole. The Bible is not merely an anthology, a conflicting collection of various opinions about religious experience. Through the texts of the various authors comes the message of the living God and the accounts of how people have and can come to know Him.

(3) These texts have a message that extends beyond the original settings in which they were given. Something about what they say lives on. Their intrinsic merit has caused them to be preserved and passed on. How this works exactly is much discussed, and we cannot solve all those debates here. But interpretation of the Bible is an important task because God speaks through Scripture and its authority emerges from its connection to Him.

This leads us to the issue of the text and meaning. Some prefer to work with a distinction between meaning and significance. *Meaning* is what the author intended to say in the original setting in which his text was produced; *significance* refers to *all subsequent uses* of the text, or what E.D. Hirsch called "anachronistic meaning." In this view, all legitimate interpretation must be tied to the author's meaning, while all significance will be an implication of that meaning. There is one interpretation of that original meaning and many applications (significances). At one level, this is a helpful distinction, but its simplicity shrouds a whole series of issues when one is dealing with the description of events that are part of a mediated chain. It is correct to distinguish between what the text said to its original audience and how it continues to speak to us. But textual meaning is not really limited to reproducing what the reader thinks the author might have meant. In one sense, the determination of meaning involves this descriptive task; but in another sense, there is a difference between description and understanding. Understanding often emerges from events and their sequel, rather than being simply inherent in the events themselves. Since Scripture is about linked events and not just abstract ideas, meaning of events in texts has a dynamic, not a static, quality.

The following illustration discloses the crucial distinction between description and understanding, while revealing the dynamic, multidimensional character of each. Imagine an Australian bushman visiting the United States on election day, November 3, 1992. What he observes in a local school are many adults putting pieces of paper in a tin box. He is able to describe accurately what actions are taking place, but he does not know the meaning of what is happening. Now the citizens of the U.S. understand that what is taking place is not some strange social ritual, but an election. They have a basic understanding of the event, but even that is not all.

Later in the evening it becomes clear that Bill Clinton has won and that America has a new President. This result reflects a deeper understanding of the event than one could have had as it was taking place. The result also is, I would argue, part of the meaning of the event of voting in the 1992 U.S. general election. Meaning emerges from an event's relationship to subsequent events (the counting of the votes cast).

Now the immediate impact of this result speaks differently depending on one's point of view. The result was a cause for joy among Clinton supporters, but a cause for gloom among George Bush followers, at least initially. Subsequently some Bush supporters argued that perhaps the result was good, because it would keep Republicans from being complacent, and if the Clinton revolution failed, it would open the door for four more Republican years in 1996. This shows how the same event can speak differently, and the same is true of texts. These additional effects show how one event can yield a variety of significant, even complementary, responses.

Even at this point we are not done. What is the meaning of Clinton's election in terms of U.S. history? We can argue correctly that it ended a twelve-year reign of Republican executive government. But that is only its meaning in the very short term. It will take years to assess its real meaning (significance) historically. With a larger time frame, we can answer the question of long-term meaning of this election much better. Again, variety of opinions may emerge. Some will surely be right, others wrong, others partially right. Such is always the case in interpreting events and the factors that contribute to our understanding of them.

Now one may object that our illustration is about events and not about a text from an author, so the point does not apply. But let us imagine a commentary on the election written on

November 4, 1992. In it the author says, "The vote yesterday was a turning point in American politics." The commentator may even elaborate on reasons why this is so from the perspective of the next day's reflection on the election. Those reasons reflect what the commentator meant. But the commentary's meaning and the reasons for it may take on more depth and value as subsequent events reveal the accuracy of the commentator's remarks. A historian citing the commentary years later may note how insightful the phrase "turning point" was, even though it may be for reasons beyond those the commentator noted. Having the perspective of the advance of history in a sequence of events, the historian can comment about both the meaning of the events and the even more apt sense in which the commentator's words were true.

Such potential for development of the meaning of events and commentary about them is especially great when the events discussed are tied to promises. Since the Bible is fundamentally about promise, the linkage of events and the meaning that develops from that promise is an inherent part of its overall message. Tracing this linkage and its development is one of the major tasks of the Bible interpreter. The biblical text should be studied in the context of the development of its story and not just mined for statements isolated from the events they portray.

The point of our illustration is that *meaning of events,* like those recorded in Scripture, is part of a dynamic sequence: meaning is influenced by the sequel of events growing out of the original event, as well as by the point of view brought to it. One can appreciate the meaning of events better as one gets more time to assess the impact of those events. But—and this is a crucial point—the event can be examined from a variety of temporal points of view or angles of perspective, each of which can contribute to an appraisal of its overall meaning. In other words, an event's meaning is not one-dimensional, but rather multidimensional.

The reality of a mediated text about events and the presence of a divine author carries with it important implications for meaning in the biblical text. These factors allow a text to speak beyond its human author, so that once a text is produced, commentary on it can follow in subsequent texts. Connection to the original passage exists, but not in a way that is limited to the understanding of the original human author. The subsequent text can develop the meaning of the original text. Now it is the nature of events in sequence that gives the possibility for commentary. But it is the presence of a divine author that gives such commentary the possibility of development, because it is built upon the pattern of God's activity and the presence of design within those events. That commentary has a privileged position because of the nature of the divine author. Since a single author stands behind the various texts and human authors of Scripture, an authorial unity remains that transcends the human authors. In fact, it is this unique dynamic that allows for revelation to progress and for God's plan to be revealed in such a way that later texts recall the promises of earlier texts.

This raises a question regarding the reuse of texts. We shall look at this phenomenon more closely in the next chapter. Here we only deal with the issue of meaning and the reuse of texts. We argue on the basis of the dynamic quality of events. To reuse a text to discuss a subsequent event is to bring that text into a new context and thus add to its meaning by associating fresh levels of reference and context to the earlier text. This adds a new angle to our prism of understanding through which the text was previously seen. It may not be so much a matter of changing meaning by altering the message, as much as adding referents and context to expand the reach of the text. To add referents is to add to or develop meaning. Change can happen by addition without subtracting from or distorting meaning. In fact failure to reuse texts in this manner relegates a text to only its original setting and makes it only an historical curiosity.

Often such reuse of a text plays off an ambiguity in the original sense, allowing it to represent a range of possible meanings. For example, the use of the term "Abraham's seed" in the Bible has an ambiguity that allows it to refer to Isaac, Jacob, or Israel in Genesis, but specifically and uniquely to Jesus in Galatians. Yet even in Galatians 3, Paul turns right around after arguing for the unique role of Jesus as "Seed of Abraham" and calls all those who believe in Jesus, both Jew and Gentile, "seed." Each of those uses is context dictated and dependent. Each use also considers the usage from a certain perspective, time frame, and worldview.

Biblical authors can often reuse texts in a second way. An original event becomes the basis and pattern for a subsequent event. God acts in similar ways in different times, so that one event comes to picture and thus explain the other. The two events mirror one another in approach and so can be linked, even when some aspects of each event differ. What is shared is the essential point or parallel that is mirrored.

This involves what is often called the typology of the Bible, though it might be better to call it pattern fulfillment. Examples include the reuse of Old Testament Exodus imagery to describe a second Exodus in the Old Testament prophets, and the use of Melchizedek, the leader-king-priest, as a type of Jesus. God indwelling the temple in the Old Testament can parallel the Spirit indwelling us. Such typology may not be limited to an original event and a single later parallel, but may involve multiple points of fulfillment. New creation imagery in the New Testament looks back to motifs found in Genesis and has realization both in the new birth of salvation (2 Cor. 5:17) and in the creation of the new heaven and new earth (Rev. 21:1).

The variety of ways meaning operates and texts are reused reveals an important point. Interpretation is not a matter of seeing one rule or approach applied to every text; it involves appreciating the variety of ways in which God weaves together His message. The Bible is like a landscape of a diverse continent. Just as there are beaches, deserts, hills, plains, valleys, mountains, islands, canyons, rivers, gulfs, lakes, and oceans, so there are a myriad of ways God links together text, message, truth, and event to reveal who He is. To appreciate what one is seeing in the biblical text, it is important to understand the kind of terrain one stands on and come to appreciate the possible variety of terrain one might encounter.

To make this point about varying perspectives and the development of meaning does not mean that an infinite number of understandings of the biblical texts exists. There is such a thing as legitimate and illegitimate meaning. But there also is such a thing as complementary aspects of meaning, where an additional angle on the text reveals an additional element of its message or a fresh way of relating the parts of a text's message.

So how do we deal with the Bible's authority? How do we handle its variety and depth?

***The Text and Readers, Part 1.*** A crucial premise of interpretation is that the Bible is designed to challenge us and our

68

worldview. That premise manifests itself in five different ways.

*First,* the Bible has a privileged position as it addresses us. Its divine quality means that it speaks with authority to the people of God across the ages. Its ability to address the ages does not mean that we simply bring texts directly into our world, because some teaching is context-limited. This context limitation may indicate that a given passage, written and intended only for a fixed time period, applies only in certain settings. For instance, Old Testament laws related to sacrifices, unclean food, or mildew illustrate that not everything in Scripture is intended to be carried out for all time. But even when the law no longer applies, it still can instruct us. In 1 Corinthians 8–10 Paul's discussion of meat and idols or of the lessons of the Exodus reveals how laws or events long past can continue to enlighten us. Determining when such limitations apply and how they are signaled is part of the more advanced study of Scripture. Such discussions are usually difficult for us, but they must be pursued in order to avoid making the Bible say more than God intends.

Other qualities of the text emerge from its privileged position. It not only informs us; it calls us. The Scripture desires our response, not just our understanding. As it challenges us, it brings us to reflection. If the Scripture is not causing us to reexamine ourselves and our relationship to the world, it probably is not being read properly. But the divine quality of the text and its complexity also give it an air of mystery. We should be slow to believe that we have figured everything out down to the last dotted "i."

A *second* issue the reality of a privileged text raises is the role of the Spirit. Some would challenge the call to humility in reading Scripture by arguing that the Spirit shows us what the text means. He is our teacher. But when two "Spirit-instructed interpreters" argue for mutually exclusive positions, a problem arises. Who brings the correct message taught by the Spirit, and how do we decide? We would argue that this question emphasizes the Spirit's teaching work at the wrong place, by stressing understanding of content. John 14–16 describes the work of the Paraclete as a ministry of convicting the world and instructing the saints through encouragement. In other words, the Spirit works in our hearts to convict us of the truth of what we read in Scripture and to encourage us with regard to how we apply what is said. There is a difference between *understanding* what the Gospel says and *accepting* it. Those who crucified Jesus understood His claims, but they rejected Him as not being from God. Our contention would be that the Spirit is primarily concerned with our responsiveness. The advantage of seeing the Spirit in this way is that it broadens the scope of reading by emphasizing the issue of response.

*Third* comes the issue of certainty and clarity in understanding the Bible as it challenges us. Given the complex depth of Scripture, the numerous points of judgment that apply to interpreting it, and the limitations we bring to the task, it is wise to recognize levels of certainty in our understanding. In calling for such an attitude, the issue is not a problem with the text or with its truthfulness, since this is a divinely inspired text. Nor is there a denial that there is such a thing as legitimate meaning for the text. The problem is realizing honestly our limitations in perceiving that truth. In recognition of our limitations, we should rank our perceptions about the text. The famous doctrine of the "clarity of Scripture" was applied by the Reformers to the central portions of its message, not to every detail of doctrine. The Apostles' Creed mentions only the most fundamental doctrines of the faith. It does not take a very careful reader to understand that God is the Creator to whom all people are accountable, that the Bible condemns sin, that it calls all people sinners, and that it presents Jesus, the Son of God, as the solution to the problem of sin. But many other matters are much discussed. There is value in ranking our level of certainty about what Scripture teaches.

Practically speaking, a scale of four categories is helpful. First are those things about which there is no doubt: the most basic fundamentals of the faith. These are matters of absolute conviction. Second are those matters where we are aware there are differences of opinion, but about which one is pretty certain of the preferred view. We would describe one's view here as a firm conviction. A third category is another case where there is a difference of opinion, but this time the feeling is that when God brings us to heaven, we may find out the other person was right. This category we would call a soft conviction. Last are those areas where we might as well flip a coin, because none of us really knows. This would be genuine uncertainty. The value of such a reading of the text is that it helps us focus on the major issues of Scripture, while being sensitive to our own limits as we examine the text. Such categories also may facilitate discussion as we consider our differences with one another.

The *fourth* point concerns the text's ability to challenge us and develops the previous category. We can always know better. The Bible is so deep that it can always make us reflect more about our worldview and our relationship to God. To feel otherwise is to argue that we possess all truth and that there is nothing left for God to teach us. It is to make ourselves into the canon.

*Fifth*, and last, are two dangers associated with interpretation—making the Bible say either too much or too little. Both errors are dangerous. Picture a scale. On one end where the Bible says too little, there results an open-ended pluralism which treats all truth as relative; on the other end, there is a type of pharisaism that has rules and doctrines for every situation with little room for much discussion about any aspect of life. Care should be exercised not to move too far in either direction.

In sum, the Bible possesses truth, has a privileged position, and is capable of speaking for itself by challenging us to see the world and ourselves differently. Our sitting before the Scripture in subjection means that both humility and transformation are attitudes to which we are committed as God seeks to call us to deepen our relationship to Him. It is the Spirit's job to convict us, and our calling is to instruct, rebuke, and encourage one another in the task, but to do so with humility and love as we discuss what the Bible means. This corporate responsibility to one another raises the issues of tradition and community.

**Readers and Worldviews, Part 2.** Another aspect of how we approach the text is the way our tradition—or often better, our sub-tradition—functions for our understanding. Interpretation is never really an individual affair, since we all are called to function in the context of community. Each of us enters community by joining different bodies, which themselves are affiliated with distinct theological traditions. Such traditions frame how we ask questions of a text. Tradition in this sense is valuable, because it helps provide perspective and a grid for understanding. Serving as a guide, and often reflecting the collective judgment of many believers over time or within a locale, a tradition gives identity and can provide an additional basis for unity. Tradition can also operate as a potential check against individual idiosyncrasies in interpretation, but it should not be an all-ruling tyrant.

There is a limit to the value and authority of tradition. A tradition is not to be equated with the authority of Scripture. It is not canon. This means that it too should be subject to Scripture. Some aspects of tradition are really matters of corporate preference, rather than something required by the Bible. And being comfortable in our community often includes matters of personal preference and taste.

The first church one of us interned in had just built a new building. The members fought for a while over the color of the carpet in the new sanctuary. Those who preferred symbolism lobbied for a red carpet, while those leaning in an aesthetic direction opted for blue. It was a debate about preference, not Scripture. Many areas we discuss operate at this level. We know of no text that clearly tells us what beat of music or what kind of instruments should be in church, yet we know of many communities that struggle over the music in the service and the perceptions associated with musical choice. These are usually debates over tradition, associations, and/or taste. Differences in doctrine are usually not so clear, but the principle remains. Tradition, though it impacts us significantly, should only be authoritative (versus merely preferred) when it reflects Scripture. This raises the issue of the testing of understanding and tradition, since sub-traditions do differ with one another about how a text is understood.

There are three elements to the testing of any view or any tradition. *First,* it needs to reflect the particulars of the text. Such reading also involves judgment, since interpretation is often a matter of deciding which meaning is more possible. To establish that a reading of the text is possible is not the same as showing that it is the most likely way to read a text. *Second,* it should be comprehensive in scope. That means that it is able to explain in a more satisfactory way than other options all the texts related to the topic. Usually if I read a text and have the feeling, "I wish this text were not here," then that means that there may be something about the way I put a doctrine together that needs attention. *Third,* there should be consistency in how the parts fit together. We will later return to the topic of the various ways texts can be related to one another. Sometimes discussion exists because different judgments are made about consistency.

Two issues often applied to such disputes need some attention. One frequent rule used to adjudicate disputes is called the "analogy of Scripture." It argues that clear texts should interpret obscure texts. Though a good rule, its application can be problematic, since clarity is often seen through the eye of the beholder. The rule, when misapplied, can flatten out texts so that they mean the same thing when perhaps their relationship is more complex.

For example, one might argue that, because Jesus is clearly the "Son of God" in terms of being God incarnate in the Gospel of John, every text that mentions the "Son of God" in the other Gospels should be read in this full sense. The clear, full text interprets the more uncertain text. But many passages in the synoptics use "Son of God" as a regal title to refer to how Jesus functions, rather than highlighting what His person is. The result of this misapplication is the reduction of the scope of the Bible's teaching about the Son.

Another problem occurs when one correlates a text that states an idea absolutely with another text that seems to offer a qualification. Two approaches to such texts are possible. One can argue that the absolute statement controls, so that one finds a meaning for the qualified text that shows it is not really an exception at all. Or one can treat the qualification as exactly that, a limitation on when the absolute statement applies.

An example of this problem is the debate surrounding the "exception" clauses on divorce in Matthew and the dispute about what immorality in these verses means (5:32; 19:9). Some, emphasizing the absolute statement, argue that the exception is not really an exception at all, but rather an historical reference to Herod's incestuous marriage outlawed by Scripture elsewhere, so that there was never any real marriage. Usually, appeals to consistency with the unqualified texts in Mark 10:11-12 and Luke 16:18 are made on behalf of this view, as well as to the practical simplicity of holding to a no-divorce view. Others, taking the second approach, argue that Jesus forbids divorce except where sexual immorality of various sorts has occurred. In such cases, divorce is permitted. In other words, the exception in Matthew is a limitation on the other passages in Mark and Luke, where no exceptions are noted. This position appeals to the common meaning of "immorality" in other contexts and also mentions how Paul seems to allow another exception in the case of desertion by an unbeliever in 1 Corinthians 7. This second view argues: if Jesus really held to no exceptions elsewhere, then how could Paul add one here? Jesus must have allowed an exception for Paul to add one.

Our goal is not to resolve this particular dispute, but simply to point out two distinct ways in which these texts can be related to one another as one discusses consistency. The resolution becomes a discussion about which approach *does a better job* of accurately relating the particulars, which best handles all the texts, and which is more consistent. Evaluative judgments are made all along the way. It will help us as a community to recognize that such judgments are being made in disputes like this.

The differences between traditions often revolve around how the various parts of the text are put together. Such differences require our attention and discussion, while also raising the question of how we listen to texts as part of various communities.

***The Text and Readers, Part 2.*** Community is healthy because it can cause each individual to examine one's own views and correct perspectives. In addition, sometimes differences in perspective are a matter of what angle is being taken in asking the question. Some disputes are a matter of genuine difference, but others, we suggest, are a matter of differing emphasis about which angle is being used to assess the question. Sometimes open discussion between communities can help each appreciate aspects of scriptural emphasis in a way they would not have considered otherwise. They still may end up with some disagreement about the relative emphasis between how the parts are related, but they also, as a result of their dialogue, may clarify where they agree, may move closer to one another, or may determine more precisely where and why their differences exist.

Interpretation of difficult texts often has a multidimensional feature. Sometimes a given tradition looks at the question from one angle only. A look at the text from another perspective may open up possibilities or allow for a fresh correlation of texts. Just as the effectiveness of instant replay in the NFL was a matter of looking at the play from the right angle or combination of angles, so also in reading the text we may improve our understanding of it by looking at it from a variety of angles. Sometimes the dialogue between traditions or between communities can help us look at texts from different angles.

We have spent a long time discussing how we approach the text and what influences that approach. The interaction of the author, the text, and its reader(s), along with the text's and the reader(s)' worldviews represented in the text and by the reader(s) impacts our understanding of the text. We have observed how we understand and the various factors that contribute to how we see texts. In the end, our approach to the text must be text-based; it must attempt to let the text speak. To be text-based members of God's community will mean dialogue between ourselves and the text and between ourselves and others. No interpreter should be an island unto him- or herself. We must approach the text in humility so it can challenge us. Sometimes that challenge to our understanding comes from others' insights into the text or from their questioning our interpretation of the text. As we embrace the text's message with humility, we will develop sensitive conviction about the truth. But we must always have an awareness of our limitations in understanding that truth, so that we have a sense of the level of conviction and clarity with which we perceive a particular truth.

# Chapter Three
# Interpreting the Bible—
# How Texts Speak to Us

O ne major aspect of the problem of defining 'literal' is that in many instances words, but not sentences, have a literal or normal meaning. Moreover, for both words and sentences context is all-important in determining meaning at any given point in an act of communication. What contexts are to be looked at, and how they are to be looked at, in the determination of meaning is very important," notes covenant theologian Vern S. Poythress.[1]

Evangelical theology has always discussed the principles by which we interpret the Bible. As a community, we share a heritage that takes the divine message of the Bible seriously. If evangelicals were asked what method of hermeneutics they use, they might reply in a variety of ways. The average believer might say that he or she reads the Bible "in a plain or normal way, as I would any book, but recognizing that God is its ultimate author." Others might say that they read it for "what it means to me." But to be done well, what would such a reading involve? Some theologians would respond that they use the "historical-grammatical method." In fact, evangelical scholars have been comfortable for some time describing their approach to interpretation as the historical-grammatical method. It means pursuing initially the meaning of the author/Author as expressed in the text with a sensitivity to its original textual setting. It means that reading for what it means to me may miss what the text meant and means. But what exactly does such a reading involve?

We will survey this approach in three categories: (1) the historical, (2) the grammatical, and (3) the literary-theological. These are three components in assembling the portrait of the meaning of Scripture, and we will examine them in three distinct subsections. Again we break up into pieces what is really an interactive, dynamic process. Think of these three sections as separate overlays that together form a picture on an overhead. This reflects the multidimensional aspect of interpretation. First, the historical level seeks to be sensitive to the message as it came to its initial audience, understanding original terms and ideas. Second, the grammatical level considers how the terminology of that message is laid out. Terms are not understood in isolation from each other but in conjunction with one another. Third, the literary-theological level highlights the fact that there is an abiding message and unity in the text, which is laid out literarily in various ways called genres. Each genre presents truth in its own way and makes unique demands for how it should be read. Reading the Bible requires an awareness of the changing nature of the terrain within the text, as well as an appreciation of the various angles used to present the truth.

A closing subsection will consider how to relate different texts to one another, by discussing the various ways the Bible interrelates passages. The category of prophecy and fulfillment receives special attention. What emerges is what we will call the "historical-grammatical-literary-theological" method. This fourfold description of hermeneutics is really what most mean when they speak simply of the historical-grammatical method. Though differences exist in how to apply the method to individual texts, there is agreement that this is the most appropriate approach to use in interpreting and understanding texts. So what is involved in this method?

## Painting the Backdrop: Historical Interpretation

The first context of interpretation is the historical one. Communication never occurs in a vacuum. A message utilizes categories of understanding the author shares with the audience. Even if the author is seeking to create new categories of understanding for his audience, the road taken to achieve this new understanding requires rearranging old categories or making fresh associations that break old barriers of understanding. For the reader, the degree of understanding the text depends in part on sharing with the author a network of background information. This includes ancient social norms, cultural expectations, historical and geographical facts, as well as a comprehension of the communication's literary form.

Sometimes the Bible is unclear to us because we do not share enough of this background information to appreciate the text. We may be unaware of how an ancient person might have felt about certain things. Because access to such data can be difficult, it is often the case that a layperson hopes the preacher or Bible teacher will supply any important background, so that the text might be clearer. This problem of "historical distance" can be a major hurdle to grasping the text's message.

Some attempt to overcome this hurdle by simply relating the text to present experience. The false assumption is that attitudes, expectations, customs, and worldviews will match across twenty or more centuries, that the biblical world is exactly like the modern world. To say as much is not to deny the possibility of common bonds between the two periods; both then and today, people experience the ebb and flow of life. We should attempt to identify with the biblical characters because we all are human, but we must be careful not to assume what is true of our customs and feelings was true of theirs.

How can we comprehend those aspects of the biblical world that strike us as so foreign when we first encounter them? How can one enter a time machine in order to traverse the vast gulf back to ancient time and perspectives?

First, we must recognize that we have incomplete access to the biblical world, because our knowledge is often limited to ancient artifacts and writings that represent only a small portion of what once existed. In one sense, we can never entirely overcome this problem of distance. We can never understand the ancient world exactly as ancient people did. But despite that limitation, we do possess a vast array of materials that show us how life was lived and help us draw closer to that world. They name, picture, describe, or reflect major historical events, ancient categories of thinking, along with ancient customs and religious ideas.

In the following discussion, we will focus on literary remains. Some of these details are present in the Bible itself, but many of them are contained in extrabiblical texts. Jewish historians, like Josephus and Philo, retell the story of Genesis through Malachi in a way that lets us see how some educated first-century Jews read many scriptural texts. Josephus even goes on to detail what happened in Israel from the end of that period to A.D. 70. Texts on Jewish religious customs and respected teachings on wisdom and religious life exist in collections known as the Old Testament Apocrypha and Pseudepigrapha. In the famous Dead Sea Scrolls of Qumran, we learn about the views and practices of a separatist Jewish community. These texts show us both the unity and variety of thought in first-century Judaism. The rabbinic rules of everyday life for the Judaism of the second century A.D. are found in the Mishnah, but some of these rules probably go back to the time of Jesus and the apostles. In addition, numerous Greco-Roman works reveal how those outside of Judaism lived in this period. Numerous documents from the various Ancient Near Eastern cultures tell us about the Sumerians, Egyptians, Assyrians, Babylonians, and other ancient ethnic groups and so illuminate details in the Old Testament.

All of the documents above reveal how the ancients lived and how they looked at the world. They did not see their world the same way. In fact, the rich diversity of ancient life at all levels is evident in these texts. Such works are not authoritative truth, but they do describe ancient life and perspective. They help form the backdrop for certain ideas referred to in the Bible. Those engaged in serious study of the Bible can benefit from learning about some of these sources and how to use them. All of us can come to appreciate how they help to open up the way people lived and thought in the ancient world.

Two examples can illustrate how this material enables us to appreciate better the message of the Bible. The first is the statement that Herod is a "fox" in Luke 13:32. In current English colloquial usage the normal figurative meaning of this term has nothing to do with a male; it refers to a female. Whatever Herod is, he is not that kind of "fox"! But even the second contemporary option refers to one who is crafty. This also is the meaning in some ancient Greek texts and in the Fathers (Plutarch, *Solon* 30.2; Dio Chrysostom in *Discourses* 74.15). However, another common ancient meaning is that a "fox" is one that destroys or is a scavenger (Song 2:15; Lam. 5:17-18; Ezek. 13:4; 1 Enoch 89:10, 42-49, 55). This meaning of destroyer fits well with the context of Luke 13, where the issue is the attempt of Herod to destroy Jesus. This is an example of where historical figurative usage coheres nicely in the context. Of course, the best ancient evidence is that which is contemporary to or is sure to predate the event being studied. It's also crucial that any extrabiblical text the interpreter might use be close to the biblical text in terms of cultural contact. Sensitivity to date and connection can keep one from making hasty associations.

A second example is the Parable of the Good Samaritan. The title even subverts the effect of the passage in its original historical context. The parable is well known. A man is overrun by robbers and left for dead. Of the three men who could help, only one does. The priest and the Levite pass on the other side of the road, while the Samaritan stops and helps the man. This is why the parable is named what it is.

But a study of ancient Judaism would show that this is precisely contrary to ancient expectation. In its original context, this story would have been shocking, since Samaritans were regarded with disdain as half-breeds, while priests and Levites were held in high regard as pious and righteous. This view of Samaritans is clear both from a text like John 4 and in the descriptions of Josephus (*Antiquities* 9.288-92; 11.340; 12.257) and the Apocrypha.

In fact, the intertestamental apocryphal Jewish work Sirach reads, "Two nations my soul detests, and the third is not even a people: Those who live in Seir and the Philistines, and the foolish people who live in Shechem" (50:25-26). The verbal insult of this ancient historical remark is unclear if one does not know ancient geography. Shechem is located next to Mount Gerizim, which is where the Samaritans worshiped and gave sacrifice to Yahweh rather than in Jerusalem. The Samaritans' distinct locale for worship and different customs resulted in strong Jewish rejection. So Sirach's attitude is that Samaritans are "not even a people." Yet it is this "nonperson" who is the example of a neighbor according to Jesus. Two thousand years of public relations on this parable has taken some of the sting from its original meaning. Jesus' story will never shock us as it did the first-century hearers. But reflection on the ancient background will help us not only see that Jesus is exhorting His listeners to be good neighbors, but realize that sometimes neighbors come in surprising dress.

But historical reading also means not being anachronistic in our approach to the text. We should be careful not to attribute to the understanding of the recipients of the text a concept that only emerges later. An example here is Genesis 3:15, what some call the "first hint of the Gospel," the protoevangelium. This understanding argues that God predicts that Eve's seed, Jesus, will crush the Serpent, Satan. Now in the context of the development of the theme of Adam's seed in the Bible, this meaning does eventually emerge from the text and is a legitimate reading of the passage. However, it is too specific for the original audience of Genesis. First of all, the early Jewish readers of the text could never have known that Messiah's name would be Jesus. What is more, in the context of the Pentateuch, the coming of a regal figure for the nation of Israel is at best only alluded to as a minor point (Gen. 49:10). Third, the specific identification of the serpent with Satan is not transparent within the Pentateuch. All these connections emerge only later in the Scripture.

So what did the text originally mean? It simply pointed to the introduction of chaos into the creation as a result of sin. Nature would now be in conflict with man. A snake, now limited by God's curse to crawl on the ground, would nip at man's heel. Meanwhile, as man attempted to defend himself, he would seek to crush the head of the serpent. Of course, this emphasis fits with the message of Genesis, explaining why God raised up Israel—a nation of grace and promise—through whom He would bless all nations. Such a message also prepares for the New Testament point of the reversal of Adam's work in the second Adam, Jesus Christ.

The point is that historically sensitive study in the Old Testament can open up additional teaching beyond issues highlighted in the New Testament's teaching about the Old. Though the New Testament develops Old Testament teaching as divine history moves on, one should not lose the teaching of the Old in the process. So historical sensitivity serves as an important potential backdrop for interpretation, but the central pieces of the portrait come from the text—the grammatical and literary contexts of the message.

## Assembling the Pieces: Grammatical Interpretation

The second context for interpretation is the combination of expression and words woven together through sentences and paragraphs. Notice that we did not speak of words alone, because words in isolation do not carry meaning, only possible meanings. The word "gross" can mean many things, depending on whether teenagers, business partners, or order forms are present. Someone has said that words are like a game of chess. They take on their sense and importance from the other words to which they are linked. A pawn is generally an insignificant chess piece, but put it in a certain position on the board and it is the most important. Words are like that, and their grammatical-literary context means almost everything. One should work through texts with special attention to the relationship of the terms to other terms in the sentence and paragraph. In addition, attention has to be paid to the work as a whole, its historical setting, and the genre of the passage. We will return later to the importance of a text's literary nature, but now we focus on terms.

Even nuances of words can shift as context shifts. A patriot as a historical term for an American revolutionary is a positive term, but speak of a German patriot in Nazi Germany who was loyal to Hitler and the nuance changes significantly. Finally, mention the term Patriot with reference to the recent Gulf War and one is not speaking of a person, but of a missile. So texts referring to an American patriot, the German Nazi patriot, or the Patriot missile will bear different meanings because of their limiting and identifying contexts. This shows how flexible terms are and how central context is for determining meaning, which, in most settings, is not random. In other words, one does not count how often a word is used in a particular way, but asks if that meaning is most appropriate in the context which is being studied. One looks for the background and concepts with which the terms being studied are associated.

Now in determining meaning there can be both accuracy and distortion in perception. If we say to you, "We have a cat," you will picture an animal that is not a dog, bat, mouse, or monkey. But you may also conceive of it as an alley cat, a Persian, or a tabby. Now you have made more of our remark than we wanted to communicate, or we may have given too little information to reveal all my remark intended to suggest. But to get our point at its most basic level, only the first set of discriminations of meaning was necessary. A general understanding of the meaning of cat is good enough, though the detail of the more specific meaning may represent a type of distortion of our sense. Someone who knew us well would know that we have a gray alley cat. They would know immediately all we may have implied and not only would appreciate the basic sense but also could supply additional detail. Our point is that often we can get a general sense of a text's teaching, but the better awareness we have to the appropriate background of the communication, the more detail we may be able to appreciate. As we sensitively incorporate more context, our understanding can deepen.

On the other hand, a general rule of interpretation is that one should not make a technical term out of a word unless the context points to such a force. Less specific meaning is usually more accurate than reading too much into a term, especially when one is historically distanced from a text.

Our cat illustration reveals other features of interpretation. The cat illustration has the advantage of allowing us, the authors, to explain to you, the reader, what we were trying to communicate. However, some degree of distortion of meaning is inevitable in the interpretation of ancient texts. We cannot ask those human writers what was meant. In fact, often a writer is not aware of all the factors that contribute to the writing and choice of terms. These factors mean there is a provisional character to all interpretation no matter how careful we are.

But this provisionalism need not result in relativity. Some distortions of meaning are trivial, while others matter a great deal. Those who understood we meant "cat" and not dog, but pictured a tabby in their mind, were not really harmed by the incorrect detail, since all we desired to communicate was the basic identity of the pet. On the other hand, had someone understood we had a bat, not a cat, they may have been unwilling to visit! In texts, the only way an interpreter can sort out understanding or the degree of potential distortion is to pay close attention to other terms in the context to confirm or further clarify a reading. If we mention fur or that a pet goes "meow," the other clues of the context confirm one identification over another. Where such additional confirmation is lacking and the disputed term is vague, care should be taken not to get too specific.

Two other features about words are important. Some words are obscure, others are broad, while others are quite precise. The Bible often uses broad terms or words, which can be referred to with more specificity or can take on additional representations as the concept is repeated later in Scripture. A great illustration of this is the concept of the servant. In Isaiah 49:3 the servant is called Israel, but in Isaiah 53, he is described with the traits of an individual. The New Testament also plays on this ambiguity. In Luke 1:54, Israel is the servant, but in Acts 8:32-33, the servant is tied to Jesus. Finally, in Acts 13:47, Paul and Barnabas describe their mission in terms of the servant by citing Isaiah 49:6. The servant figure describes various representatives of God. It is not one person but several, though one—Jesus—is a particularly key aspect of fulfillment for the term. He is its realization in a way others are not. Note how each context reveals the diversity in the usage. One context does not guarantee or dictate how the term is used in another context, though it may help to explain the relationship between the various uses.

In fact, there is also an ancient historical concept at work in this theme as well. It is the idea of the "one representing the many" or "the many in the one." Jesus as servant can be seen as the servant par excellence, a faithful, individual representative of what the nation Israel had been called to be. In turn, Paul and Barnabas can be seen to be "in Jesus" and thus take on a servant role like His. We have similar figures today as when the president speaks for all of his country's citizens or when a team of lawyers speak for one client.

A second characteristic of terms is that the same idea can be said in different ways. Biblical concepts or themes often involve more than one term. So to limit looking for a concept by looking for the presence of a specific term can often result in underdeveloping the theme in Scripture. An example is that Jesus as Lord (Acts 2:30-36) and Jesus as Head (Eph. 1:19-23) are two ways to portray Jesus' ruling authority over the church. Both titles are associated with imagery from Psalm 110:1, which is a regal (or royal) psalm. Note how in this example, the presence of imagery about being exalted and seated at God's right hand (Ps. 110:1) helps to fill out the portrait of a "head" (a regal, ruling image). To talk about Jesus' kingship or lordship includes discussing His headship. In fact, Paul may have chosen to use the term "head" to avoid confusion in Greek contexts in which he preached about what kind of ruler Jesus was as He sat at God's right hand. Here historical background study and the study of how a term is used may help us be sensitive to the reason for such usage. Putting all the elements together, the imagery suggests that Jesus transcended the political rule of Rome. In fact, Jesus said as much in John 18:36, when He declared, "My kingdom is not of this world." That was because His kingdom is the kingdom of God. Or, as Jesus said elsewhere, "Render therefore to Caesar the things that are Caesar's, and to God the things that are God's" (Matt. 22:21, RSV). Whatever type of rule Jesus possessed, it did not represent a current, direct threat to Roman rule. Its reach into people's lives went beyond political authority by heading for the heart. Historical features set the backdrop that are a context for interpretation, while words in their grammatical context reveal the pieces of the puzzle. One factor remains to be considered. One must put the pieces together in light of the whole, both in terms of the variety of literary genre used to present the biblical message, as well as the theological unity of that message. So we turn to the literary-theological aspect of reading.

## Unifying Message and Story: Literary-Theological

*Be Genre Sensitive.* The study of genre moves us into the area of interpretation that helps us unify the pieces of the message, even though that unity is achieved through the use of a wide variety of literary means. We can recognize these genres because we can also see them in the larger ancient world as well. One should think of this aspect of interpretation as being like the Olympics, a grand occasion made up of a variety of sports. Though it is all sport, each game is played by its own rules and has its own expectations about how to play the game. The variety of literature is the same way. It all has a message, but it conveys that message in a variety of ways and with a variety of expectations. To try to play basketball with soccer's rules will never work, though both use a ball and require foot speed. Or think of musical instruments, they all make music, but in different ways with different sounds. One cannot play the violin like a piano or drums; nor should one expect a violin to sound like either a piano or the kettledrum! In the same way, to read the poetry of the Psalms like a historical book is to miss the emotional and pictorial impact of the message, though both genres convey reality about people's experience with God. To transform the imagery and setting of the Psalter into mere theological proposition is also to take the passion and lifeblood out of its veins.

We will briefly survey the six major genres of the Bible to try to point out their dominant characteristics. Each one tells the biblical story in its own way. By story we mean the presentation of events, pictures, and/or ideas about God and humanity in an organized sequence. The point is: be genre sensitive as you study the text.

**1. *Theological narrative.*** Here we refer to the historical books of the Old and New Testaments—Genesis through Esther and Matthew through Acts. These books tell a *story with plot about events*. They discuss events which involve God's interaction with humanity. But they do so with themes, characters, an unfolding story line, and conflict. These elements all interact with each other to make up the story and provide contact with life. The characters often represent not just individuals in history but types of people. The story itself is usually centered around promises or hope that people have in their relationship with God. Conflict arises because an obstacle gets in the way of that hope. Interaction between character, plot, and conflict surfaces themes and lessons about walking with God. A theological narrative is more than a collection of past events and facts. It is the story of people's lives expressed in terms of hope and disappointment.

For all the triumph of the Exodus, there is a tragic note to the end of Moses' life, since he is not able to enter the Promised Land at the end of the Pentateuch. The hope of reaching the land lives on and the story continues in Joshua, but there is a note of pain as disobedience prevents Moses from sharing in the moment of triumph. All he gets is a glimpse of its reality. Disobedience often cheats us of a fuller experience of promise. Here is a major lesson of the narrative in terms of life, but there are others as well. Though we have a wonderful taste of God's involvement now, it is but a glimpse of what we often could have if our obedience were more complete. Moses also came to realize that in God's plan, he was but a table setter. Others would experience the fullness of God's promise in ways he would not. But he came to be content in the wonderful servant role God had called him to have.

Subgenres within narrative literature include miracle accounts, parables, and discourse material. They too have their own ways in which they should be read. Miracles also have a representative quality by picturing within the event the power of God over forces that oppose humanity (Luke 5:17-26; 11:14-23). Parables often picture through stories theological truth or ways to live (Luke 10:25-37; 15:1-32; 16:1-13). Discourses can be read more like epistles, the communication of teaching in logical sequence, though even within this subgenre there can be the heavy use of figures and imagery.

**2. Poetic literature.** The poetical books and some portions of the prophets are theological song. It is *story from the heart.* Hymnic material is less frequent in the New Testament, but some does exist (e.g., Luke 1:68-79). This is story with emotions worn on the sleeve. Psalms picture events that become representative to the reader. Though a reader's experience differs from the psalmist in detail, he or she still can identify with the hymn's attempt to communicate one's experience and emotions before God.

It is important to recognize the representative quality of this material. Such literature often had a concrete setting in the life of the psalmist. What is interesting is that the language is often so symbolic that we cannot be sure of the details of that experience. But the mere placing of the psalm into the Psalter (or into the Bible for other hymns) demonstrates that the people of God recognized that what is expressed here is something all God's people could share in and identify with. Whether in praise, pain, or both, the psalmist's experience, often unknown to us, can still be shared and taught. Through the combination of emotions and theological reflection comes understanding.

Most of the psalms are "laments," where the pain of disappointment in life pierces the heart. The psalmist verbalizes the pain and the anger before realizing that God does care about, and is sovereign over, these events. Other psalms, "songs of praise," are outright acclamations of God, pure joy in a high octave. Still others, "regal psalms," reveal promises about the king of Israel and express the hope that he will be all that God promised. The unique realization of this ideal kingship comes in Jesus Christ in the context of His two comings. Other psalms, "psalms of the righteous sufferer," depict the suffering of the people of God or an individual at the hands of those who reject God. Here again the psalms portray the heart of a certain kind of person. Once more as well, Jesus becomes in the New Testament an example of the "righteous sufferer" par excellence, and by doing so models our walk in the midst of a hostile world.

In sum, the psalms come in various subtypes (or "forms"), the understanding of which helps to reveal the message. But one should never ignore the emotion that comes in its graphic imagery. It is that element, along with the possibility of identifying with the psalmist, that gives the psalms their power. To interpret sensitively is to explain the imagery and to retain a sense of its emotion.

*3. Wisdom literature.* This genre's texts, like Proverbs, Ecclesiastes, and James, contain short sayings of generalized approaches to life, *story in generality.* They often are not designed to be understood as true in every particular moment, since some proverbs are internally in tension (Prov. 26:4-5). But they do serve, again often through emotively driven pictures, to motivate one to live with a sense of responsibility and accountability before God. Wisdom calls the reader to avoid the traps that often lead into destructive relationships and ways of living. It can be helpful to trace a particular theme through the book, rather than to focus on one proverb at a time, in order to appreciate the breadth and variety of advice on a theme. Thus one can examine with profit the wise man, the fool, money, labor, and the lazy. Or one can examine the seductions of sin with profit by collecting all the references to the theme and then considering each one in turn. Often these proverbs are contextless. That is, the proverb before or after it is not relevant to its meaning. Such detached proverbs are more profitably studied as collected clusters on the same theme, than within a flow of a literary context.

*4. Prophetic literature.* The Old Testament prophets and prophetic sections of other books are not primarily prediction, though there is some. Rather, they are *story of confrontation and fresh perspective.* They are designed to subvert spiritual complacency and declare accountability to God, while affirming the presence, promise, and judgment of God. The prophets set forth an image of a different world order from the one the people of God currently experience. In doing so, they remind the people that God is in control, that judgment will come to the unrighteous, and that God holds all accountable for how they live and treat others. In this genre, rebuke and exhortation dominate. The prophets rely heavily on symbolic imagery to make their points. Such imagery makes the prophets difficult to read if one does not appreciate the background of the metaphors. Their message appeals for righteous character and warns of the consequences for relating to others unjustly. At the heart of their preaching is the revelation of divine values and virtues. Thus the prophets also drive for the heart and shun the importance of rules or routine, opting to look instead at motive. As with the Psalms and poetic literature, lessons for the modern reader here are not necessarily found by paralleling the particular circumstances the prophet addresses, but in considering the attitudes that are displayed in the midst of such events.

**5. Epistolary literature.** This genre of the New Testament is *story with explanation,* or teaching discourse. Like the discourse sections in a narrative, the epistle is the most explicitly propositional of all the genres. Whereas the message of non-discourse sections in narrative emerges through characters, plot, conflict, dialogue, and interaction, here the teaching is expressed more directly. Often these letters provide the most natural reading for us, if we understand most of the theological terminology used. It is amazing to read these letters and realize that they were originally addressed to everyday people, not theologians. Of course, in the case of Paul's letters, his audience often had the advantage of having heard him teach and preach on these themes, so they knew the force of his terms, including the technical ones. Still, we read in 2 Peter 3:16 that Paul's letters are often hard to understand.

In sorting out the use of terms in this genre, it is often important to stay within the usage of the given human author being studied before considering how other authors use a term. For example, Paul's use of *righteousness* in his epistles is often limited to what theologians describe as the doctrine of justification, or God's declaring us righteous through the work of Christ in response to faith, or to what many people call "getting saved." But in Matthew the term *righteousness* means the display of righteousness in our actions, or what theologians label "ethical righteousness." Such ethical righteousness has nothing to do with getting saved, but rather has to do with the response to God's grace. The example is a reminder and variation of a point made earlier: terms are determined by their context. In this material it is the meaning of terms and the grammatical-syntactical relationships between sentences that bear a great deal of the burden in interpretation.

**6. Apocalyptic literature.** Found in Daniel, Revelation, portions of Zechariah and Isaiah, along with portions of Jesus' eschatological discourses (Matt. 24–25; Mark 13; Luke 17:20-37; 21:5-38), this genre is by far the most cryptic in the Bible. This is *story which views the present through the lens of heavenly perspective, conflict in the world, the future, and end times.* Apocalyptic is forward-looking literature, penetrating the corridors of time and eternity through visions, dreams, and journeys into the counsels of the heavens. It is heavily symbolic literature, which is why its force is often so debated. This literature deals with the basic conflict between God and the world, but also comforts those in suffering by reminding them that one day God will restore righteousness and order to the earth. Because of the difficulty of its imagery, and its relevance to the wider topic of this book, we will discuss this genre in some detail.

In the Book of Revelation, much of the imagery echoes concepts presented in the Old Testament. In fact, though no verse in Revelation appears with an introductory formula marking its wording as from the Old Testament, allusions to ancient Scripture can be found many times on any page. These allusions convey a link to Old Testament teaching and hope, which serves to underline the perception that Revelation details the climactic chapter of the story of the promise of God.

To argue that apocalyptic literature is heavily symbolic is not to argue that it is non-referential. There is a reality present in the imagery, even though that imagery may seem strange. In fact, one of the many points of unusual imagery (like the blood-drinking harlot riding a seven-headed monster in Revelation 17) is to communicate graphically through pictures. The image of the harlot and monster portrays the grotesqueness of the sinful world system which Revelation condemns. It reveals that this system horrifically stands opposed to God and will manifest itself eventually in a worldwide rebellion against God's people. Its presence necessitates Christ's return, which will bring about its fall. The picture is supposed to yield a response like, "what an ugly looking scene! Who would want any association with her?" This scene portrays the death of believers. How will God react? He will react by crushing her in judgment.

Commentators debate about how to understand apocalyptic images, what they represent, and how they relate exactly to future events. Some attempt to explain the text by using the method of "literal interpretation." Others stress their "figurative" quality. But lack of agreement about what these labels actually mean shows the diffculty of appealing to them as the key to interpreting such biblical texts. Imagery can legitimately represent reality in various degrees of detail and by various means. It can be specific, general, or even representative, and can be expanded while maintaining a basic unity of sense. Some specific textual examples may help us sort through whether such labels really help us appreciate the complexity of this genre.

For instance, should we simply substitute things like helicopters and modern weapons for the imagery of locusts, scorpions, and other such images in Revelation 9:3? Is the imagery of Revelation always this specific? Should we assume the prophet saw something like a motion picture of the future in his vision and then attempted to explain it in terms of images he understood? Or did he see a picture precisely in the images he gives, images which paint reality rather than describing it? Which description of those options is "more literal"? Is it the one that focuses on how it might look to us, so we explain what he meant in words and images very different from the prophet's terms and images? Or should one focus on how it looked to the prophet and how it appears in the ancient text? We would thus attempt to understand his words in their literary character, both by examining the image in context and the Old Testament images and background(s) it evokes.

Is literal versus figurative the best way to approach this debate? Imagery like the harlot and monster clearly shows that at least sometimes representative portrayal, not a motion picture, is present. The interpretations of the various visions within Daniel also indicate that the imagery of the text is representative of reality *and* evocative of earlier biblical imagery, while looking to the future, genuine vindication of God's people. The message is *both* real and figurative. It looks to the future not by detailing all that will happen in the future with movie-like imagery, but by emphatically and artistically declaring that such a comprehensive deliverance will happen. It deals with reality though imagery.

For instance, consider the locusts of Revelation. One wonders if a past interpreter of this text, say a seventeenth-century man or the original first-century reader holding to imminence, could have made such an explicit identification of locusts with helicopters? Was the literal meaning of this text totally inaccessible to its original recipients? If this world remains until A.D. 3000, what might the locusts become and could we ever know it now? It is possible that such specific identification is implied by such imagery, but it is not very likely. If the internal interpretation of these texts helps us unlock them and if the lessons of history teach us anything about their interpretation, then we must be sensitive to the literary character of their portrayal of history.

So why refer to locusts? Perhaps one point among many in this text is to depict the presence of moving destructive forces on the earth connected with Satan, without intending to communicate any more detail about what such forces might actually look like. The imagery calls forth the picture from Joel 2. Through this parallelism with the Old Testament imagery, the awareness emerges that here is an allusion to the arrival of the terrible Day of the Lord, that is now related to Christ's return which brings final vindication of the saints and judgment for all. The reality the text communicates is that such judgment is horrible, like going through a swarming plague of locusts, however it eventually manifests itself in history.

Recalling our cat illustration, we know that one can communicate at a general level without filling in all the details. Apocalyptic imagery seems often to operate at this basic level, since its imagery and its internal interpretations seem to reveal a representative approach. The key to apocalyptic literature is to determine the roots—at a general level—of the imagery that is evoked.

On the contrary, other apocalyptic images have a specific, even Israelite, feel to them: the 144,000 (Rev. 7) or the allusion to 42 months (Rev. 13:5), which is similar to the language of Daniel 12:11. Or take the seventy weeks of Daniel 9:24-27, where Jerusalem and the temple are described. Promises made here are not yet realized in our time. Since God keeps His commitments, something more in terms of fulfillment can be anticipated. Such uncompleted promises within apocalyptic literature look forward to fulfillment. On the other hand, references in Revelation 20 to the first and second resurrection are not symbolic, but specific, distinct, sequential, and descriptive. These various examples show that some details in apocalyptic literature are not symbolic images, but name concrete realities in the world of the writer. They appear to present a worldview where Israel is present, since many of them point us back so vividly to the world and reality of Old Testament hope.

Still other Old Testament images, while reused, have a fresh force explicitly noted in the new context. For example, Gog and Magog in Revelation 20 refer explicitly to the four corners of the earth (v. 8), rather than to specific national entities as in the Old Testament (Ezek. 38–39). Such a shift in imagery is noted by not just citing the Old Testament and its imagery but by also filling in the details explicitly in the new context.

This mixture of highly symbolic and directly descriptive imagery, along with the presence of fresh referents in some other contexts, makes interpreting the Book of Revelation difficult, even though it clearly refers ultimately to future reality. Interpretation of apocalyptic is not a matter of literal versus figurative/allegorical approaches, but of how to identify and understand the reference of the figure in question. Often the case is that more narrowly defined images of the Old Testament have been expanded to cover a wider scope in Revelation, but not at the expense of the original emphasis of the term; rather, such expansion is in addition to the original image. On the other hand, other texts merely evoke the Old Testament and suggest that to understand the image one can simply look at the earlier text.

Another example of this literal/symbolic difficulty is the debate over the identity of Babylon in Revelation 17. This text shows how multilayered the associations are in an apocalyptic passage and how focusing on only one element may limit its understanding. Should one appeal to Jeremiah 51 and take it literally as Babylon rebuilt, so that the center of the world system in the end will be where Iraq is now? Or is it a cipher for a rebuilt Rome as the reference to seven hills of Revelation 17:9 suggests? Which context helps us identify what is taking place, the Old or the New? Are the two associations in conflict or can they form a unity? Even dispensationalists have not agreed here. Perhaps ultimately a choice between the two contexts is not necessary. This is one of the few texts in Revelation that offers an interpretation with its image. As such, it is a key to the book.

The beast in Revelation 17 is composed of seven heads representing various kingships (or national dynasties in all likelihood). The representative imagery characteristic of Revelation is clearly present. No nation *is* a beast, especially a multiheaded one. The interpretation tells us that five heads have fallen, one is and one is to come for a short time. Then comes an eighth figure related to, but distinct from, the seventh. Those who try to limit Revelation's teaching at this point to a period contemporary to John, referring this remark to past Roman history, have an awful problem explaining whom the five heads on the beast represent in terms of past Roman kings. There is no historical list that fits with John's time period! To simply read Revelation as a reference to history in John's time seems not to work; it is a futurist document.

But what kind of futurist image is present? We would suggest that this image refers to the sweep of history. The beast depicts each worldwide dynasty of biblical times: Egypt, Assyria, Babylon, Medo-Persia, and Greece are the five fallen kings. The sixth, Rome, is "the one that is," thus honoring the allusion to seven hills in Revelation 17:9. The seventh, the one to come for a short time, may well be from a region unidentified in the text, as is also the eighth king, the beast. If one asks why the text skips some world dynasties, such jumping of periods and time is not unusual in prophecy. The story simply picks up with the resumption of God's program in association with Christ's return.

The principle for reading the details in this way is careful, contextual study of the imagery within the text. As with other genres, such a reading honors interpretation in context, with the immediate context having priority. Taking the image as a whole, the interpreter can see that each head represents a new period located in a different capital. The world empire's center is always shifting, though each succeeding era is organically related to the previous ones.

Among the many points of the image, we highlight three. First, there is a genealogical and organic relationship between the various dynastic empires of the world that have stood opposed to God. In fact, the "beast from below" image suggests an appeal to the Leviathan image of the Old Testament, the opponent of God and the consummate scriptural image for evil. This conflict is not only cosmic in scope, but it has been ongoing in duration! This connection also raises the point that the conflict transcends human opponents. As Paul says in another context, our struggle is not against flesh and blood (Eph. 6:12).

Second, one day that "beast" will manifest itself in a horrible, climactic worldwide rebellion against God and His people. Death will be everywhere, and the beast and harlot will be slaying believers. Such a reading fits the cosmic scope of other imagery in the book as well. Those who associate the image with Babylon are right in that it is the greatest Old Testament picture of such a power. That is why the beast is called Babylon. Those who associate it with Rome are right because Rome was the current manifestation of that beast in the time of John the writer. And yet the beast's imagery reminds us that its real existence is from long ago. So Rome and Babylon both apply, and yet the beast is more than either national identification. But neither Rome nor Babylon is likely to be the final location of this worldwide opposition, given the shifting nature of the location of the eras represented by the heads of the beast. The text is both specific and indefinite at the same time. It describes what the beast is specifically, but not where it will ultimately reside.

Third, there is an organic relationship between evil in John's generation and its culmination in the end. Everyone who identifies with God is urged not to identify with what is represented in the evils of the beast. What is required in the interim, in light of what the future brings, is faithfulness to God and His people, since ultimately vindication of the saints will come. The message applies to John's audience and to the future.

This third reading could be incorrect. In fact, identifying the beast with rebuilt Babylon or Rome here may be correct, as might another interpretation of the text. Yet, our reading demands attention and reflection, because it tries to deal with the imagery from within the context of the book's own interpretation of itself and with a sensitivity to apocalyptic genre. We admit that the imagery here is difficult, but the goal of interpretation is to be as faithful as possible to the imagery in its context. Regardless of who is right on the issue of locale, we would still argue that the three themes—the genealogical character of the beast, the final worldwide rebellion it brings, and the connection between the beast and the present—are among the important points in the passage, and those who hold to different details might also agree with our statement of these central concerns.

All the genres considered together reveal the vast variety of terrain that the Bible contains. One should understand how each genre operates and study it accordingly. Above all, sensitivity must be maintained for each context in which a text falls. One must be sensitive to four levels of context in interpreting the Bible—the historical, grammatical, literary, and theological. The interaction of these contexts raises the issues of different ways to read the text and how to relate different passages to one another.

## Ways of Reading the Bible and Relating Different Texts

To think about the process of reading is to consider how one should engage the text. From what has been said, one thing should be very clear. It is important to let each context of a passage speak to its meaning. In particular, it is crucial that each interpretation be sensitive to the passage's own genre and thematic, literary categories before integrating it with the message of other texts given in other settings. This simply allows the story of the Bible to progress while remaining sensitive to how the story is told. It is also sensitive to what kind of terrain a given part of the story is using to advance the journey through the message.

If we're not careful, we can read a text in a way that dilutes another text's message. Sometimes what happens is that an early text is regarded as so clear that a later text simply is read in its terms. But this can flatten out meaning, so that progression in the story is lost. When progress or development of the story occurs, it is indicated by other features in the later context that show the theme's development, even though some terms of the text match terms used earlier in Scripture (e.g., Gog and Magog in Revelation 20). But there is another way to flatten out the text as well. It is to argue that the later text redraws the lines of the earlier text in such a way that what the second text means is what the first text always meant. The effect of this type of reading is also a reduction in the depth of the biblical message. This approach also loses the sense of progress in the story.

An example of how this occurs in both directions is to compare how some handle the theme of the kingdom of God in the New Testament. Some, noting texts that clearly place the kingdom of God in the future, argue that this theme refers only to what the Old Testament pictured it to be, an earthly kingdom. On this basis some commentators claim that either there is no present form of the kingdom today or the present heavenly form of the kingdom has nothing to do with Old Testament kingdom promise. This position holds that to argue for a present form of the kingdom is to contradict the Old Testament texts about its arrival in the future. This approach to eschatology understands the kingdom as residing totally in the future. This limitation is the error of reading the New Testament solely in light of the Old.

On the other hand, some have argued that the texts on the presence of the kingdom mean that the kingdom has already arrived. This has been called *realized* eschatology. The promise of the future has come fully now; Jesus is the presence of fulfillment, so what He brings must come in totality. Texts about the kingdom's futurity are really nothing but extensions of what is already here. This present reality is merely projected toward eternity. Old Testament texts about the kingdom are then focused on, if not limited to, their meaning for this current form of the kingdom. This approach errs by reading the New Testament back into the Old.

The biblical characteristic of viewing events from a variety of perspectives shows us that one can make points from a "both-and" perspective without denying either side of the present-future relationship. It is possible to get fulfillment "now" in some texts, while noting that "not yet" fulfillment exists in other passages. In fact, in some texts fulfillment can be initial or partial, as opposed to being final and total. As a result, one can speak of *inaugurated* eschatology without denying either what the Old Testament indicates about a future, earthly kingdom or what the New Testament asserts about the arrival of the kingdom as part of fulfillment in the first coming of Jesus. To call such eschatology inaugurated is only to say the process of fulfillment has commenced; there is more – even much more – to come.

Such "already-not yet" tensions are not surprising. They reside in our description of salvation itself. I am saved now when I trust Jesus, but God is going to complete that salvation in the future. In one sense salvation has arrived; in another I await it. In the cases of both salvation and the kingdom of God, one should pay attention to which side of the relationship is being highlighted in any given text. To note the presence of one aspect of the relationship is not to deny the other part of its realization. "Already-not yet" teaching links the plan of God into a unified whole. It allows one to see both continuity and discontinuity in the outworking of God's promises.

There is another dimension of reading that needs attention. It is that a story can be read from different angles, drawing on differing amounts of context to tell the story. The best illustration for this concept is to think of reading a mystery or going to see a movie about a murder. The first time through as the event is being experienced without knowledge of the end, one is caught in the grip of the drama of trying to decide "who done it." The story unfolds a step at a time and the perspective and expectations are limited by one's partial knowledge. Only at the story's end are all the pieces brought together. If one is observant, though, he or she can sometimes put together the solution to the crime before the story unwinds.

On the other hand, in reading the story or seeing the movie a second time, one sees differently. Now all the tension of the story is reduced, but also connections are seen that were missed the first time through. Note that the story is exactly the same, but it is perceived and evaluated on different terms because of better knowledge or because of the different angle taken in viewing the whole. *Both* ways of relating to the story are legitimate ways to encounter it and to consider it. To return to our previous illustration, it is a little like assessing the Clinton election on November 3, 1992 versus election day 1996 or any other subsequent date in history.

Now as one thinks about event and text in Scripture, one can think through the same kind of analogy. A difference in approach can impact how the text is read. If one views the event of Scripture in its immediate context as event, then one views the event portrayed from the limited perspective of how it was originally experienced. Often the characters' reactions reflect a perspective that is less knowledgeable than the reader of Scripture today has, since that reader knows the whole story. Connections, though they have the potential to exist, are not transparent in that original time frame. In fact, often events seem disjointed and expectations meet with surprises along the way. But when one examines the story in the light of all the events, the connections can emerge more explicitly and be established with greater clarity. Things that seemed distinct at first glance have a closer relationship than one might have initially imagined. This is like seeing the movie for a second time. Regardless of which angle one takes in viewing the story, both angles are appropriate ways to look at the event.

Our earlier illustration of Genesis 3:15 with the image of Eve's seed and the serpent is an example of this distinction. In the near context of Genesis the emphasis would be on the chaos that sin introduced into the creation, while in the context of the canonical story that tension is resolved through the work of Jesus Christ.

One can also suggest that this helps to explain the difference in perspective between the synoptics and John. The synoptics tell the story of Jesus by highlighting how the disciples experienced His ministry. The emphasis is on their lack of understanding and the struggle they had in grasping who He was. It tells the story of Jesus "from the earth up," working from categories the reader can identify with and then showing how Jesus goes beyond those expectations. It is like reading the story for the first time.

John writes from the other angle, highlighting the story in light of his total understanding about Jesus. In fact, at points he notes for the reader that at the time of the events the disciples did not understand the significance of certain actions (John 2:22; 12:16). Only after Jesus was resurrected did they put the pieces together so that they understood who Jesus really was.

John's portrait is "from heaven down," starting with and exalting Jesus as Word Incarnate from the very beginning. It is interesting that Christians often like the Gospel of John because of its explicitness, but that unbelievers often relate well to Matthew, Mark, or Luke because the non-Christian can identify more easily with its developing portrait of Jesus.

Now what is important here is that each angle on the account is legitimate and carries an aspect of the total canonical message. The Scripture complements its message, not by having one Gospel, but four, so portraits exist from a variety of angles. A sensitive reader will let each story and angle speak rather than flattening them all out into one message where each text says exactly the same thing. But if one pursues such a unified, canonical reading, it is done with sensitivity to the contribution each piece makes to the whole. Rather than laying each account on top of each other to make them say one thing, they are placed together in locked pieces, so that the full portrait and its elements can be observed.

***Three Levels of Reading.*** In sum, texts of the Bible can be read in three ways. First, they can be read at a *historical-exegetical level*, where the issue is the context of the event viewed as a fairly self-contained unit. Though this perspective is a limited one, it can have value in highlighting the immediate impact of an event. Sensitivity to this level of reading will preserve the sense of progress in the story and allows one to appreciate how the story builds as time passes and revelation progresses.

Second, a text can be read in the context of the whole book in which it falls. We can call this a *biblical-theological reading,* provided we do not confuse it with the normal way one speaks of biblical theology, which usually refers to all the writings of a given writer or period. To put it another way, one can read Romans trying to deal with it as a reader in Rome might have, that is, without assuming that the Roman reader had access to 1 Corinthians (or any other of Paul's letters) to help him figure out Paul's meaning. Romans was originally conceived to stand on its own. Now usually this second level of reading will be very close in meaning to the first level, but in longer books this will not be the case. The promise of Abraham's seed in the early chapters of Genesis focuses on Isaac. For Abraham, the most important aspect to the seed promise was its start. Only as the

Genesis story moves through the generations do Jacob and his sons emerge as the seed. Only in light of all of Genesis do we see the nation of Israel as the seed. The refocusing of the seed uniquely on Jesus is nowhere explicit in the context of Genesis. Only the movement of the story of promise beyond Genesis begins to show the possibility for such narrowing in the concept of the king as representative of the nation. But that move takes us to the third way to read the biblical text, at a *canonical-systematic level.* This reading takes the passage in light of the whole, either through all of an author's writing, through the lens of a given period, or, most comprehensively, in light of the whole of the canon. Now the story of the seed takes on added dimension as Jesus becomes the seed who brings *the* promise. Abraham's promise is linked with the one to David (see Luke 1–2 [esp. 1:31-35, 67-79]). Jesus as Christ—the promised king of the line of David—fulfills promises to Abraham and bestows the Spirit of God. Jesus brings the initial manifestation of the kingdom (see John the Baptist's announcement of the "one to come"). By linking Spirit and kingdom, Davidic regal hope is tied to the promise of the Spirit in the new covenant, as well as to the hope of Abraham. The entire discussion assumes a context of promise and fulfillment, so it is the realization of one fundamental promise to Abraham that is being realized. Even then, with Jesus as the turning point, we are not done. For those who are "in Christ" also become "the seed," as Galatians 3:29 shows. The Bible loves to give many dimensions to a single theme. To discover those dimensions is like the joy and amazement one gets from seeing light split into many colors as it passes through a prism.

Another theme that draws on this type of dynamic reading is the development of kingdom texts in the Bible. The journey moves from its formation in promise to Israel and David to its culminating description in terms of millennium and then the new heaven and new earth. The Old Testament mostly discusses the promise of a kingdom on earth (2 Sam. 7:8-16), with the exception of brief remarks in Daniel that suggest a heavenly origin (esp. Dan. 2 and 7). The New Testament develops these heavenly elements of the hope (Eph. 2:4-7; Phil. 3:20; Heb. 12:22-24), culminating in the Millennium and then the new heaven and new earth (Rev. 20–22). When Revelation is read *canonically-systematically,* its message refracts back on Old

Testament kingdom texts to show that the promised kingdom is fulfilled in part within the Millennium and the new heaven and new earth. What Old Testament promises have not been fulfilled yet will be fulfilled in the future. As the Apostle Peter suggests, there is much detail about the career of Jesus and the outworking of promise declared in the Old Testament (Acts 3:21). To appreciate how the entire story unfolds and which promises belong where, one must read the text *historically-exegetically*, *biblically-theologically*, and *canonically-systematically*.

All three levels of reading are appropriate, though ultimately the canonical-systematic reading brings the pieces of the Bible's message together. To consider carefully how God's plan is unified, how fulfillment works, and how the parts of the Bible relate to one another, we must turn to our final topic of concern—the variety of ways that promise and fulfillment link together. What are the various ways the New Testament uses the Old?

***The Use of the Old Testament in the New.*** We have already cleared much ground for this discussion. As has been made clear, promise and prophecy are not always a matter of exclusively direct prophetic texts, where the Old Testament passage refers only to one event or person in one setting. Fulfillment in Jesus can be prepared for by establishing the pattern of God's activity in one age and then reenacting it again later. Sometimes such reenactments occur more than once. Concepts like the Servant of God, the Righteous Sufferer of the Psalms, and the Seed of Abraham operate in this manner. Such prophecy is both prophetic and typological. In the "patterned" design of the event lies the prophecy. But prophecy is only a subset in the larger topic of how the New Testament uses the Old.

There are different kinds of use or combinations of use: some are prophetic, others are illustrative, while others are explanatory. Some texts mix these categories together. Some texts like Daniel 7:14 are *directly prophetic*, having in mind only one referent. For example, there is only one "Son of Man," who returns in judgment.

Texts that reflect pattern can be called *typological-prophetic*. They present the realization of a pattern or the emergence of someone who again fulfills a given role. That makes it a type.

But the escalation normally associated with Jesus' fulfillment of the pattern reveals its prophetic character. Escalation means that He fulfills it to a degree greater than others before Him, pointing to His unique and often culminating position within the pattern. Most of the regal promises tied to David's descendants culminate in an escalated fulfillment in Jesus. For example, the New Testament's uses of Psalms 45, 89, 110, 118, and 132 belong here. What was hoped for from any king of David was realized (or will be realized) in Jesus. The fact that He fulfills such promises in a unique way reveals that He is the key and culmination of the pattern. John the Baptist as an Elijah-prophet is another example of such usage. In fact, a significant number of the New Testament uses of the Old Testament fit into this category.

Other texts merely make an illustrative comparison. They involve an *analogical* use. When Paul alludes to the Exodus in 1 Corinthians 10:1-13 or the author of Hebrews looks back at the concept of rest in Psalm 95, they are making comparisons between the divine acts of old and current events.

Some texts relate to promise by noting either its realization or termination. They serve to explain relationships within promise.

Some texts assert the *cancellation* of previous revelation. The law of circumcision is explicitly canceled as texts in Acts 15 and Galatians indicate.

But other texts indicate *substitution*, at least for a given period. The parable of the tenants indicates that the vineyard of promise is given to others and is taken from those who had tended it, namely the nation of Israel. But the nature of such substitution needs to be defined by additional texts on this theme. Romans 11 makes it clear that there comes a time in the future when Israel is grafted back in, and Acts 3:18-21 makes it clear that when Jesus returns He will complete the remaining prophetic promises of the Old Testament.

This kind of qualification means that some themes and texts have a *complementary* relationship. The additional inclusion of some in the promise does not mean that the original recipients are thereby excluded. *The expansion of promise need not mean the cancellation of earlier commitments God has made.* The realization of new covenant hope today for Gentiles does not mean that the promise made to Israel in Jeremiah 31 has been jettisoned. Cancellation of promise only occurs where it is explicitly stated. Chapters 5 and 6 in this volume will develop this point.

Given the variety of possible ways the Old Testament can be cited within the New, the relationship between the Testaments on given themes must be handled on a case-by-case basis. Rules that apply in every case before each text is examined preempt the discussion and ignore the variety of possibilities. In this area, one size does not fit all cases.

Texts are not always associated by means of simple identity, since the progress of promise, issues of genre, and the presence of the developing themes (e.g., seed) allow ideas to deepen and develop. Nor is the relationship always a matter of substitution. For example, the nature of God's promises and program prohibit merely substituting the church for Israel (Acts 3:18-21). Neither does simple analogy always work because some texts develop themes in contexts where promise and fulfillment clearly reside (Acts 2; Heb. 8–10). Texts frequently have a complementary relationship (often by appeal to pattern), so that later realizations of that pattern can occur when Jesus returns. Fulfillment can be "already-not yet," that is, partial and then full. To sort out whether fulfillment is inaugurated, realized, or still anticipated, one must study each passage with sensitivity to the various aspects that contribute to the textual message: historical, grammatical, literary, and theological. Each passage should be allowed to speak on its own terms and should be studied with sensitivity to the various angles from which the text can be read. One must also be aware of the various ways texts can be associated with one another.

## Conclusion

Interpretation is the product of how we speak to the text and how it speaks to us. However, the text occupies the privileged position. We sit in submission to it. Scripture's role is to transform us daily as we address it and look for it to challenge us. But our dialogue does not occur in a vacuum, nor should our deliberations be private. Others read the text with us. Though we do not always agree with others on what the Bible says, these differences reflect our limitations in understanding. Sometimes our dialogue with others helps us see our own blind spots. As Scripture says, "Iron sharpens iron" (Prov. 27:17). These realities call for humility, even as we seek to gain perspective and conviction from the truth of Scripture. Indeed, the Spirit works to convict the world and encourage His children.

In the end, Scripture tells the story of God's pursuit of humanity. The Bible presents not just His message, but His action on our behalf. In His message He declares His relationship to us and His involvement with us. That message contains promise, reveals the possibility of relationship, and guarantees human accountability to God. The text of Scripture also discloses His authority and program. The activity of Jesus Christ stands at its center. He is the ultimate possessor of promise and the mediator of blessing.

Scripture constructs a worldview. The Word is not just about a random series of events, facts, doctrines, or propositions. Nor is it even a picture of different groups all with equal access to God. There is no relativism in Scripture about how one enters into relationship with God. Rather, the Bible speaks to relationships, whether healthy or crippled, and calls the reader to enter into blessing on God's terms through Jesus or else be left on the outside, subject to the story's divine outworking. Ultimately, Scripture is about God's promise realized in Jesus. Everyone is accountable to Him who is our Creator. In the message of Scripture, we find how God created and entered the world of humanity. God tells us just how He did it, does it, and plans to do it. He invites us to join Him in the journey. The task of hermeneutics is to listen carefully and humbly for His voice, so we might walk with Him.

# Chapter Four
# Dispensations in Biblical Theology

The idea that the history of the Bible is divided into different dispensations was not invented by dispensationalists. It is in fact a matter that has long been recognized in Christian theology. This stems from the fact that the Bible itself uses the word dispensation in speaking about different arrangements which God has instituted in history in the process of bringing about the salvation of the world.

### The Word *Dispensation*

We are using the word *dispensation* to translate the Greek word *oikonomia*. Tertullian, a North African Christian in the early third century who set much of the theological vocabulary for the Latin-speaking church, used the Latin word *dispensatio* to translate *oikonomia*. From that Latin term, our English word *dispensation* is derived.

**General Sense.** In ancient Greek culture, an *oikonomos* was a servant in charge of a household. *Oikonomia* referred to his office or activity of managing the house. However, these words were soon used more broadly for any type of management or administration. Not only an estate manager but even a cook could be designated as an *oikonomos*. Public and political offices from Roman procurators to city treasurers, and even managers of bath houses, were addressed by this title.[1]

The management activity of an *oikonomos* usually involved financial transactions requiring a careful accounting of funds received and disbursed. This reference to money and finance carries over into our English word economy which transliterates the Greek *oikonomia*. The words *steward* and *stewardship*, which also translate *oikonomos* and *oikonomia*, carry this notion of financial responsibility while extending the sense of accountability to non-financial matters as well.

In the Greek translation of the Old Testament (the Septuagint), the individual who was put in charge of the palace by the King of Judah was called an *oikonomos* (see 1 Kings 4:6; 16:9; 18:3; 2 Kings 18:18, 37). And his *oikonomia*, his management responsibility, extended over everything having to do with the palace, from physical maintainance and furnishings to accommodating guests and coordinating daily activities. His chief obligation was to the king, to make sure that the palace was suitable to the needs of the king and his family. If his service was found unacceptable, a change in *oikonomia* occurred with the appointment of a new *oikonomos* (see Isa. 22:15-25).

In the New Testament, we find evidence of the general use of *oikonomos* and *oikonomia*. In Romans 16:23, Paul conveys greetings from Erastus, the *oikonomos* of the city of Corinth. This probably means that he was the treasurer or the chief financial officer of the city. (The fact that he was a Christian testifies to how quickly Christianity was penetrating Roman society.)

Jesus used these terms in some of His parables. In Luke 12:42 He introduces a parable concerning a steward (*oikonomos*) who was responsible to see that all the other servants were properly fed. The performance of the steward was subject at any moment to review by his master, with the possibilities of promotion for a job well done, or punishment and even termination for dereliction of duty. In Luke 16:1-13, Jesus tells the story of an unjust business manager (*oikonomos*) who is called in for an evaluation by the owner of the business. The evaluation concerned the manager's *oikonomia*, that is, the way in which he conducted business, including an audit of the books. The result was a change in *oikonomia* with the discharge of that particular manager and presumably the appointment of a new one.

From these various sources we can summarize the general sense of *oikonomos* as any type of manager or administrator. The term *oikonomia*, which we translate *dispensation*, referred generally to the activity of a manager and the overall organizational arrangement in which that activity was carried out. Its sense can properly be conveyed by words such as *administration, arrangement, order, plan*, and *management*.

***Theological Sense.*** The parables of Jesus about stewards and their responsibilities are not just stories about the difficulty of finding good help. Jesus told the parables to teach about the coming kingdom of God. They speak of a relationship between God and Israel (especially the leaders of Israel) which is called into account in the judgments preceding the coming kingdom. Through this teaching, the word *oikonomia*, which conveyed the notion of a management arrangement, acquired a theological sense—that is, it came to designate the relationship between God and the world.

The Apostle Paul uses both *oikonomos* and *oikonomia* to describe God's relationship to the world. Most of these uses refer to Paul's own office as an apostle of Jesus Christ. God, the Master of the world, entrusted to Paul, along with others, the apostolic responsibility of proclaiming a new revelation. Paul referred to this revelation as the mystery (or mysteries) of God and Christ (1 Cor. 4:1-2; Eph. 3:2-6; Col. 1:25-29). Church officers could also be seen as part of this ministerial arrangement (a bishop should be thought of as "God's steward" [Titus 1:7]). And Peter extends the concept to include all Christians (they are all stewards, *oikonomoi*, of the grace of God [1 Peter 4:10]).

In Ephesians 3:9, Paul speaks of the dispensation (*oikonomia*) of the mystery of Christ. Reading this in light of verses 4-6, we see that this use of the word dispensation refers to a new order, a new arrangement in the overall relationship between God and humankind. Here is the theological sense of dispensation which is most important. It is broader than the other theological senses (the notion of individual ministry responsibilities) while including them in its scope. The relationship between

God and human beings should be thought of as a dispensation, a management relationship which He has instituted. It is also a dispensation which is new in time, having been set up through the death, resurrection, and ascension of Jesus Christ, replacing an arrangement which had previously been in effect. This, of course, implies that the previous arrangement should also be thought of as a dispensation, an implication which Paul makes explicit elswhere in Galatians 3:23–4:7.

As Paul discusses this new dispensation in his letters, three things stand out about it: (1) It is structured by certain features of a new covenant which God inaugurated to fulfill and replace the covenant He made with Israel at Sinai; (2) no distinctions of race, gender, or class are being drawn in the bestowal of blessings from this new covenant—they are given to all who believe in Jesus Christ; and (3) the new dispensation is being revealed in the community that gathers in the name of Jesus Christ, the church.

We will have more to say about the specifics of this dispensation later in this chapter and in the chapters to follow. But here we need to ask, what is the significance of calling God's relationship with human beings a dispensation? How does the general sense of *oikonomia* carry over into its theological sense? Or to ask it another way, what does a dispensation imply about God's relationship to the world?

First of all, to speak this way—as Paul does—emphasizes *the sovereignty of God* over human affairs. Just as the master of an estate, the owner of a business, or the CEO of a corporation exercises the foundational authority of designing and structuring his or her business and hiring and appointing persons to delegated levels and positions of authority, so God is sovereign in the design and organization of the affairs of the earth. "God is dispensing or administering [the world's] affairs according to His own will."[2]

Secondly, seeing the relationship between God and the world as a dispensation emphasizes *purpose and overall planning.* Management activity has some vision or plan, some purpose in view. Likewise, any dispensation which God institutes with human beings has an internal design and purpose. Just as management communicates its vision to carry out its purpose, so we see that God reveals the structure and design of the dispensation which He institutes. But there is more. Businesses and other organizations may from time to time go through restructuring or reorganizing. There are many reasons why this may be so, but it does not happen haphazardly. Some overall purpose guides the restructuring process to move the business forward. Likewise, the Bible speaks of God reorganizing the relationship of human beings to Himself, changing from one dispensation to another. There is a divine purpose which guides this process of dispensational change, pointing to an ultimate goal which God has in view.

Third, a dispensation is *an ordered set of relationships.* In understanding any particular dispensation, one would need to know what are the fundamental relationships that form its distinctive structure. In a business organization, this means knowing what the management structure is, what the organizational plan looks like, what the various departments do, and how one's own job description fits into this overall arrangement. Likewise, seeing God's relationship with humanity as a dispensation implies order and structure in the way people relate to Him and to each other. As Paul expounds the present dispensation, the primary management position is held by Jesus Christ. There are stewardships which He has appointed (apostles and other ministers) and gifts which He has bestowed by the Holy Spirit (such that all believers are stewards of the grace of God). But primary emphasis is put on the fact that in contrast to the preceding dispensation, the present arrangement places all believers, regardless of cultural or political background, on the same level as members of the household of God.

Fourth, along with the structure of relationships come *responsibilities and requirements.* When these responsibilities are carried out and the requirements are met, the plan for that dispensation is accomplished. This in turn contributes to the overall purpose which guides the history of the dispensations. Concerning the present dispensation, the New Testament teaches that all of us in Christ have stewardship responsibilities entrusted to us by God. Offices in the church such as that of apostle and bishop (pastor) are stewardships specifically mentioned in Scripture. But this could be extended to various forms of ministry as well. To each of us, however, is given the stewardship (*oikonomia*) of the grace of God. We are instructed in the administration of this grace according to the law of Christ, or law of the Spirit, which makes reference to the commandments of Christ handed down to us through His apostles. This brings us to the practical matter of the Bible's teaching on Christian living.

Finally, as we noted above, to view God's relationship to the world dispensationally is to raise the prospect of *dispensational change.* Such restructuring is rooted in the overall purpose of God. It is an actual factor in the way in which He accomplishes His ultimate purpose. To speak of dispensational change, however, is to speak of dispensational history, or the history of dispensations. God's purpose is accomplished historically. He works out His will through history in successive administrative arrangements all progressing toward the ultimate fulfillment of His purpose.

In summary, by using the word dispensation (*oikonomia*), the Bible presents a way of understanding God's relationship with human beings in terms of arrangements (dispensations) which He has instituted in the course of history. He manages the way in which human beings are to relate to Him and to one another through these arrangements which He has set up. The church is the new dispensation which God has organized through the death, resurrection, and ascension of Jesus Christ. It differs in important respects from the dispensation that was in place prior to Christ. And yet it is not wholly different. This dispensation is the fulfillment of the previous one, and as we will see, it looks forward to a future arrangement in which all the promises and covenants of God will be completely and eternally fulfilled.

The dispensational relationship between God and the world is an important feature of biblical theology. Dispensational terminology is central to the New Testament understanding of the church. And it is particularly used in explaining the church's relationship to the Old Testament, to the pivotal events of Jesus' ministry, and to the overall plan and purpose of God yet to be accomplished at the return of Christ.

In order to better understand the notion of dispensations, we will examine them in relation to other structural notions of biblical theology such as salvation history, divine/human covenants, and the kingdom of God. What follows is the beginning of such a study. The following chapters will explore the dispensational nature of the biblical covenants and the kingdom of God in more detail.

## Dispensations in Biblical History

*New Testament Dispensationalism and Salvation History.*
Salvation history or history of redemption are terms used by
theologians today to refer to the history of God's interventions
on behalf of His people to deliver or save them: such as His
protection of Noah; His promises to, and personal care of, the
Patriarchs (Abraham, Isaac, and Jacob); and His many interventions on behalf of the people of Israel, including the deliverance through the Exodus. Salvation history specifically refers to
the history of God's relationships with human beings as recorded in the Bible. It is one of the major categories of biblical
theology. As one reads through the Bible in a chronological
fashion, one notes that the later writings refer to the earlier
narratives. Thus, later reports of God's actions on behalf of His
people indicate to the reader a pattern of relationships —
relationships based on promises made earlier in history. To
understand the theology of the Bible, a person needs to recognize and grasp this structure of salvation history.[3]

The New Testament presents Jesus Christ as the climax of
salvation history in both His first and future comings. His ministry fulfills the pattern of divine human relationships and becomes the basis for securing those relationships eternally. His
death, resurrection, and ascension mark the turning point in
the progress of history into the eschatological age. His future
return brings the process to consummation.

In the New Testament epistles of Ephesians, Colossians, and
Galatians, the words *oikonomia* and *oikonomos* are used in
reference to a new arrangement between God and human beings that came into existence in salvation history. The sense of
historical newness or historical change is emphasized in these
texts by temporal words and phrases marking a contrast between the present and the past. In Ephesians 3, where Paul
speaks of the *dispensation of the mystery,* he says that "*in
other generations* [the mystery, and hence its dispensation]
was not made known . . . as it has now been revealed." He then
adds that the dispensation itself was "for ages . . . hidden in
God" but that it is "*now*" revealed "through the church."

These remarks carry forward the argument given in the previous chapters of Ephesians in which Paul explains the historical
significance of the death, resurrection, and ascension of Jesus

Christ. In chapter 2, he notes that "formerly," "at that time," Gentiles were "separate from Christ, excluded from the commonwealth of Israel, and strangers to the covenants of promise." Then in verse 13 he states, "But now in Christ Jesus you who formerly were far off have been brought near by the blood of Christ."

This is not just a statement about unbelievers coming to faith. It concerns the very nature of the dispensational structure identified in the third chapter. Furthermore, it is a statement about changes that God introduced in history through the sending of His Son. This ties the notion of changing dispensations directly to the concept of salvation history, the history of redemption which God brings to fulfillment through His Son Jesus Christ. A previous arrangement (dispensation) between God and human beings which maintained a division between the races in the experience of divine blessing has now been replaced or superseded by a *new* dispensation in which there is no racial distinction in the bestowal and experience of certain promised blessings now being given. The racial subordination of Gentiles had been a structural feature of the Mosaic covenant. But Paul argues in Ephesians 2:14-15 that through the death of Jesus Christ, that structural subordination has been removed. In the new humanity, all races have direct access to God the Father through the Son by the Holy Spirit. God is dwelling in this new temple—this assembly from all races—bringing peace among the peoples with the peace they now have with God.

These remarks in Ephesians 2 are in turn related to Paul's prayer in Ephesians 1:18-23. Here he speaks of the power of God present in the church. This power was manifested in the resurrection of Jesus Christ from the dead (note the temporal phrase, *"when* He raised Him from the dead," v. 20). Upon His ascension into heaven, this power was given to the church ("[when He] seated Him at His right hand in the heavenly places . . . He put all things in subjection under His feet and gave Him as head over all things to the church, which is His body, the fullness of Him who fills all in all"). Paul prays that the church might comprehend what God has done. But our point here is to recognize that this blessing, which is historically related to the death, resurrection, and ascension of Jesus Christ, is part of a new arrangement (dispensation).

These thoughts are repeated in somewhat abbreviated fashion in Colossians 1:24-29 where Paul speaks of the *oikonomia* given to him by God to preach "the mystery which has been hidden from the past ages and generations; but has *now* been manifested to His saints." He then speaks of "the riches of the glory of this mystery among the Gentiles, which is Christ in you, the hope of glory." Again he is speaking of a change in God's relations with human beings which has taken place through Jesus Christ, of which the most obvious feature is the blessing of the indwelling of Christ to Gentile believers.

Paul outlines in Galatians the historical relationships between the revelation of the promise to Abraham, the dispensation of the Law (the Mosaic Covenant), Jesus Christ, and the present relationship of the church to God through Jesus Christ. Historical markers are present throughout the argument. The Law came 430 years after the promise was given (3:17). It did not invalidate or replace the promise; it was given *"until* the seed should come to whom the promise had been made" (v. 18). This "seed" is Jesus Christ (v. 16), who had only recently appeared in history. Paul then speaks of "faith in Jesus Christ" — that faith whose content is specifically the historical Jesus from Nazareth — which has come into existence in history: *"before* faith came, we were kept in custody under the law, being shut up to the faith which was *later* revealed . . . the Law has become our tutor to lead us to Christ . . . but *now* that faith has come, we are *no longer* under a tutor" (vv. 23-25).

This concept of being "under the Law" for a time is repeated in the analogy of the supervision of children. The child is under "managers" (manager here is the word *oikonomos*) *"until the date* set by the father" (Gal. 4:2). This situation of being under the *oikonomos* is compared to our situation of being "under the Law" (v. 5). And the date at which the child is released from his *oikonomos* (that is, released from the dispensation of guardianship to receive his full standing of sonship) is compared to that "fullness of time" at which God's Son came "that we might receive the adoption as sons."

It is unmistakable that in Paul's theology, there have been at least two dispensations (arrangements) between God and human beings in history. They are not simultaneous arrangements existing side-by-side through the course of history, but successive arrangements, one being replaced by the other in time.

And the time of dispensational change has occurred in conjunction with that great event of salvation history: the incarnation, death, resurrection, and ascension of Jesus of Nazareth, the Christ.

One other use of *oikonomia* by Paul should also be considered. In Ephesians 1:9-10, he says that the divine purpose for the "fullness of times" concerns a *dispensation,* an arrangement, structured by "the summing up of all things in Christ, things in the heavens and things upon the earth." It is plausible that this dispensation is the same one of which he speaks in Ephesians 3:9. As we have already noted, that dispensation (the one which has been in existence since the ascension of Christ) had been the subject of both Paul's prayer in 1:15-23 and his remarks about Jews and Gentiles in 2:11-22. With the present dispensation receiving so much attention in the rest of the letter, it would be reasonable to interpret Ephesians 1:10 as an introductory reference to it. Also, the union of all things in Christ, mentioned in 1:10, can be related to what Paul says in Ephesians 2:11-22 and 3:6-9 about the present dispensation. In Colossians 1:19-20, speaking again of the present dispensation, Paul says that "it was the Father's good pleasure . . . through Him to reconcile all things to Himself . . . things in heaven and things on earth." And in Galatians 4:4, he says that Christ was born in "the fulness of time."

Though the language of Ephesians 1:10 may relate to what Paul says elsewhere about the present dispensation, the possibility that Ephesians 1:10 refers to a yet future dispensation cannot be ruled out. The themes of present blessing and future inheritance are presented in verses 13-14. And it is clear that the present arrangement (dispensation) is a downpayment on blessings that will be fully realized in the future. Though existing blessings will differ from those in the future, the difference is one of degree not of kind.

It is quite possible that Paul has this future inheritance in mind when he speaks of the dispensation which God has planned for the fullness of times. The present dispensation is an arrangement in which the blessings of that inheritance have been inaugurated. The present arrangement is not the culmination of the divine plan, but it is both the revelation and the guarantee that that plan will yet be realized.

In Paul's theology, this future arrangement — the future reception of our inheritance—coincides with the return of Jesus Christ, the future culminating event of salvation history. He writes in Colossians 3:4, "When Christ, who is our life, is revealed, then you also will be revealed with Him in glory" (cf. Phil. 3:20-21; 1 Thes. 1:10; 4:13–5:11; 2 Thes. 1:6–2:14; 2 Tim. 4:1). The inheritance of Israel is also included as a feature of this salvation history which culminates at the coming of Christ (Rom. 11:26). As a result, the next dispensational change—the change to the arrangement of the future inheritance—coincides with the next great feature of salvation history. For Paul, dispensational theology and salvation history are interrelated.

***The Dispensations of Biblical History.*** We have seen that Paul uses the terminology of *oikonomos* and *oikonomia* to distinguish at least two and possibly three successive dispensations. Jesus' teaching that the coming kingdom of God would involve stewardship changes also shows the appropriateness of dispensational terminology to characterize his view of present and future. Could we use the word dispensation for other periods of history as well? Could it be used throughout the entire history of redemption, to characterize God's relationship with human beings from creation to eternity?

It certainly seems appropriate to use the word dispensation in this extended fashion. And in fact it has been used in this way by many in the history of Christian theology. Irenaeus, bishop of Lyons in the late second century, used the term dispensation repeatedly to refer to arrangements which God had set up in history. In the third book of his five volume *Against Heresies,* he follows Paul in distinguishing between the dispensation of the law set up through Moses and the new dispensation of liberty, the covenant instituted through Christ.[4] Then he periodizes biblical history according to covenants instituted through Adam, Noah, Moses, and the new covenant through Christ.[5] The last two correlate with his use of the term dispensation. This shows the natural way in which dispensation can be extended in the periodization of biblical history.

Augustine spoke of the periods of world history as distinguished by differing dispensations.[6] Elsewhere, he favors dividing history as successive millennia, a notion popular in the early church, although just how early theologians made their divisions differed from one person to another. Augustine divided the millennia from Adam to Noah, from Noah to Abraham, from Abraham to David, from David to the Exile, from the Exile to Christ, and from Christ onward including his own day.[7] Augustine's two periodization schemes do not entirely match, but they show the comprehensive scope he must have had in mind when he spoke of the various dispensations of world history.

Moving forward to more recent times, we can see that many theologians and biblical scholars from the Reformation era to the nineteenth century used the idea of a history of dispensations to set forth the structure of biblical history. Covenant theology, which began formalizing in the late sixteenth century, readily adopted this notion to explain differing historical manifestations of the covenant of grace. The Westminster Confession spoke of "various dispensations" which administered the covenant of grace.[8] After that time, dispensational divisions of biblical history became very common in British biblical studies. The following charts show a comparison of some of these schemes offered at that time. The chart on page 118 gives a comparison of writers from the seventeenth through early twentieth centuries, while the chart on page 119 compares the schemes of writers belonging specifically to the dispensationalist tradition.

One could say that throughout the history of the church certain divisions of biblical history have been commonly recognized: Creation to the Fall; the Fall to the Flood of Noah; the Flood to Abraham; Abraham to Moses; Moses to Christ; the first coming of Christ to the Second Coming. Each of these periods of biblical history have been and can be characterized by some interpreter as a dispensation. At the same time, we recognize that biblical history is more complex than this simple periodization would allow. The time between Moses and Christ (the history of Old Testament Israel) can certainly be subdivided in a number of ways: the Exodus, the sojourn in the wilderness, conquest under Joshua, the time of the Judges, Saul, David, Solomon, the divided kingdoms, the Exile and return. The word dispensation is flexible enough in its meaning that it could be properly applied to any of these different historical *arrangements*. Further subdivisions could also apply to the tenure of each of the patriarchs, each of the judges, or the rulership of each of the kings. In fact, as we saw earlier, different

# REPRESENTATIVE DISPENSATIONAL SCHEMES[1] (17th to 19th Centuries)

| Hugo Grotius (1583–1643) | Johannes Cocceius[3] (1603–69) | Herman Witsius[2] (1636–1708) | Francis Turretin[4] (1623–87) | Peter Poiret (1646–1719) | Isaac Watts (1674–1748) | John Fletcher (1729–85) | Patrick Fairbairn (1805–74) | John Cumming (1810–81) | Andrew R. Fausset (1821–1910) |
|---|---|---|---|---|---|---|---|---|---|
| Dispensation of Promise | Old Testament Dispensation Part 1: Promise | Old Testament Dispensation Part 1: Adam to Noah | Adam to Abraham | Infancy to the Deluge | Innocence / Adamical | Gentilism | Patriarchal | Adamic / Antediluvian | Innocence / Adamical |
| | | Part 2: Noah to Abraham | | Childhood to Moses | Noachical | | | Noachian | Noachical |
| | | Part 3: Abraham to Moses | Abraham to Moses | | Abrahamical | | | Abrahamic | Abrahamic |
| Dispensation of Law | Part 2: Law | Part 4: Moses to Christ | Moses to Christ | Adolescence to the Prophets | Mosaical | Judaism | Mosaic | Mosaic | Law |
| | | | | Youth to Christ | | Gospel of John the Baptist | | | |
| Dispensation of Gospel | New Testament Dispensation Part 1: Gospel | New Testament Dispensation Under various periods (7) | New Dispensation | Manhood | Christian Dispensation | Perfect Gospel | Christian | Christian | Christian Part 1: Spirit |
| | | | | Old Age | | | | | Part 2: Epiphany |
| | | | | Renovation (millennium) | | Prophetic Gospel (millennium) | | Millennium | Part 3: Final |
| | Part 2: Glory | | | | | | | Eternal State | |

1. Except for the first four, these dispensational outlines can be found in Arnold Ehlert, "A Bibliography of Dispensationalism," *Bibliotheca Sacra* 101-03 (1944–46). Compiled at a time when "dispensationalism" and "covenant theology" were polarizing through mutual criticism, Ehlert purposely omitted the dispensational schemes of early covenant theologians. He did not omit all covenantalists, as can be seen from some of his entries (e.g., Charles Hodge). However, dispensational distinctions made by theologians of the covenant tradition must be included as part of the general practice of dividing Scripture into a series of dispensations.
2. See Herman Witsius, *The Economy of the Covenants*, Trans. by Wm. Crookshank (London: 1822), 307–24.
3. Charles Sherwood McCoy, "The Covenant Theology of Johannes Coccevs" (Ph.D. diss. Yale Univ., 1956), 177.
4. Francis Turretin, *Institutio theologiae elencticae* 12.7. This outline was adopted by Charles Hodge. See his *Systematic Theology*, 3 vols. (N.Y.: 1874), 2:373–77.

## DISPENSATIONS IN THE DISPENSATIONAL TRADITION

| J.N. Darby (1808–82) | J.H. Brookes[2] (1830–97) | E.W. Bullinger[3] (1837–1913) | C.I. Scofield[5] (1843–1921) | I.M. Haldeman (1845–1933) | Wm. Graham Scroggie (1877–1958) |
|---|---|---|---|---|---|
| Paradisaical State[1] | Innocence | Innocence | Innocency | Edenic | Adamic |
| Conscience[1] | Conscience | Patriarchal | Conscience | Antediluvianm | Antediluvian |
| Noah | Patriarchs | | Human Government | Patriarchal | Noachian |
| Abraham | | | Promise | | Patriarchal |
| Israel 1. Law 2. Priest 3. Kings | Law | Law | Mosaic | | Sinaitic 1. Mosaic 2. Gideonic 3. Davidic |
| Gentiles | | | | | |
| Spirit/Christian Church | The Lord | Grace | Grace | Messianic | Christian |
| | Grace | Judicial[4] | | Holy Ghost | |
| Millennium | Millennial Age | Millennial | Kingdom | Restitution | Millennial |
| | | Glory | | Eternal State | Final |

1. Darby taught that these situations were not "dispensations." See Larry Crutchfield, *The Origins of Dispensationalism* (Lanham, Md.: Univ. Press of America, 1992), 67–75.
2. From James Hall Brookes, *I Am Coming*, 7th ed. (Glasgow: Pickering and Inglis, n.d.). The outline given by Arnold Ehlert, "A Bibliography of Dispensationalism," *Bibliotheca Sacra* (1945), 327, and reproduced in C. Ryrie, *Dispensationalism Today* (Chicago: Moody, 1965), 84, is the same in structure but different in nomenclature. Brookes attributed that outline to W.C. Bayne of McGill University. Brookes agreed with the structure but changed the nomenclature. The final outline is much closer to that eventually adopted by Scofield.
3. The dispensational schemes from Bullinger to Scroggie can be found in Ehlert, "A Bibliography of Dispensationalism."
4. The Day of the Lord.
5. This outline has been adopted and followed by many including Arno C. Gaebelein, H.A. Ironside, and Lewis Sperry Chafer.

stewardships under King Hezekiah warrant distinction as different dispensations.

This flexibility accounts for the variation seen in the charts on pages 118 and 119 where different theologians attempted to divide biblical history. Even dispensationalists have not agreed on the number of dispensations in biblical history, and in our sampling (p. 119) only three historical transitions were uniformly recognized as major dispensational changes.

Nevertheless, we can propose a way of dividing the dispensations of biblical history by following three basic principles: (1) begin with the structure of New Testament dispensationalism; (2) keep the basic dispensational scheme as simple as possible; and (3) be flexible with the notion of a dispensation so as to be able to see greater simplicity or greater differentiation than the working dispensational scheme allows. Let me explain this last point. The Bible itself draws continuities and distinctions throughout the history of revelation. One needs to be flexible enough to speak of both dispensational continuity and differences, depending on what aspect of biblical history is being looked at. For example, from one perspective, the dispensation of the Mosaic covenant can be regarded as a whole; yet from another perspective the same period of history is surveyed by noting a difference between the dispensation of the monarchy and the dispensation of the Judges. Flexibility in drawing dispensational distinctions will enable different interpreters of Scripture to work together in a constructive fashion as they seek to understand and explain biblical revelation.

With these principles in mind, let's construct the dispensations that distinguish biblical history. We begin first of all with Pauline dispensationalism, which uses explicit terminology and structure foundational for dispensational thought. As noted above, this yields us at least dispensations of the past and present, and possibly a third of the future as well. If we stick with Paul's terminology we would label these (1) the dispensation of the law, (2) the dispensation of the fullness of times, and (3) the dispensation of the mystery.

The first, "dispensation of the law," comes from Paul's illustration of the law as an *oikonomos* (Gal. 4). However, the term *law* is used in different senses by Paul, one of which is a reference to the Mosaic covenant as such. It would be preferable to title this dispensation "the dispensation of the Mosaic covenant" to avoid confusion that has arisen over Scofield's unqualified use of the term law in his title of that same dispensation (see the chart on p. 119). Though Scofield's designation has become very popular, one can see from the chart that other dispensationalists have referred to that dispensation as Mosaic. This avoids the implication that Paul was teaching antinomianism (lawlessness) by declaring the end of the law dispensation. Some may also wish to term this dispensation "the theocratic dispensation," since the Mosaic covenant primarily concerned the constitution of Israel as a theocracy, a political state governed by God.

Whether or not it is proper to understand the "dispensation of the fullness of times" in Ephesians 1:10 as future (a point which as noted above is debatable), there is no doubt that Paul expects future changes in the relationship between God and human beings at Christ's return. Romans 8:18-25 looks forward to the time when the children of God stand on the renewed and redeemed earth in resurrection bodies. In 1 Corinthians 15, Paul anticipates that time after the resurrection when the Son "delivers up the kingdom to God the Father" and God will be "all in all." Just prior to that time is a situation in which the reigning Christ puts "all His enemies under His feet," including death. This may be that millennial order which John envisions in Revelation 20. As a result, we anticipate in biblical theology a future dispensation which can be subdivided into two recognizable arrangements: the millennial kingdom of the returned Jesus Christ, and the eternal order of resurrection life on the redeemed earth. Some may wish to simply designate these as two future dispensations: the Millennium and the new earth. Or, following Ephesians 1:10, we could envision both phases, millennial and eternal, as the Final, or Zionic, dispensations.[9] The principles of simplicity and flexibility should guide us here.

The mystery referred to in the "dispensation of the mystery" (Eph. 3:9) is the relationship of Jews and Gentiles to Christ and to one another. This relationship is the distinguishing characteristic of the church. Consequently, one might just as well call this dispensation the "dispensation of the church" or the "ecclesial dispensation." One might also call it the "dispensation of the Spirit," since Paul contrasts the coming of the Spirit to the stewardship of the Law in Galatians 4. Either title (or some other) will do. For purposes of consistency, however, we will refer to it hereafter as the "ecclesial dispensation."

From this analysis of Pauline dispensationalism, it may be suggested that we see three dispensations: the Mosaic or theocratic dispensation, the ecclesial dispensation, and the Zionic or final dispensation which includes both the millennial and eternal kingdoms.

With regard to dispensations prior to the theocratic dispensation, we should follow the principles of simplicity and flexibility. In Galatians 3, Paul speaks of the time before the Law (before the Mosaic covenant) during which the Promise (Abrahamic promise) had been given. But he never speaks of the dispensation of promise as Scofield does. In Romans 5:13, Paul speaks of the time before the Law from the standpoint of sin's existence in the world. Sin was in the world before the Law, but it was counted as transgression after the giving of the Law. In this discussion of sin as transgression, the Mosaic dispensation is compared to the situation from Adam to Moses, implying that we see that whole period under a common arrangement or dispensation. Paul then goes on to speak of the new situation since the coming of the Spirit (Rom. 7–8). The contrast of Law and Spirit is essentially the same as that given in Galatians 3–5, where Paul distinguishes these situations as two different dispensations: the Mosaic and the ecclesial. This leads us to see the structure with respect to sin in Romans in closer harmony with Paul's dispensational divisions than his introduction of the notion of promise in Galatians 3.

As a result, we would suggest seeing the situation before the time of the Mosaic covenant as a unified, patriarchal dispensation. Patriarchs seems best suited as a title. This patriarchal dispensation includes God's relationships of blessing, judgment, and covenant with the various families of the earth including notable individuals such as Abel, Cain, Seth, Enoch, Noah, Noah's children, and Abraham, Sarah, and their descendants: Isaac, Jacob, and his twelve sons. A next major dispensation begins when God makes the covenant at Sinai with the twelve tribes of Israel.

Following the principle of flexibility, we can certainly allow other dispensational divisions to be drawn during this period of history. Some will want to highlight the prefall conditions of Eden as a peculiar arrangement. Others will want to distinguish conditions before and after the Flood of Genesis 6–9. Yet at the same time, there is a consistency to the actions of God with humanity that draws these conditions together as the foundational relationships to the later dispensations that present the Mosaic and new covenants.

In conclusion, we have four primary dispensations in biblical history: Patriarchal, Mosaic, Ecclesial, and Zionic dispensations.

| |
|---|
| **PATRIARCHAL** to Sinai |
| **MOSAIC** to Messiah's Ascension |
| **ECCLESIAL** to Messiah's Return |
| **ZIONIC** 1. Millennial 2. Eternal |

***Dispensations and Covenants.*** As Paul explains in Ephesians 3:4-10, the present dispensation (which he calls the dispensation of the mystery) relates Gentiles with Jews as "fellow-heirs and fellow-members of the body, and fellow-partakers of the promise in Christ Jesus through the Gospel" (Eph. 3:6). The word *promise* had previously been used in Ephesians 2:12 in a context in which Paul was developing the same thought about the co-relationship of Jews and Gentiles in Christ. In that passage he speaks of the *covenants of promise* to which Gentiles had been strangers but are strangers no longer (2:12, 19). These covenants belong to Israel as the parallel phrases in 2:11-12 make clear. This means that in Pauline dispensationalism, the past and present dispensations are to be understood as ways of relating to covenants.

The connection between covenant and promise had been drawn in Galatians 3:17, where reference is made to the covenant that preceded the Law (Mosaic covenant) in which God granted a promise to Abraham. Paul sees the Gospel of Jesus Christ as rooted in this promise covenanted to the Patriarch (Gal. 3:8, 16). He also sees that covenant as encompassing Gentiles in its prophetic scope (3:8). Gentiles who now believe in Jesus Christ are heirs of that covenant promise (3:28-29).

The new dispensation then is a new arrangement in which blessings promised through the Abrahamic covenant are being bestowed. However, in order for the bestowal to take place in its present manner (being granted equally to Gentiles as well as Jews), changes in other covenants had to take place.

In Ephesians 2:14-15, Paul argues that in order for Gentiles to be brought into an equal place of blessing with Jews, Christ "broke down the barrier of the dividing wall, by abolishing in His flesh the enmity, which is the Law of commandments contained in ordinances." The dividing wall was that portion of the temple which separated Jews from Gentiles. Its presence was a structural feature of the Mosaic covenant. In this passage, it symbolizes that covenant as a whole, referenced as "the Law of commandments contained in ordinances."

In biblical theology, the end of the Mosaic covenant correlates with the establishment of the new covenant. Paul presented himself as a minister of the new covenant (2 Cor. 3:6). And it is through newly inaugurated blessings of the new covenant that the dispensational change in Ephesians 2–3 has come about.

Paul writes that those who have believed the Gospel message have been "sealed in [Christ] with the Holy Spirit of promise" (Eph. 1:13). The word promise here is picked up again in 2:12 as "covenants of promise." The plural *covenants* indicates that more than one covenant is in view. We have already seen that the Abrahamic covenant is for Paul a covenant of promise. When we recall that the indwelling Holy Spirit was a specific promise of the new covenant (Isa. 59:21; Ezek. 36:27), it would seem that the linkage of 1:13 and 2:12 through the word *promise* indicates that the new covenant is rightfully included among the covenants to which Gentiles have been brought near. Even more than that, though, the new covenant blessing inaugurated with Christ's ascension is the blessing which characterizes the arrangement of the new dispensation. Ephesians 2:22 describes Jew and Gentile being built together in Christ as "a dwelling of God in the Spirit." The peace by which the new dispensation is characterized (Eph. 2:15) is the fruit of the indwelling Holy Spirit (Gal. 5:22) — the fulfillment of new covenant promise.

The covenants of promise rightfully include the covenant made with David. Note that the new covenant is not mentioned by name in Ephesians but is evident by reference to its characteristic features (note also forgiveness of sins in Eph. 1:7 and the knowledge of God in Eph. 3:19 and 4:13 [cf. Jer. 31:34]). Likewise, the elements of the Davidic covenant are also present in Ephesians, indicating that it is similarly intended within the covenants of promise mentioned in 2:12.

God had promised David concerning his descendant, "I will be a father to him and he will be a son to me." He promised to establish the kingdom of his son forever and to always maintain his loving-kindness with him. He also predicted that this son would build a house (a temple) for the Lord (2 Sam. 7:12-15). Jesus is presented in Ephesians 4:13 (as elsewhere in Paul's writings and the New Testament generally) as the Son of God. He is the Beloved (Eph. 1:6), a title which is connected with Son in the Father's descriptions of Him at His baptism and transfiguration (Matt. 3:17; 17:5; Mark 1:11; 9:7) and which recalls associated promises of sonship and everlasting loving-kindness in the covenant with David. Ephesians 1:20-22 has Him seated at the right hand of God with "all things in subjection under His feet." This recalls the promise of an established kingdom in the language of Psalms 2 and 110. And finally, Ephesians 2:14-22 pictures this one as constructing "a holy temple in the Lord," a Davidic covenant activity. And furthermore, this very same activity is the structural feature of the new dispensation — the building of Jew and Gentile together as partakers of Patriarchal and new covenant blessing.

As we have seen, transition from the past dispensation to the present involves covenantal change. The past dispensation was characterized by the Mosaic covenant; the present dispensation is characterized by certain blessings of the new covenant which have appeared in an inaugurated form. Both dispensations are ways of relating to the promises of the Patriarchal and Davidic covenants (given in a yet earlier dispensation). We will elaborate on this matter in greater detail in the next chapter. But from this very fact of covenantal continuity and change, the progressive and advancing nature of dispensational transition can be seen.

***Dispensations and the Kingdom of God.*** In Colossians 1:26, Paul speaks of the mystery of God which "has now been manifested to His saints." It is evident from the context of Colossians 1 that this is the dispensation Paul speaks of in Ephesians 3. It is noteworthy that this arrangement is also referred to in Colossians 1:13 as "the kingdom of His beloved Son." The words *beloved* and *Son* are used of Jesus in Ephesians, as we have seen, recalling the Father's designations at His baptism and transfiguration and looking back to the promises of the Davidic covenant. (In fact, the designation *Thou art my beloved Son* in Luke's account of the baptism of Jesus [Luke 3:22] is unmistakably a reference to Davidic covenant promise quoted in Luke 1:32-33: "He . . . will be called the Son of the Most High; and the Lord God will give Him the throne of His father David.) This, of course, fits with what we have already said about Davidic covenant fulfillment in Ephesians 1 and 2 (cf. Ps. 110:1). Jesus is seated at the right hand of God, "far above all rule and authority and power and dominion," with "all things in subjection under His feet."

This notion of the kingdom of God is tied directly to the person and work of Jesus, especially His ascension into heaven. As we have seen, this is exactly the point of dispensational change in the theology of Ephesians. We will address this more fully in a later chapter. But it is important to note that dispensational theology and kingdom theology are integrally connected. The change from the past to the present dispensation is coordinate with an appearance of the eschatological kingdom of God. Certain features predicted of the eschatological kingdom are present in the new dispensation, including a ruling Messiah and the phenomena of peace among and between His Jewish and Gentile subjects (Eph. 2:15, 17).

In biblical theology, the eschatological kingdom is the arrangement in which all covenantal promises are fulfilled. The present dispensation, however, is only an inauguration, a down payment (Eph. 1:13) on those promised blessings. Consequently, just as covenant blessings are yet to be fulfilled in their fullness (v. 14), so likewise the kingdom of God's Son has yet to receive its full revelation.

Whereas in the dispensation of Colossians 1:13 we have already been transferred into the kingdom, in Colossians 3:4 we expect that "when Christ . . . is revealed, then [we] also will be revealed with Him in glory." There is an appearance of the kingdom that is yet future, tied to the return of Christ (1 Cor. 15:23-28; 2 Tim. 4:1). It constitutes the dispensation that is likewise yet to come.

## Conclusion

A dispensation is an administrative or management arrangement. The Bible uses this term to describe God's relationship to the world. Not only is God's present relationship to the world described as a dispensation, but the Bible also compares and contrasts this present relationship with past and future dispensations as well. From this we understand that God's relationship with human beings consists of a history of successive dispensations.

These dispensations can be described as ways of relating to biblical covenants. They can also be seen as progressive stages of salvation history which finds its fulfillment in the revelation of the eschatological kingdom of God. As a result, understanding these biblical dispensations is crucial to understanding the history and theology of the Bible.

Understanding the Bible dispensationally is especially important for understanding God's relationship with human beings today. It helps us focus on those distinctive relationships He institutes today and the explicit responsibilities He gives us. In other words, interpreting the Bible dispensationally focuses especially on this dispensation, clarifying what the church is and what are the principles of Christian living and the nature of Christian responsibility. Dispensational interpretation helps the reader of Scripture understand the comparisons and contrasts which the New Testament draws to earlier history and to the time of the Lord's return when it describes our present situation as the church of Jesus Christ.

# Chapter Five
# The Structure of the Biblical Covenants: The Covenants Prior to Christ

The word covenant, *berit* in Hebrew and *diatheke* in Greek, is used in the Bible to refer to a variety of formal or legal agreements. These agreements, from individual wills, business contracts, territorial deeds, to national constitutions, define relationships between people. Since the term *dispensation* also speaks of a relational arrangement between people, it is easy to see how these terms conceptually overlap. When it comes to theological relationships—that is, to relationships between God and human beings—the notions of dispensation and of covenant are definitely interrelated. As was noted in the last chapter, Paul's perception of the dispensational change brought about by Jesus Christ was linked to and explained by covenantal changes which Jesus instituted. Consequently, a study of the covenants God has instituted with human beings and the history of their development will inform our understanding of dispensations and the progressive nature of dispensational change.

## The Noahic Covenant

The word covenant first appears in the Book of Genesis, where it is used to formalize divine promises of blessing. These covenants stand in contrast to divine judgments against human rebellion and sin, judgments bringing destruction and death. The greatest of these judgments is found in Genesis 3, where God cursed the earth, expelled Adam and Eve from a land of blessing, and decreed their death. The flood of Genesis 6–8 is also a dramatic judgment on human sinfulness, introduced by the lament in 6:5-7.

> Then the Lord saw that the wickedness of man was great on the earth, and that every intent of the thoughts of his heart was only evil continually. And the Lord was sorry that He had made man on the earth, and He was grieved in His heart. And the Lord said, "I will blot out man whom I have created from the face of the land, from man to animals to creeping things and to birds of the sky; for I am sorry that I have made them."

These judgments call into question the plan of creation. As God made the heavens and the earth, and filled the earth with life, repeatedly the refrain sounded, "it was good" (Gen. 1:4, 10, 12, 21, 25, 31). The Bible says that when He created humankind, "God blessed them; and God said to them, 'Be fruitful and multiply, and fill the earth, and subdue it; and rule over . . . every living thing that moves on the earth' " (v. 28). Human rebellion jeopardized that blessing to the point of bringing the human race and most of life on the earth to the point of extinction. Individually, all people faced death. Collectively, entire families, tribes, and cultures along with terrestrial life itself could be lost.

However, against the certain and menacing storm of divine judgment, we hear the words, "But Noah found favor in the eyes of the Lord" (Gen. 6:8). And in Genesis 6:18, the Lord formalizes a *covenant* to Noah, promising to preserve his life and the life of every kind of creature taken into the ark. The word *covenant* is used again in Genesis 9:9-17 of God's promise never again to destroy life on the earth through flood.

Whether viewed as two separate covenants or one and the same, these promises confirm the divine intention expressed in creation (Gen. 1–2) that there be an earth inhabited by life, filled with a humanity in communion with God. Furthermore, the formal nature of the covenant emphasizes that intent, pointing the way for a plan of redemption in which it will be accomplished.

## The Abrahamic Covenant

***The Contents of the Covenant.*** The Genesis narratives concerning Abraham begin with a promise from God to bless him and to bless all peoples on earth through him. This promise is further expanded into a collection of promises, all contributing to the notion of blessing. Included are the following:

1. God will bless Abraham (Gen. 12:2; 22:17)
2. Abraham will mediate God's blessing to others (to all nations) (Gen. 12:2-3; 18:18; 22:18)
3. He will also mediate God's curse (Gen. 12:3)
4. Abraham's name will be great (Gen. 12:2)
5. He will become a great nation (Gen. 12:2; 18:18)
6. God will give to him and to his descendants the land of Canaan (Gen. 12:7; 13:14-17; 15:7-21; 17:8)
7. Abraham will have innumerable descendants (Gen. 13:16; 15:4-7; 17:4-7, 15-21; 22:17)
8. This covenant will be established with Abraham's descendants (Gen. 17:7, 19, 21)
9. God will be the God of Abraham and his descendants, and they will be His people (Gen. 17:7-8)

Like the Noahic covenant, the Abrahamic covenant stands in contrast to the judgments of God on human sin and presents anew the plan of creation. This can be seen in the way that important elements in the creation of humankind are repeated in the blessing to Abraham: the multiplication of human beings, the provision of a special dwelling place on the earth (a land of blessing), and a peaceful relationship between God and humanity.

The Abrahamic blessing also reaches the ethnic and national dimensions of human existence. Genesis 10–11 shows how human life developed into various nations. Genesis 11 reveals how sin spread to the national level and how divine judgment exacerbated tensions between the nations. The promise to Abraham in Genesis 12, however, offers to bless nations. The blessings will come to one nation, descended from Abraham, and will then be mediated to all other nations as well.

Consequently, God affirmed the ethnic and national plurality of humanity. In promising to bless all peoples through Abraham, He did not follow the path He took with Noah. He did not propose to destroy all save Abraham and his immediate family, leaving Abraham the new progenitor of the race. On the other hand, the promise to bless all nations does not identify any particular nation except one which will be descended from Abraham. That nation, of course, will be Israel, the one which takes its name from Abraham's grandson, Jacob, who was renamed Israel by God. With the exception of Israel, nothing prevents the disappearance of certain nations in the course of history, and nothing precludes God reworking or recombining the ethnic and political structure of humanity through the course of its history. Nevertheless, the blessing envisioned in this covenant does see a plurality of nations.

The nature of the blessing which comes upon the nations would presumably be similar to the blessing which is promised to the nation of Abraham's descendants: numerous people, territorial possessions, and a peaceful relationship with God. These features present in a national form the blessings which God pronounced upon all humankind when He created them. But now, they are promised *first* to Abraham *and then* through him to the other nations on earth.

The blessings promised to Abraham are holistic, that is, they cover the whole of human life and experience: physical, material, social, personal (including mental and emotional), political and cultural, and religious. Once again this shows that this covenant affirms the plan of creation, for it offers blessings that extend through the whole scope of life as God created it.

The religious blessing (seen in God's promise to be their God and they to be His people) is the key to the others for it was the breach between God and humanity that brought about the loss of other blessings in the first place. The restoration of a peaceful relationship with God requires an act of reconciliation, of redemption, of forgiveness. Such an act is implied in the very fact that God approached Abraham to bless him. But it is revealed more directly in the promise of an abiding relationship between God as the God of His people and His people as the people of God. Just what that act of redemption would be required further revelation. Later we come to see that it is none other than the atoning death of Jesus Christ.

131

***The Nature of the Covenant.*** From the beginning in Genesis 12:1-3, the blessing to Abraham is presented as a collection of promises. No single passage contains all of the various elements. As the narratives progress, one or two aspects may receive special focus and more specific elaboration, and new promises may be added. It is clear, however, that they are meant to be taken together as one collective promise.

In two passages the term covenant is used to formalize the promise (that is, the collection of promises) as a legal agreement between God and Abraham (Gen. 15:18; 17:2, 7-21). Studies on the form of the Abrahamic covenant indicate that it is a grant covenant rather than a bilateral contract (as in a business contract or a treaty). That is, it follows the legal form used in the ancient Near East to ensure the integrity of a gift from one person to another, often from a master to a servant (or from a king to a subject). As such, the grant covenant is *unconditional,* for it guarantees the gift to the master's servant and his heirs.[1]

The way in which Abraham received the covenant also supports that covenant's unconditionality. In Genesis 15, the Lord repeats His promise to Abraham, and Scripture tells us that in spite of circumstances that made the promise seem impossible, "Abraham believed in the Lord; and He reckoned it to him as righteousness" (15:6). Further revelation is given to Abraham about how the promise would be fulfilled, and then in a formal ceremony, complete with accompanying sacrifices, "the Lord made a covenant with Abram" (15:18).

In Romans 4 and Galatians 3, Paul argues that Genesis 15 is foundational for understanding the promissory nature of the Abrahamic covenant. The blessing was not given to Abraham because he performed certain works. Rather, he received it through faith. God gave Abraham a promise. Abraham believed God. God counted him righteous and formalized the promise to him as a grant covenant.

A grant covenant does not, however, exclude obligations from the overall relationship of a recipient to his master. Disobedience or disloyalty are punishable offenses. The punishment may take away the enjoyment of the grant temporarily (as in the case of imprisonment) or permanently (through capital punishment). Yet the unconditional nature of the grant covenant guarantees the legal possession of the gift even during the period of such punishment. In the case of capital punishment, the grant covenant guarantees the inheritance of the gift by the recipient's heirs.

Certainly, Abraham was obligated to serve God faithfully and loyally. In Genesis 17:1, the Lord commanded him, "Walk before Me, and be blameless." In Genesis 18:19, the Lord states that He chose Abraham, "in order that he may command his children and his household after him to keep the way of the Lord by doing righteousness and justice; in order that the Lord may bring upon Abraham what He has spoken about him."

There are some occasions when Abraham seems to fall short of being "blameless." He left, for a while, the land in which he was told to dwell. And on two occasions, he was not completely honest about his relationship with Sarah, so that he almost caused his wife to commit adultery, not to mention the possibility of losing her completely to another man's harem. Nevertheless, Abraham is generally described in Genesis 26:5 as one who "obeyed Me and kept My charge, My commandments, My statutes and My laws." His obedience in offering up Isaac at the Lord's command is rewarded by an oath that the Lord will surely fulfill His promise to Abraham and to his descendants (Gen. 22:16-18).

The fact that God gives commandments to Abraham does not make His covenant with him a bilateral contract, one in which God's blessings are wholly dependent upon Abraham's (or his descendants') obedience. As Paul notes in Romans 4:1-5, God's relationship with Abraham is not contractual such that the blessing is offered to him as a wage. The grant covenant relationship is more like a bequest, with the blessing taking the form of a gift.

Others have observed that even in the structure of the Lord's commands to Abraham, the stress is on the intention to bless.[2] Many passages repeat the promise without accompanying obligation (see Gen. 12:7; 13:14-17; 15:1-7, 18-21), and even speak of the gift as everlasting (see Gen. 13:15; 17:7, 13, 19).

On the other hand, Abraham's obedience to God's commandments does function as *the means* by which he experiences God's blessing on a day to day basis. These commandments function as *conditions* for Abraham's *historical experience* of divine blessing, for as he obeys God, God blesses him more and more. But these obligations do not condition the fundamental intention to bless Abraham. They condition the *how* and the *when* of the blessing.

This is perhaps best seen in the Genesis 18:18-19 passage where in the strongest language possible, the Lord declares that "Abraham *will surely become* a great and mighty nation, and in him all the nations of the earth *will be* blessed." And then He adds, "For I have chosen him, in order that he may command his children and his household after him to keep the way of the Lord by doing righteousness and justice; *in order that the Lord may bring upon Abraham what He has spoken about him.*"

If the Abrahamic covenant was a bilateral covenant, verse 18 could not be stated in this factual way. Acts of disobedience on the part of Abraham or his descendants would be sufficient grounds for refusing the promised blessing. But in fact, God promises to fulfill the blessing in spite of human disobedience. Even after a long history in which descendants of Abraham failed "to keep the way of the Lord by doing righteousness and justice," the New Testament presents Jesus Christ as the present and future fulfillment of the Abrahamic covenant.

This does not mean that the commandments of the Lord are inconsequential or irrelevant to the promise. They function as means of experiencing blessing, which shows that God is concerned with holiness, with "righteousness and justice." He is just as concerned with human obedience as He was at the Creation or at the time of the Flood. But there is an unconditional intention to bless which will resolve the problem of human disobedience in a manner yet to be revealed. The fact that this will happen is seen in the unconditional promise that He *will be* their God and that they *will be* His people. It is also seen in the fact that He accepts the heirs on the basis of faith and that He promises to be with them and to help them. The final resolution will later be revealed in the promise of a new covenant. In the meantime, He accepts Abraham and his believing descendants into this covenant of blessing, training and disciplining them through commandments and ordinances.[3]

***The Abrahamic Covenant and the Bible.*** In Genesis 17:7, God promises to establish the covenant with Abraham's descendants (defined as the line of Isaac in 17:21 and then as the line of Jacob in 27:27-40) *throughout their generations for an ever-*

*lasting covenant.* The abiding nature of the Abrahamic covenant provides the ultimate revelation of its unconditionality.
While God imposes various obligations on Abraham's descendants, biblical history records numerous failures on their part
in meeting them. Nevertheless, this covenantal relationship remains in force through the generations, guiding the history of
redemption to a blessed conclusion.

The declaration of Genesis 17:7 extending the covenant to all
subsequent generations is significant. It means that the history
of Abraham's descendants (through Isaac and Jacob) must be
understood theologically from the standpoint of this covenant.
Since the rest of humankind is also envisioned in the promises
to bless or curse all other peoples, the Abrahamic covenant
consequently sets forth the foundational relationship between
God and all humankind from Abraham onward. This means that
to understand the Bible, one must read it in view of the
Abrahamic covenant, for that covenant with Abraham is the
foundational framework for interpreting the Scripture and the
history of redemption which it reveals.

**The Abrahamic Covenant and the Narratives of Isaac and
Jacob.** The foundational nature of the promise certainly gov-
erns the narratives of Isaac and Jacob which, in the Book of
Genesis, follow the narratives of Abraham. Twice to Isaac (Gen.
26:1-6, 19-26) and three times to Jacob (Gen. 27:18-29; 28:10-
16; 35:6-15) the promise is officially confirmed. Isaac is told
that the promise is being given to him for the sake of, or on the
basis of, the oath given to Abraham (Gen. 26:3, 5, 24). Likewise, when the promise is transferred to Jacob, God identifies
Himself to Jacob as the God of Abraham and of Isaac (Gen.
28:13). The following elements of the promise appear in these
texts:

1. God will bless them (Gen. 26:3, 24; 27:27-29)
2. They will mediate God's blessing to others (Gen. 26:4;
   27:29; 28:14)
3. They will mediate God's curse (Gen. 27:29)
4. God will give to them and to their descendants the land
   promised to Abraham (Gen. 26:2-4; 28:13-15; 35:12)
5. God will give them innumerable descendants (Gen. 26:4,
   24; 28:14; 35:11)

6. God will be their God (seen in His promises to be with them) (Gen. 26:3, 24; 28:15)

This last affirmation — that God will be with them — is striking, especially in the case of Jacob where it is tied to the promise of return to the land (Gen. 28:15). Also we should note that when the promise is transferred to Jacob, his mediation of blessing to other peoples and nations is interpreted as His rulership over them (Gen. 27:29). When the blessing is then transferred to Jacob's sons, this specific feature of rulership is given to Judah (Gen. 49:8-10),[4] where it anticipates the Messiah. This shows that the rulership of Messiah has its origin in the Abrahamic promise to bless all peoples.

The narratives of Isaac and Jacob reveal an important theme about the transference of the Abrahamic covenant. Physical descent from Abraham does not in itself guarantee inheritance of the covenant. Ishmael, a legitimate son of Abraham with the rights of firstborn, is passed over in favor of Isaac. The process of selection also extends to Isaac's descendants as Esau is passed over in favor of Jacob. Both Ishmael and Esau are blessed by God, but they are blessed as outsiders to the covenant. They are blessed *because of* Abraham, Isaac, and Jacob. They are included among the families of the earth, not within the "you" in whom the families of the earth are blessed.

The theme of selectivity in the inheritance of the covenant is important in the biblical history of redemption. The choice of Isaac over Ishmael reveals the process of divine election. It is not necessarily a choice here between condemnation and blessing but rather between mediating the blessing and receiving it through mediation. The choice between Jacob and Esau, however, is especially instructive for Jacob's descendants — the generations of Israel. Jacob is chosen to receive and mediate the covenant, for he is a man of faith who truly desires the Abrahamic covenant (his sinfulness notwithstanding). Esau disregarded his birthright. He is portrayed as an unbeliever (Heb. 12:16-17). Consequently, the inheritance of the covenant passed him by. At his repentance, he is granted a blessing, but it is not that of a covenant heir. He is blessed because of the covenant heirs Isaac and Jacob, not as one of the heirs himself.

In summary, the descendants of Abraham, Isaac, and Jacob were chosen by God to receive the covenant. All others, including other descendants of Abraham and Isaac, have the opportunity to receive blessing through the mediation of the elect line. Furthermore, the successive election of the patriarchs and their response to God in faith reveal two important principles for the history of Israel: (1) further selectivity in the physically elect line is possible; and (2) the true heirs are those who believe in God, those who receive the covenant from Him by faith.

***The Abrahamic Covenant in the History of Israel and the Nations.*** We note here that in setting forth the history of Israel and the nations, the Scriptures testify to the *abiding nature* of the Abrahamic covenant. We will reserve comments on how the blessings of the covenant were received for the discussion of the Mosaic covenant in the pages that follow, for the Mosaic covenant provided the dispensational structure in which Israel experienced the Abrahamic blessing.

Numerous references to the Abrahamic covenant in the rest of the Scriptures underscore its foundational nature for the generations following the patriarchs. At the beginning of the Book of Exodus, the statement is made, "God remembered His covenant with Abraham, Isaac, and Jacob. And God saw the sons of Israel, and God took notice of them" (Ex. 2:24-25). Even though the word covenant had not been used when the promise was transferred to Isaac and to Jacob, this Scripture teaches that the promise given to them must be understood precisely in this legal manner. Furthermore, this statement in Exodus 2 is positioned as an interpretive remark for all the events of the Exodus. The covenant with the patriarchs (Abraham, Isaac, and Jacob) is the formal, foundational relationship which explains God's actions toward Israel and toward Egypt during this time.

Our observation is confirmed by the Lord's remarks in Exodus 6:3-9 which refers explicitly to His covenant with the patriarchs and highlights two of the subsidiary promises: the land of inheritance and the promise to be their God. The promise to the patriarchs to establish this covenant with their descendants undergirds the whole conversation. The phrase, "I have remembered My covenant," is further explained: "I am the Lord, and I will bring you out from under the burdens of the Egyptians, and I will deliver you from their bondage. I will also redeem you with an outstretched arm and with great judgments."

Throughout Exodus and Deuteronomy, and to a lesser extent in Numbers and Leviticus, there are numerous *explicit* references to the patriarchal covenantal relationship, either using the term covenant as such or by reference to the oath sworn to Abraham, Isaac, and Jacob. It is also heard in repeated references to God as the God of Abraham, Isaac, and Jacob. Added to this is the fact that this literature presents an extended discussion of two of the subsidiary promises of the patriarchal covenant: the Promised Land and God's relationship to Israel as their God and theirs to Him as His people. Repeatedly, these matters are mentioned as promises made *to the patriarchs.*[5]

The fundamental and abiding nature of the Abrahamic covenant as the constitutive relationship between God and Israel is reaffirmed through explicit statements in narratives of later Israelite history and in wisdom and prophetic literature. In 1 Chronicles 16, portions of two psalms are historically situated in the celebrations of David upon the arrival of the ark of the Lord in Jerusalem. In the praises being offered are the words:

Remember His covenant forever,
The word which He commanded to a thousand generations,
The covenant which He made with Abraham,
And His oath to Isaac,
He also confirmed it to Jacob for a statute,
To Israel as an everlasting covenant,
Saying, "To you I will give the land of Canaan,
As the portion of your inheritance,
When you were only a few in number,
Very few, and strangers in it" (1 Chron. 16:15-19).

The psalm goes on to recount the Exodus from Egypt. Like the Books of Exodus and Deuteronomy, this passage views the entire chain of events making up the Exodus from the perspective of the covenant with Abraham. (Psalm 105 is the extended version of this psalm; it concludes with the phrase, "For He remembered His holy word with Abraham His servant; And He brought forth His people with joy, His chosen ones with a joyful shout.") But the Chronicler places this psalm in the setting of David's capture of Jerusalem from its long intractable Canaanite inhabitants (the Jebusites), expressing praise to God

138

with the phrase "Remember His covenant forever . . . which He commanded to a thousand generations." Accordingly, the Chronicler sees those events in Jerusalem at the time of David as fundamentally based on the Abrahamic covenant (and specifically related to that covenant's promise of the land of Canaan).

In 2 Kings 13:22-23, the writer interprets the Lord's grace to Israel during the reign of Jehoahaz as fundamentally based on the covenant with Abraham. These were the days of the divided monarchy. The northern tribes, retaining the name Israel, were led by a succession of idolatrous kings. Jehoahaz was no different, except that he did call upon the Lord to deliver Israel from the harsh oppression of the Syrians. The Scripture reads: "But the Lord was gracious to them and had compassion on them and turned to them because of His covenant with Abraham, Isaac, and Jacob, and would not destroy them or cast them from His presence until now." The last phrase extends this covenantal loyalty to the time of the writer (around the time of Israel's exile). Consequently, the Abrahamic covenant is seen as the fundamental relationship between God, Israel, and Judah through the history of the two monarchies.

As the time of the Exile drew near, the prophets' interpretations of the coming judgment made frequent reference to the Abrahamic covenant. On the one hand, warnings about the impending judgment are conditioned with offers to bless with covenanted promises.[6] On the other hand, as judgment becomes sure, the covenanted blessings are predicted for a yet future day.[7] The important point is that the covenant of promise made with the patriarchs continues as the fundamental defining relationship between God and Israel, even though extreme judgments eliminate for a time the present experience of blessing (or at least the most visible aspects of that blessing).

## Summary

The Abrahamic covenant clarifies the way in which God will fulfill for humanity the blessing promised to Noah for all flesh. A principle of mediation has been introduced, beginning with Abraham and transferring to his descendants who are selected and accepted by God. From the mediator(s), the blessing passes to others (both to subsequent mediators and to outside recipients who seek it by faith — or in the language of the covenant, who bless God and Abraham or the mediators descended from him).

The blessing is not fully detailed in the Genesis narratives but subject to further revelation. However, the blessing is set forth against the background of earlier curses of death and destruction, curses which threaten the divine plan of creation. Consequently, the promised blessing appears to offer the hope of redemption from those curses and the restoration of the favor shown in creation. The blessing is a renewal of *life* as revealed in the creation itself and seen in the repetition of certain themes pronounced at the creation of humankind.

The revelation of these and some other aspects of the blessing shows it to be holistic, that is, it covers all aspects of human experience. Included within the blessing and foundational to all other aspects is the relationship between humanity and God. The Abrahamic blessing offers the hope of reconciliation with God, the restoration of proper worship, and divine-human fellowship. In later revelation, we see that this blessing includes the atonement of Christ, rectification of human sinfulness leading to full communion with God, and resurrection to immortality and everlasting life.

The Noahic and Abrahamic covenants reveal aspects of the overall plan of redemption and set forth a foundational structure for the subsequent relationship between God, humanity, and life on the earth. This foundation is established in an unconditional divine determination to bless. It is revealed both in the patriarchal narratives themselves and in the repetitive reaffirmation of the covenant through the progress of revelation. As we continue our study of the covenants, we will see this foundation confirmed, clarified, and expanded. We will also see that progressive confirmation and expansion taking place in a succession of new dispensations which come into existence as subsequent covenants are revealed, inaugurated, and fulfilled in human experience.

## The Mosaic Covenant

***The Contents of the Mosaic Covenant.*** As Israel is poised to enter the land promised in the patriarchal covenant, Moses recalls a special relationship which God established with them at Sinai (Horeb). He states:

140

The Lord our God made a covenant with us at Horeb. The Lord did not make this covenant with our fathers, but with us, with all those of us alive here today. The Lord spoke to you face to face at the mountain from the midst of the fire, while I was standing between the Lord and you at that time, to declare to you the word of the Lord; for you were afraid because of the fire and did not go up the mountain (Deut. 5:2-5).

Due to the mediatorial role of Moses on this occasion, this covenant is often called the Mosaic covenant. As noted in the passage just quoted, it was a special covenant which had not been made with the patriarchs. Yet, it was given to Israel because of the relationship with God granted to them by the patriarchal covenant. Recalling the events of the Exodus and the covenant at Sinai, Moses states:

Out of the heavens He let you hear His voice to discipline you; and on earth He let you see His great fire, and you heard His words from the midst of the fire. *Because He loved your fathers, therefore He chose their descendants after them.* And He personally brought you from Egypt by His great power, driving out from before you nations greater and mightier than you, to bring you in and to give you their land for an inheritance, as it is today (Deut. 4:36-38).

We have already seen that the Books of Exodus and Deuteronomy contain many references to the Abrahamic covenant. These references establish the fact that not only the event of the Exodus and wilderness sojourn as a whole, but also the specific establishment of the covenant at Sinai are all based on the fundamental covenant with Abraham. Reconfirming the gracious character of the patriarchal grant, the Lord first bound that generation of Israel to Himself by faith (Ex. 14:31), and *then* He established a covenant with them to bring into their day-to-day history an experience of the blessings promised to the patriarchs.

The dependence of the Mosaic covenant upon the Abrahamic covenant is seen in a comparison of their respective blessings. The blessings of the Mosaic covenant (see Lev. 26; Deut. 6–11; 28) restate the promises of the Abrahamic covenant.

1. God will bless them (Lev. 26:4-12; Deut. 7:13-15; 28:3-12)
2. God will multiply them (Lev. 26:9; Deut. 6:3; 8:1; 28:11)
3. God will give them this land (Lev. 26:5; Deut. 6:3; 8:1; 9:4; 28:11)
4. God will make them a great nation (Deut. 7:14; 28:1, 3)
5. God will be their God and they will be His people (Lev. 26:11-12; Deut. 7:6-10; 28:9-10)
6. God will confirm His covenant with these particular descendants of the patriarchs (Lev. 26:9)

The only difference in the way the blessings are stated is that the general promise, "I will bless you," is given more specific content as physical, material, and national prosperity.

With Israel poised to enter Canaan in holy war, little is said in these texts about the promise to mediate blessing to the nations. The mediation of divine curse, however, is readily apparent. God is using Israel to judge the nations in Canaan. But the promise to mediate blessing is not forgotten. Balaam prophesies in Numbers 24:9, "Blessed is everyone who blesses you, and cursed is everyone who curses you." As late as Jeremiah 4:1-2, Israel is admonished that if they return to the Lord (in accordance with the Mosaic covenant), "then the nations will bless themselves in Him, and in Him they will glory."

***Nature of the Mosaic Covenant.*** Since these blessings are already promised in the covenant with Abraham, what is the purpose of stating them in the form of a covenant at Sinai? Is the Mosaic covenant any more than a restatement of the covenant with the patriarchs?

The difference between the two covenants is seen first of all in Moses' statement that the covenant made at Horeb (Sinai) was *not* made with the patriarchs (Deut. 5:3). Second, the two covenants have different forms. Whereas the covenant with Abraham was a grant covenant, the Mosaic covenant follows the form of a Suzerain-vassal treaty, that is, a treaty between a king (Suzerain) and his subjects (vassals). This kind of covenant is not a grant to a particular subject but a bilateral agreement between the king and the nation subject to him in which the king promises to allow his subjects to enjoy life under his beneficent reign in return for their loyal service to him. Conversely, he threatens to punish those who disobey his laws. The

Mosaic covenant follows this treaty form. In fact, the structure of a typical Suzerain-vassal treaty can be detected in the literary structures of Exodus and Deuteronomy (practically all of Deuteronomy follows this structure):

*Elements of a Suzerain-Vassal Treaty*
1. Identity of the King (Ex. 20:2; Deut. 1:1-6)
2. Historical Relationship between the King and the People (Ex. 20:2; Deut. 1:6–4:49)
3. Stipulations, the Laws of the King (Ex. 20–31; Deut. 5–26)
4. Blessings and Curses (Lev. 26; Deut. 27–30)
5. Witnesses (Deut. 4:26; 30:19; 31:28)
6. Ceremonial Meal (Ex. 24:9-11)
7. Filing of the Treaty (Ex. 25:16; 40:21; Deut. 31:25-26)

It is important to note that the blessings of a Suzerain-vassal treaty are *conditioned* on the fulfillment of the stipulations. Also cursing is a real possibility should the laws be transgressed. This in turn helps to clarify the significance of the Mosaic covenant.

The Abrahamic covenant promised blessing in the indefinite future. God simply said, "I will bless you." Furthermore, the blessing itself was partly indefinite, allowing for further specification. The Mosaic covenant offered a specific generation of Abraham's descendants the opportunity of experiencing very specific aspects of that blessing (see Deut. 28) in the definite present, the here and now. But that blessing was dependent on Israel's obedience to the law of the covenant. Disobedience to the law would not only remove the experience of blessing, but would bring God's curse upon them — the radical contrary of a blessed life (see the curses listed in Deut. 28).

The Mosaic covenant, then, had a function similar to the commandments given to the patriarchs. Their obedience was the means to experience covenant blessing in their personal lives. The Mosaic covenant functioned in this way on behalf of a *nation* of Abraham's descendants.

However, we should also note that the first three commandments concern the people's exclusive faith and trust in the Lord. They are commanded to be a people of faith in the Lord, and then they are commanded to live a life of obedience to His will. Like Abraham and the individual patriarchs, so now the nation as a whole would receive the covenant grant by faith and would experience in their own historical situation the blessings God would bestow upon them.

It is important, at this point, to remember that the Abrahamic covenant is the fundamental relationship. The Mosaic covenant is dependent upon it. This means that even though a certain generation (or generations) fails the terms of the Mosaic covenant and experiences the curse instead of the blessing, the opportunity still exists for a renewed offer of blessing to that generation or later descendants of Abraham.

Statements within the literary structure of the Mosaic covenant verify this point. In Deuteronomy 4, that portion of the covenant immediately preceding the Ten Commandments and additional laws, Moses warns Israel of the consequences of not following God's commandments.

> I call heaven and earth to witness against you today, that you shall surely perish quickly from the land where you are going over the Jordan to possess it. You shall not live long on it, but shall be utterly destroyed. And the Lord will scatter you among the peoples, and you shall be left few in number among the nations, where the Lord shall drive you (vv. 26-27).

Yet, he then predicts that the Lord's blessing will eventually be restored.

> But from there you will seek the Lord your God, and you will find Him if you search for Him with all your heart and all your soul. When you are in distress and all these things have come upon you, in the latter days, you will return to the Lord your God and listen to His voice. For the Lord your God is a compassionate God; He will not fail you nor destroy you *nor forget the covenant with your fathers which He swore to them* (vv. 29-31).

Note the reference to the covenant which God swore to the patriarchs. Because of this foundational covenant, complete failure by one generation may be replaced by blessing on a future one.[8]

This relationship between the Mosaic and Abrahamic covenants helps explain the combination of warnings and promises given by the prophets especially as the destruction of Jerusalem and the exile of the nation drew near. Jeremiah 11:1-5 declares a curse against those who do not obey the laws of the Mosaic covenant, the covenant which was given "to confirm the oath which [God] swore to [their] forefathers [Abraham, Isaac, and Jacob]" that they would be His people and dwell in the land. Jeremiah summarizes the message of all the prophets as a message of repentance in order to enjoy the patriarchal blessing (25:4ff). But as a result of continued disobedience [to the Mosaic law], Jeremiah predicts the coming destruction and exile. And yet he later prophesies, " 'For behold, days are coming,' declares the Lord, 'when I will restore the fortunes of My people Israel and Judah.' The Lord says, 'I will also bring them back *to the land that I gave to their forefathers,* and they shall possess it.' " Ezekiel also explains the destruction and exile of the nation as a judgment in keeping with the terms of the Mosaic covenant, but like Jeremiah he predicts a future restoration to blessings promised to the patriarchs (Ezek. 20:1-44; 36:17-38).

The patriarchs who received the Abrahamic covenant received it by faith. To be sure, they were chosen by God. Abraham was chosen and received the promise that blessing and mediation of blessing would be granted to his descendants. However, God reserved the privilege of selecting some from among the entire number of physical descendants to receive this covenant. Those who received it did so by faith.

Since the Mosaic covenant is a form of the Abrahamic covenant, we should expect that the granting of blessing requires believing recipients. However, the Mosaic covenant was given to Israel *as a nation,* which raises a problem: What if the nation is mixed, including believers and unbelievers, those who worship and trust in God and those who trust in themselves or in false gods? What if some of them despise the covenant as did Esau?

The histories of Israel and Judah and the warnings and admonitions of the prophets reveal two related principles that speak to this concern. One is that God's covenant response to the nation varies depending on its overall character. When Israel as a whole is characterized as a nation of faith and trust in the Lord, God blesses them with the blessings of the Mosaic covenant. For example, at the Red Sea He delivered them from death, preserved their lives, and set them on a course to inherit the land promised to the patriarchs. For their part, "the people feared the Lord, and they believed in the Lord and in His servant Moses" (Ex. 14:31).

The people who crossed the Jordan feared the Lord; they trusted in Him and acted in obedience to His commands on the basis of their faith. And He gave them the land promised to their forefathers. At the end of the conquest, they affirmed together:

> Far be it from us that we should forsake the Lord to serve other gods; for the Lord our God is He who brought us and our fathers up out of the land of Egypt, from the house of bondage, and who did these great signs in our sight and preserved us through all the way in which we went and among all the peoples through whose midst we passed. And the Lord drove out from before us all the peoples, even the Amorites who lived in the land. We also will serve the Lord, for He is our God. . . . We will serve the Lord our God and we will obey His voice (Josh. 24:16-18, 24).

To that generation, the Scripture says that "the Lord had given rest to Israel from all their enemies on every side" (Josh. 23:1). Joshua also testified, "not one word of all the good words which the Lord your God spoke concerning you has failed; all have been fulfilled for you, not one of them has failed" (Josh. 23:14).

In 1 Samuel 7, at the end of the time of the Judges, "the sons of Israel removed the Baals and the Ashtaroth and served the Lord alone" (v. 4). They confessed, "We have sinned against the Lord," and they cried to the Lord to save them (vv. 6-8). And the Lord delivered them and granted peace in the land (vv. 9-14).

The reigns of David and Solomon established the worship of the Lord in Israel, so that in the reign of Solomon it was said:

> Judah and Israel were as numerous as the sand that is on the seashore in abundance; they were eating and drinking and rejoicing. Now Solomon ruled over all the kingdoms

from the River to the land of the Philistines and to the border of Egypt; they brought tribute and served Solomon all the days of his life . . . and he had peace on all sides around him. So Judah and Israel lived in safety, every man under his vine and his fig tree, from Dan to Beersheba, all the days of Solomon (1 Kings 4:20-21, 24-25).

However, when Israel as a whole was characterized as a faithless nation, they experienced the curses rather than the blessings of the covenant. At Sinai, while Moses was on the mountain, the people made an idol saying, "This is your god, O Israel, who brought you up from the land of Egypt" (Ex. 32:4). In response, the Lord told Moses, "Now then, let Me alone, that My anger may burn against them, and that I may destroy them; and I will make of you a great nation" (Ex. 32:10). This proposed judgment was similar to that which the Lord carried out on all humanity in the days of Noah, and it is directly related to Israel's lack of faith in the Lord. God's later decision not to carry out this threat leads to a revelation of His character as "compassionate and gracious, slow to anger, and abounding in lovingkindness." However, lest there be any doubt, he quickly adds that, "He will by no means leave the guilty unpunished." (See Ex. 34:6-7.)

The Book of Judges gives the story of Israel's struggle with faith and the tentativeness of divine blessing. In Judges 2:10, we read that after the death of the generation which entered the land under Joshua, "there arose another generation after them who did not know the Lord, nor yet the work which He had done for Israel." They were an unbelieving generation who

forsook the Lord, the God of their fathers . . . and followed other gods from among the peoples who were around them, and bowed themselves down to them; thus they provoked the Lord to anger. . . . And the anger of the Lord burned against Israel, and He gave them into the hands of plunderers who plundered them; and He sold them into the hands of their enemies around them, so that they could no longer stand before their enemies. Wherever they went, the hand of the Lord was against them for evil, as the Lord had spoken and as the Lord had sworn to them, so that they were severely distressed (Judges 2:12-15).

From the end of Solomon's reign through the history of the kings of Israel and Judah, the people struggled with faith in the Lord. In spite of notable exceptions, both nations came to be characterized as an unbelieving people, nations that forsook the Lord by putting their trust in other gods. Eventually this brought the ultimate curse of death, destruction, and expulsion from the land of blessing. In 2 Chronicles 36:11-21, we read how Zedekiah, the last king of Judah, following the pattern of those who reigned before him

> did evil in the sight of the Lord his God; he did not humble himself before Jeremiah the prophet who spoke for the Lord. . . . But he stiffened his neck and hardened his heart against turning to the Lord God of Israel. Furthermore, all the officials of the priests and the people were very unfaithful following all the abominations of the nations; and they defiled the house of the Lord which He had sanctified in Jerusalem. And the Lord, the God of their fathers, sent word to them again and again by His messengers, because He had compassion on His people and on His dwelling place; but they continually mocked the messengers of God, despised His words and scoffed at His prophets, until the wrath of the Lord arose against His people, until there was no remedy.

Because the nation as a whole was characterized as an unbelieving, faithless people, the wrath of God came upon them. They were cut off from the blessings promised to Abraham and his descendants, for those blessings were to be received by faith in the Lord. Under the terms of the Mosaic covenant, when the nation was a nation of faith, trusting in the Lord and walking in His ways, they were blessed with the dispensational form of the Abrahamic blessing offered in the Mosaic covenant. When they were a nation that rejected the Lord, characterized by unbelief, putting their faith in and walking in the ways of other gods rather than the Lord, they did not receive the Lord's blessing. They were viewed by God as "not My people and I am not your God" (Hosea 1:9).

Consequently, we see that in the Mosaic dispensation, God related to Israel as a nation, a collective group of people who could be characterized on the whole as either a people of faith or an unbelieving people. But there is another principle, the principle of the remnant of faith. God's treatment of the nation as a whole takes into account those individuals who truly place their faith, confidence, and trust in the Lord. They are the true recipients of the Abrahamic grant, meaning that not only do they receive the Lord's blessing, but they mediate it to the rest.

The presence of a large majority of believers within Israel leads to the characterization of the nation as one of faith. However, the fact that the nation as a whole is treated as a believing, faithful people does not mean that every member of it is thereby deemed a believer and consequently justified as was Abraham. Rather, the presence of a large majority of individuals who are believers and consequently justified, creates a situation in which the Lord bestows national blessings upon the collective whole.

When the nation as a whole is characterized by unbelief, the Lord nevertheless maintains a remnant of faith within it. In the days when Ahab and Jezebel ruled Israel and led the nation into the worship of Baal, the covenant curses of famine and trouble fell upon the nation. Elijah felt that he was the only worshiper of God left among the people. But the Lord revealed to him that He had 7,000 who revered the Lord (1 Kings 19:14, 18).

As the judgment of God comes upon the nation which as a whole is characterized by unbelief, the remnant maintains its trust in the Lord. Their lives are founded upon the Rock of Israel, finding security in Him even as destruction breaks out around them (Isa. 28:16). The blessing covenanted to them is an eschatological hope that the wrath of God falling upon the nation will function as a purifying, refining fire which will usher them—the remnant of faith—into the covenanted blessing.

> But who can endure the day of His coming? And who can stand when He appears? For He is like a refiner's fire and like fullers' soap. And He will sit as a smelter and purifier of silver, and He will purify the sons of Levi and refine them like gold and silver, so that they may present to the Lord offerings in righteousness. Then the offering of Judah and Jerusalem will be pleasing to the Lord, as in the days of old and as in former years. . . . "For behold, the day is coming, burning like a furnace; and all the arrogant and every evildoer will be chaff; and the day that is coming will

set them ablaze," says the Lord of hosts, "so that it will leave them neither root nor branch. But for you who fear My name the sun of righteousness will rise with healing in its wings; and you will go forth and skip about like calves from the stall" (Mal. 3:2-4; 4:1-2; cf. Isa. 1:24-26).

This theme is repeated often in the prophets. The Lord will leave a remnant of those who take refuge in Him (Zeph. 3:12-13), who truly rely on the Lord (Isa. 10:20-23). They will be His sheep, and He will reign over them (Micah 2:12; 4:6-8). They will be holy and will be blessed with the blessing promised to the patriarchs (Isa. 4; Micah 7:18-20; Zech. 8:11-13). At that time, they will fully constitute the nation of Israel, so that Israel will indeed be a nation wholly constituted by faith and trust in the Lord and consequently wholly blessed by Him.

The remnant of faith, which through the judgments of God's wrath emerges to become the eschatological nation, is also the object of prophecies of a new covenant which look beyond the Mosaic dispensation for the fulfillment of the grant made to the patriarchs, a theme which takes us forward in our study of the covenants. They are also the people to whom an everlasting kingdom is given in the apocalyptic visions of Daniel—the saints of the Most High. That theme in turn will lead us to a later chapter where we trace the biblical teaching on the eschatological kingdom of God.

## The Fulfillment of the Mosaic Covenant

As a bilateral treaty, the Mosaic covenant can be said to be fulfilled successively in the history of each generation of the descendants of the patriarchs. It is a covenant which concerns the concrete, present relationship of Israel and Judah to God. In each generation, God manifests the blessing or the curse (or aspects of both) in response to the faith and obedience (or unbelief and disobedience) of the people. However, predictions begin to arise in the latter prophets that the Mosaic covenant will be replaced by another covenant which will fulfill the intention God revealed in the Abrahamic promise. Consequently, in addition to its ongoing historical fulfillment, we will speak of a final fulfillment of the Mosaic covenant which the New Testament sees as taking place in Jesus Christ.

## The Mosaic Dispensation

Before leaving this discussion of the Mosaic covenant, we need to note what it has to say about the history of dispensations. The relational arrangement of the Mosaic covenant is identified by the Apostle Paul as that dispensation which preceded the one in which we now find ourselves. Our study up to this point indicates that when it was instituted, the Mosaic dispensation marked a change from the way God related to the patriarchs. A covenant was made which had not been in existence in the days of the patriarchs. It set up an arrangement by which God would relate to the descendants of the patriarchs as a nation, distinguishing them from other nations on earth. It was not, however, *utterly* different from the patriarchal dispensation which preceded it. In fact, the Mosaic dispensation was a dispensation of the blessing promised to the patriarchs. The promises covenanted to Noah and Abraham (which also take in the plans and intention for humanity revealed in the creation narratives) form the structural continuity between these dispensations. But dispensational change comes as God institutes a new arrangement for realizing those blessings.

At the same time, the Mosaic dispensation is a *progression* in dispensational history. It sets up a *national* religious cult for the relationship between God and His people. The Mosaic covenant also offered an extensive revelation of the will of God in the giving of the Law, and it provided the means for blessing an entire nation and, through them, all peoples on the earth.

## The New Covenant

*The Contents of the New Covenant.* Among the prophecies of Isaiah, Jeremiah, and Ezekiel regarding the future restoration of patriarchal covenant blessings after the exile of Israel and Judah are predictions of a new covenant which will replace the covenant made at Sinai. This new covenant will have a purpose similar to the Mosaic covenant — that is, to bring the blessing of the Abrahamic covenant back into the present experience of a generation or generations of Israel. However, whereas the Mosaic covenant was set forth with stern warnings of national failure and liability to the curse of God's judgment, the prophets speak more optimistically of the new covenant.

151

***A New Heart Indwelt by God's Spirit.*** One reason for the optimism is that the new covenant will be constituted by a divine operation on the human heart. This will be a unilateral act of God which will render the recipient faithfully devoted to God and obedient to His law.

Jeremiah speaks of this gracious act of God as the writing of the law on the heart. " 'But [in contrast to the Mosaic covenant] this is the covenant which I will make with the house of Israel after those days,' declares the Lord, 'I will put My law within them, and on their heart I will write it' " (Jer. 31:33). The act of writing the law on their hearts is an act of making the law of God the internal principle of the life and conduct of His people. God is saying that by divine action He will overcome the distance between external divine commands and internal human rebellion. He will make them to be the kind of people He wants them to be. As a result of writing His law directly into their hearts, He says, "I will be their God, and they shall be My people" (Jer. 31:33); and "they shall all know Me, from the least of them to the greatest of them" (v. 34).

This action is anticipated in the promise at the end of Deuteronomy, that in the restoration—after the consummation of the curses of the Mosaic covenant—God would circumcise the hearts of His people. He had already commanded them to circumcise their own hearts (Deut. 10:16; cf. Jer. 4:4; 9:25), a metaphor which speaks of rendering themselves holy, set apart to God (physical circumcision was a sign that as a people they were holy, set apart to God). Yet warnings were given that they would fail, invoking the curses of that covenant even to the point of expulsion from the land of inheritance. In contemplating their return to a state of blessing (in accordance with the patriarchal covenant), Deuteronomy 30:6 predicts, "The Lord your God will circumcise your heart and the heart of your descendants, to love the Lord your God with all your heart and with all your soul, in order that you may live."

In Jeremiah 32, the divine operation on the human heart is described as instilling the fear of the Lord: "I will put the fear of Me in their hearts so that they will not turn away from Me" (v. 40). This is also described as giving them a different heart toward God: "I will give them one heart and one way, that they may fear Me always, for their own good, and for the good of their children after them" (v. 39).

The theme of a new heart is picked up by Ezekiel: "I shall give them one heart, and shall put a new spirit within them. And I shall take the heart of stone out of their flesh and give them a heart of flesh, that they may walk in My statutes and keep My ordinances, and do them" (Ezek. 11:19-20). This is repeated in Ezekiel 36:26: "I will give you a new heart," with the associated promise of the indwelling Holy Spirit. The indwelling Holy Spirit will be the agent by which the writing of the law on the heart is accomplished and the new heart is thereby formed. "And I will put My Spirit within you and cause you to walk in My statutes, and you will be careful to observe My ordinances" (Ezek. 36:27). Isaiah combines both concepts of Word and Spirit in predicting the covenant which the Lord will make when He comes as redeemer to Zion: " 'And as for me, this is My covenant with them,' says the Lord: 'My Spirit which is upon you, and My words which I have put in your mouth, shall not depart from your mouth nor from the mouth of your offspring, nor from the mouth of your offspring's offspring,' says the Lord, 'from now and forever' " (Isa. 59:21).

***Forgiveness and Cleansing from Sin.*** A second reason for the prophets' optimism about the new covenant as contrasted with the old is that God will grant His people forgiveness and cleansing from all sin. In Jeremiah, the Lord declares, "I will forgive their iniquity, and their sin I will remember no more" (31:34; cf. Ezek. 16:62-63). In the Book of Ezekiel He states: "Then I will sprinkle clean water on you, and you will be clean; I will cleanse you from all your filthiness and from all your idols" (36:25). Having been cleansed from idolatry, the people will be confirmed in faithfulness to the Lord. God will be their God, and He will bless them with the blessings promised to Abraham.

***Resurrection and Everlasting Life.*** Finally, the new covenant offers the ultimate blessing, promising resurrection from the dead (Ezek. 37:1-23). It is the ultimate blessing because it overturns the curse of death pronounced upon all humankind in Genesis 3. It is the promise of life immortal, which is *truly life*, the redemption of the creation plan. In Ezekiel 37:12, the Lord's promise to "open your graves and cause you to come up out of your graves" is linked to the promise to "bring you into the land of Israel." The resurrection with a view toward the inheritance of the Promised Land is accomplished by the Holy Spirit, as He says in 37:14, "And I will put My Spirit within you, and you will come to life, and I will place you on your own land" (see also the vision of vv. 1-10, where the Spirit comes into the dead). On one hand the indwelling of the Holy Spirit and inheritance in the land of promise look back to 36:22-38. On the other hand, though, it also looks forward to 37:15-28, where God dwelling in His people and the people dwelling in their land are called "a covenant of peace" and "an everlasting covenant" (37:26).

The promise of resurrection from the dead and immortality had been revealed in the prophecies of Isaiah as a blessing which would follow the great day of the Lord's judgment. He writes:

> And the Lord of hosts will prepare a lavish banquet for all
> peoples on this mountain. . . . And on this mountain He
> will swallow up the covering which is over all peoples,
> Even the veil which is stretched over all nations.
> He will swallow up death for all time.
> And the Lord God will wipe tears away from all faces,
> And He will remove the reproach of His people from all
> the earth; for the Lord has spoken.
> And it will be said in that day, "Behold this is our God for
> whom we have waited that He might save us.
> This is the Lord for whom we have waited;
> Let us rejoice and be glad in His salvation."
> (Isa. 25:6-9)

As the Abrahamic covenant had promised that *all peoples* would be blessed in Abraham and his descendant(s), so the blessing of resurrection from the dead is accordingly granted to all peoples.

Elsewhere, the resurrection is promised especially to the remnant of Israel. Isaiah promises that after the great day of judgment:

> Your dead will live;
> Their corpses will rise.
> You who lie in the dust, awake and shout for joy,

For your dew is as the dew of the dawn,
And the earth will give birth to the departed spirits
   (26:19-21).

Daniel, also, in a vision that parallels the one in which the saints of the Most High inherit an everlasting kingdom, prophesies that "many of those who sleep in the dust of the ground will awake, these to everlasting life, but the others to disgrace and everlasting contempt" (12:2).

Ezekiel, however, identifies this blessing as an aspect of the *new covenant* which God will make with His people. It is a blessing which correlates with the special way in which God will dwell in and with His people, sanctifying them and bestowing upon them His blessings forever.[9]

***The Nature of the New Covenant.*** The blessings of the new covenant show it to be a grant-type covenant rather than a bilateral contract or treaty. Consequently, its superiority over the Mosaic covenant, which it replaces, is readily apparent. Like the Mosaic covenant, it offers to bring the blessings of the Abrahamic grant into the daily experience of God's people. But the new covenant fulfills the intention of the Abrahamic grant by *granting* the experience of these blessings to Israel. It will supersede both the Mosaic and patriarchal dispensations by even *granting a faithful, loyal, and obedient heart* to God's people, eliminating the gap between the promise of future blessing and the present daily experience of it. In the new covenant, God will confirm His people in faith and obedience. It will be the supreme manifestation of grace. For He will give to His people that which He commands from them, and He will command that which He gives.[10]

Like the Abrahamic covenant, of which it is the fulfillment, the new covenant grant will be received by faith. New covenant promises appear in Jeremiah and Ezekiel as the hope extended to the remnant of Israel and Judah, those who wait upon the Lord to fulfill to them the covenant blessings as they live in a time when judgment and curse have come upon the nation as a whole.

***The New Covenant and the Abrahamic Covenant.*** The divine operation upon human hearts—complete forgiveness of sins—and resurrection from the dead are blessings which expand the notion of *blessing* in the Abrahamic covenant. We are now to understand that the fulfillment of the promise "I will bless you" (Gen. 12:2) will include the indwelling of the Holy Spirit in their hearts and the internalization of the divine will into human volition. The blessing will also include forgiveness and cleansing from sin, with the implication that curses of divine judgment, both actual and possible, will be removed from the experience of God's people. And the fact that those curses are completely removed is seen in the promise of immortal life.

While resurrection from the dead is undoubtedly new, we should not assume that God had never before conditioned the hearts of His people, that His Spirit had never before indwelt them, or that He had never before forgiven them of their sins. However, the new covenant makes these blessings a constitutive *abiding* feature of God's relationship to His people. They will be given to *all* the people ("from the least of them to the greatest," Jer. 31:34) *forever* ("from now and forever," Isa. 59:21).

Furthermore, there is a qualitative advance in the experience of these blessings under the new covenant. Forgiveness is comprehensive and eternal. And the indwelling of God's Spirit produces complete sanctification. The point is that the new covenant promises a complete elimination of sin forever. It will be the fulfillment of the heavenly decree seen in Daniel's vision: "to finish the transgression, to make an end of sin, to make atonement for iniquity, to bring in everlasting righteousness" (Dan. 9:24).

The relationship of the new covenant to the Abrahamic covenant is also seen in the way the new covenant promises restate the blessings already revealed in the Abrahamic covenant. Promises belonging to the patriarchal covenant and cited in predictions of the new covenant are:

1. God will bless them (reference is made to the blessings of peace and prosperity specified by the Mosaic covenant, a specification of the general promise to bless in the patriarchal covenant) (Isa. 49:9-10; Jer. 32:42-44; Ezek. 34:26-29; 36:8-9, 29-36)
2. God will give them the land promised to the forefathers (Isa. 49:8; 54:3; Jer. 32:37, 41; Ezek. 11:17; 34:27; 36:24, 28; 37:12, 14, 21, 25-26)

3. God will multiply their descendants (Jer. 31:27; Ezek. 36:10-12, 37-38; 37:26)
4. God will make them a great nation (Jer. 31:36)
5. God will make them to be His people and He will be their God (Jer. 31:33; 32:38; Ezek. 11:20; 34:24, 30-31; 36:28; 37:23, 27)

The specific promise made to the patriarchs to bless all peoples through them is not explicitly stated in these texts. However, we have already seen that certain promises, such as resurrection from the dead, are predicted for all peoples in other prophecies. The universal extent of blessing is implied in the Jeremiah and Ezekiel texts in the promise to grant Israel peace with the nations (Jer. 32:37; 33:16; Ezek. 34:25, 28). This is also implied in the term *covenant of peace,* which is sometimes used to refer to this new covenant (Isa. 54:10; Ezek. 34:25; 37:26). In this peace, all the nations will know the Lord and fear the Lord (Isa. 59:19; Ezek. 37:28).

Peace with the nations was a feature of the Davidic covenant, a covenant which we have yet to examine. Consequently, it should not be surprising that as the new covenant incorporates the promise of peace with the nations, it does so in conjunction with the fulfillment of the Davidic covenant. In Isaiah 55:3-5, the promise of an everlasting covenant (also called a covenant of peace, 54:10, which will manifest God's "everlasting lovingkindness," 54:8) accords with "the faithful mercies shown to David" in which he will lead the nations and reconcile them with Israel in the worship of the Lord.

In Isaiah 49, the Servant of the Lord will be given "for a covenant of the people" (v. 8). This servant is identified as Israel in verse 3. However, in verse 5 he is one Israelite who will bring the rest of Israel back to the Lord. Restoration to the land (v. 8), prosperity and the multiplication of descendants (vv. 10-21) are among the patriarchal promises to be fulfilled through the ministry of this servant. Most interpreters recognize a messianic ministry in view here. The fact that the servant is given as "a covenant of the people" ties the promise of a new covenant (which is given precisely to fulfill these Abrahamic promises) with the fulfillment of the Davidic covenant. (We will have more to say about this later.) We also should note that in this passage we have some information on how the new covenant will fulfill the promise to bless the nations. In verse 6 we read: " 'It is too small a thing that you should be My servant to raise up the tribes of Jacob, and to restore the preserved ones of Israel; I will also make you a light of the nations so that My salvation may reach to the end of the earth.' " The covenant promise in this passage connects with other prophecies predicting Gentile blessing.

The promise of a new covenant shows the abiding nature of the Abrahamic covenant since the new covenant will be given precisely to bring the Abrahamic covenant promise to fulfillment. At the same time, the meaning of "blessing" promised to the patriarchs is expanded to include the indwelling of the Holy Spirit in the people and a divine operation on human hearts to make them holy. The blessing is also now seen to include immortal, everlasting life through the resurrection from the dead. The fact that the promise of spiritual renewal is set side-by-side with promises of physical and material prosperity (including bodily resurrection from the dead) shows that in biblical theology, physical and spiritual blessings should not be thought of as contradictory or mutually exclusive.

Even though these promises are given at a time of great conflict with Gentile nations — so that the restoration theme is often given in conjunction with statements of retribution on Gentile powers — the theme of mediating blessing to all the nations is not absent. It is noteworthy, however, that this theme of blessing the nations is discussed in texts that tie the new covenant to the Davidic covenant. It will not be surprising that most of what the Old Testament has to say on the blessing of the nations will be found in prophecies speaking of the eschatological kingdom of God.

***The Dispensation of the New Covenant.*** The new covenant is prophesied as a new arrangement for the experience of patriarchal blessing. As we saw in the last chapter, Paul speaks of a new dispensation of the Spirit which follows the dispensation of the Mosaic covenant. When we examine Pauline teaching on the new covenant in the next chapter, we will see that this new dispensation of the Spirit is precisely an inauguration of the new covenant.

From the standpoint of the Old Testament, the new covenant was expected to bring the patriarchal blessings to everlasting fulfillment. Nevertheless, the dispensation of the new covenant could not be an *utterly* different dispensation from that which preceded it. Its purpose and its continuity with preceding dispensations lie in the patriarchal covenants. The dispensation of the new covenant will be a progressive advance over the Mosaic dispensation. It will bring a greater revelation of God and will expand (not replace) the meaning of "I will bless you." This expansion will occur through a decisive reversal of the divine curse on humanity by raising the dead — renewed and sanctified, willing and obedient people — in fellowship with God, innumerable, dwelling on the earth and in His presence forever.

## The Davidic Covenant

David, the second king of Israel, is presented in Scripture as a man of faith in the Lord. He is described as a man after God's own heart (1 Sam. 13:14); one who "did what was right in the sight of the Lord, [who] had not turned aside from anything that He commanded him all the days of his life, except in the case of Uriah the Hittite" (1 Kings 15:5). With the exception noted, he is presented in Scripture as one who exemplified the relationship with God expected in the Mosaic covenant.[11]

At the high point of David's reign — after he had conquered Jerusalem and had renovated it as the City of David, after bringing the ark of the Lord into the city (but before "the case of Uriah the Hittite") — David proposed to build a "house" (temple) for the Lord. The Lord blessed David by giving him a promise. The Lord would build David a house (a dynasty), and one of his sons would build the temple for the Lord.

***Contents of the Davidic Covenant.*** This promise is developed as a cluster of promises found chiefly in 2 Samuel 7 and 1 Chronicles 17, but reiterated and supplemented in Psalms 89, 110, and 132. There are two main parts: the promises concerning the establishment of David's house and the promises concerning the intimate relationship between God and David's descendant.

***The Promise to Build the Davidic House.*** The central and primary promise is that of building the house of David. This is explained by the Lord's promise to establish the kingdom of David's descendant, a promise which is repeated four times in 2 Samuel 7, as well as in 1 Chronicles 17, alternating the terms *kingdom* and *throne* for literary emphasis (2 Sam. 7:12, 13, 16; 1 Chron. 17:11-12, 14). Three times in each passage, the promised kingdom is said to be forever. Second Samuel 7 emphasizes the continuity of *Davidic rulership* by using the phrases, "your house," "your throne," and "your kingdom." First Chronicles 17 stresses the establishment of *the descendant's kingship within God's kingly rule* over Israel and the nations, by setting in parallel the phrases "his throne shall be established forever" and "I will settle him in My house and in My kingdom forever" (1 Chron. 17:14).

God's promise to build the house of David is repeated in other passages as well. Psalm 132:11 states:

> The Lord has sworn to David,
> A truth from which He will not turn back;
> "Of the fruit of your body I will set upon your throne."

The 89th Psalm, written most likely during the exile of Judah, repeatedly recalls God's covenant promise to (1) establish David's descendants and (2) establish David's throne (vv. 4, 29, 36-37). Like Psalm 132:11, the promise is viewed as grounded in the very truthfulness of God Himself (Ps. 89:1-3, 14, 24, 28, 33, 35).

### The Promise of a Special Relationship with David's Son.

The second major part of the Davidic promise concerns the relationship between God and the Davidic king. "I will be his father and he shall be My son" (1 Chron. 17:13; cf. 2 Sam. 7:14). Likewise, in Psalm 89:26-27 we read:

> He will cry to Me, "Thou art my Father,
> My God, and the rock of my salvation."
> I also shall make him My first-born,
> The highest of the kings of the earth.

This language reveals the intimacy which will exist between the covenant king and the Lord, and it also shows the security of that relationship. The Lord declares that His loving-kindness will abide with this king, the Lord's adopted son (2 Sam. 7:15;

160

1 Chron. 17:13; Ps. 89:24, 28, 33). For his part, the king trusts in the Lord, and by faith he receives the promises of this covenant. In the bond of the Father's love for him and through his reciprocal trust in the Lord, the kingdom of the Son is established over all and forever.

The promise that "he shall build for Me a house" (1 Chron. 17:12; 2 Sam. 7:13) also shows the Son's loving response to the Father. The house spoken of here is the temple of God, the new mode of God's presence among His people. As such, the temple would function as a historical fulfillment of the Abrahamic blessing declared to Jacob, that God would be *with* His people, thus constituting them as His people and revealing Himself to be their God.

The promise to David was that his son would establish the mode by which God would be present among his people, and by which the people in turn would worship God. We first see this in Solomon when he builds the temple of God.[12] The Lord accepted it as the mode of His presence among His people by filling it with His glory (1 Kings 6:12-13; 2 Chron. 7:1-4). Solomon presented the temple to the people as the central place for worship in Israel. In this way, the king supported and affirmed the worship of God. In 1 Chronicles 17:12 and 2 Samuel 7:13, the phrase "and I will establish his throne forever," is linked to the phrase, "He shall build for Me a house." This shows that the establishment of the king's throne goes hand-in-hand with the king's establishment of the worship of God.

Building and maintaining a temple is a priestly act. Pagan priests maintained shrines for the worship of their gods. Levitical priests were also known to maintain shrines (in violation of the Mosaic covenant, see Judges 18). Since the Davidic king builds and maintains the house of God, it is not surprising that he is described in Scripture as a kind of priest. In Psalm 110:4, we read:

> The Lord has sworn and will not change His mind,
> Thou art a priest forever
> According to the order of Melchizedek.

Melchizedek was the king of Salem and "priest of God Most High" who blessed Abraham (Gen. 14:18). David's conquest of Jerusalem, the former city of Salem, gave him the ancient throne of Melchizedek. Although the city had fallen into idolatry since the time of Melchizedek, David — the new Melchizedek — restored the worship of the one true God. Furthermore, as king not only of Jerusalem but of all Israel, he made Jerusalem the religious center for the whole nation. As he brought the ark of the Lord into the city, the Scripture describes David as dressed in priestly attire leading the priests in joyful celebration (2 Sam. 6:14-15, 18-19). As the king-priest (Melchizedekian order) he made plans for the construction of the temple, and he exercised his authority over his priestly subjects, the Levites, by reorganizing them for service in the house of God when that house would be built (2 Chron. 23:18; 29:25-30; 35:2-6; Ezra 3:10; Neh. 12:24).

There should be no doubt that the Melchizedekian priesthood is part of the Davidic covenant. Like the Abrahamic covenant, the Davidic covenant is a collection of promises. The term *covenant* first appears at the end of the Samuel narratives (2 Sam. 23:5), looking back at the promises which God has given to David and his descendant(s). In Psalm 110:4 the position is promised on divine oath. The oath of God primarily functions in Scripture to guarantee a covenant relationship.[13] Finally, there is no doubt from a New Testament perspective that the Melchizedekian priesthood is an office given to David's son as part of his inheritance. As we will see in the next chapter, Hebrews connects the roles of covenantal sonship and Melchizedekian priesthood in the one ministry of Christ.

The priestly role of the Davidic king accords well not only with his function of mediating the relationship between God and the people but also with his intimacy with the Lord. God promises that His loving-kindness will always abide with him. Even the warnings of punishment for sin, punishment "with the rod and . . . with stripes" (Ps. 89:30-32; 2 Sam. 7:14) carry the expectation of an abiding relationship.

***The Nature of the Davidic Covenant.*** Although 2 Samuel 7 and 1 Chronicles 17 do not use the term covenant, we do find it in later passages. David testifies in 2 Samuel 23:5, "He [the Lord] has made an everlasting covenant with me, ordered in all things, and secured." Solomon also speaks of the promise as a covenant (1 Kings 8:23), and it is interpreted as such by later writers. The psalmist quotes the Lord as saying:

I have made a covenant with My chosen;
I have sworn to David My servant. . . .
My lovingkindness I will keep for him forever,
And My covenant shall be confirmed to him (Ps. 89:3, 28).

In the narratives of the later kings of Israel and of Judah, we read:

Do you not know that the Lord God of Israel gave the rule over Israel forever to David and his sons by a covenant of salt? (2 Chron. 13:5)

Yet the Lord was not willing to destroy the house of David because of the covenant which He had made with David and since He had promised to give a lamp to him and his sons forever (2 Chron. 21:7).

Like the covenant with Abraham, the covenant with David is a grant covenant. It is the formal establishment of a grant or gift to David, the servant of the Lord. It consists of promises to David, and is often referenced in just that way, as the promise of the Lord to David (2 Sam. 7:28; 1 Kings 2:4, 24; 5:12; 8:20, 24-25, 56; 9:5; 2 Kings 8:19; 1 Chron. 17:26; 2 Chron. 1:9; 6:10, 15-16; 21:7). As a covenant of grant, the Davidic covenant is unconditional. David, a man of faith, receives these promises believing that God will fulfill them. God declares His intention to carry out these blessings to David as an act of His grace. Accordingly, conditions are absent when the promise is revealed to David (2 Sam. 7; 1 Chron. 17). And God's intention to fulfill the promise is repeated in the subsequent history of the Davidic kings despite many acts of disloyalty on their part (see 1 Kings 11:11-13, 34-36; 15:4-5; 2 Kings 8:19; 2 Chron. 21:7; 23:3).

However, when the covenant is transferred to Solomon, it is placed in a conditional form. David announces:

He [the Lord] has chosen my son Solomon to sit on the throne of the kingdom of the Lord over Israel. And He said to me, "Your son Solomon is the one who shall build My house and My courts; for I have chosen him to be a son to Me, and I will be a father to him. And I will establish his kingdom forever, *if he resolutely performs My command-ments and My ordinances, as is done now"* (1 Chron. 28:5-6).

In his subsequent charge to Solomon, David reveals a new promise which is conditional in nature and which had not appeared in the list of promises in 2 Samuel 7 or 1 Chronicles 17:

Be strong, therefore, and show yourself a man. And keep the charge of the Lord your God . . . so that the Lord may carry out His promise which He spoke concerning me, saying, *"If your sons are careful of their way, to walk before Me in truth with all their heart and with all their soul, you shall not lack a man on the throne of Israel"* (1 Kings 2:2-4).

The conditional promise of *not lacking a man on the throne of Israel* is repeated twice more by Solomon (1 Kings 6:12; 8:25; cf. 2 Chron. 6:16) and reconfirmed by the Lord (1 Kings 9:4-9; cf. 2 Chron. 7:17-22). It also appears in Psalm 132:12 where it is juxtaposed with the unconditional promise of *placing a descendant upon his throne* (v. 11). God's promise to raise up a descendant is unconditional. But a continuous, uninterrupted reign is not. That is conditioned upon the faithfulness of the Davidic kings.

The conditional form of the Davidic covenant given to Solomon parallels the conditional form of the Abrahamic promise given to Israel as the Mosaic covenant. As we have seen, the Mosaic covenant did not compromise the original intention expressed in the Abrahamic covenant. Rather, it made possible a historical experience of the Abrahamic blessing in the specific form of Mosaic covenant blessing. God's intention to bless descendants of Abraham is firm, but whether or not He will give certain blessings to a particular generation of those descendants at a specific time in history was conditioned by the terms of the Mosaic covenant. Even so, Israel experienced many blessings from God throughout the history of the Mosaic covenant despite examples of covenant unfaithfulness. And as we have seen, God's unconditional intention to bless was often reconfirmed throughout that history as a promise to be realized in the future.

The same is true regarding the Davidic covenant. God promised David that He would establish the kingdom of his son(s). But when a specific son was chosen, so that the possibility of inheriting the promise was narrowed to the descendants of that son of David, the promise was conditioned on covenant faithfulness. God's intention to fulfill the Davidic promise remained firm, however, as can be seen in the narratives of the succession of Davidic kings. Disobedience to the Mosaic law brought various kinds of punishments. Yet the Lord maintained the Davidic throne because of the grant covenant made to David (see 1 Kings 11:11-13, 34-36; 15:4-5; 2 Kings 8:19; 2 Chron. 21:7; 23:3). Eventually, when the Lord judged the Davidic house, vacating the throne of David (see the curses in Jer. 22:28-30; 36:30-32), the conditionality of an uninterrupted line was clearly demonstrated.

For a long time, David did in fact lack a man to sit on the throne of Israel. However, prophecies about a future Davidic king and the rebuilding of the house of David reaffirmed the ultimate intention of God's covenant to David. Repeating the language of the Davidic covenant, the prophets declared that the Lord would raise up a descendant of David (Isa. 9:6; Jer. 23:5) and establish his kingdom (Isa. 9:7; 16:5; 28:16). He will be a shoot or branch off the stump of the fallen tree (Isa. 11:1; Jer. 23:5; 33:15), the rebuilt tabernacle of the fallen house of David (Amos 9:11-12). Much of prophecy concerns the character of this future Davidic king: He will be righteous and will rule with righteousness and justice (Isa. 9:7; 11:3-4; 16:5; 28:17; Jer. 23:5; 33:15), and he will be wise, filled with the Spirit in wisdom, piety, and the knowledge of God (Isa. 9:6; 11:2; Jer. 23:5). As a result of his wisdom and righteousness, he will completely fulfill the condition placed on the sons of David, so much so that Jeremiah speaks of the promise of not lacking a man to sit on the throne as sure as the everlasting fulfillment of the Noahic covenant (Jer. 33:14-26).

## The Relationship of the Davidic Covenant to the Other Covenants of the Lord

The Davidic covenant established Davidic kingship as crucial to the fulfillment of the blessings of Abraham. This requires closer examination, and it will lead us to investigate the relationship between the Davidic covenant and the Mosaic and new covenants since, as we have seen, they are forms in which the Abrahamic covenant has been and will be fulfilled.

***The Davidic Covenant and the Abrahamic Covenant.*** At the beginning of the group of promises given to David in 2 Samuel 7 and 1 Chronicles 17 are two promises which are part of the Abrahamic covenant. First, the Lord says, "I will make you a great name" (2 Sam. 7:9; cf. 1 Chron. 17:8). To Abraham, the Lord had said, "I will make you a great nation . . . and make your name great" (Gen. 12:2). The promise of the great name has now passed specifically to the Davidic king. His name will be great. And since he is the king, the ruler of the nation, the greatness of his name translates into the greatness of the nation. Consequently, we see how under his rule the Abrahamic promise of the great nation and the great name come together.[14]

This connection between blessing on the king and blessing on the nation appears to guide the literary structure of the text as well, for following the promise of the great name is a reference to the Abrahamic promise to establish Israel "in their own place" in peace and security (2 Sam. 7:10-11; 1 Chron. 17:9-10). The promise that they will "not be disturbed again, nor will the wicked afflict them any more" looks to a time beyond the curses of the Mosaic covenant, to the time in which the Abrahamic blessing will be ultimately fulfilled. It is important to note that in these promises the ultimate fulfillment of the Abrahamic covenant coincides with the ultimate fulfillment of the Davidic covenant. In other words, the final fulfillment of the Abrahamic promise of blessing in the Promised Land will take place under the rulership of a Davidic king.

Here is the relationship between the Davidic and Abrahamic covenants. On the one hand the Davidic covenant is *part* of the blessing of the Abrahamic covenant. A blessed king from the line of David is one way in which the promise to bless descendants of Abraham will manifest itself. On the other hand, the Davidic covenant provides the *means* by which the Abrahamic blessing will be fulfilled for all descendants. The blessing for the many will be mediated by the rulership of the one, the king. Through his action, enemies of the blessing will be subdued, the nations will be pacified, and Israel will be established in the worship of God.

We can see this in the reigns of David and Solomon. David established peace and security for Israel by fighting the wars of the Lord, driving the enemies of God's people from the land of promise. Solomon ruled over the surrounding nations in a hegemony which maintained the peace and brought prosperity to Israel. First Kings 4:20-21 describes the situation in the language of the patriarchal covenant.

> Judah and Israel were as numerous as the sand that is on the seashore in abundance; they were eating and drinking and rejoicing. Now Solomon ruled over all the kingdoms from the River to the land of the Philistines and to the border of Egypt; they brought tribute and served Solomon all the days of his life.

The security of this peace was rooted in Israel's proper worship of God. The monarchy contributed here by overseeing the construction and maintenance of the temple. As highest priest (of the order of Melchizedek), the king was to lead Israel in the worship of God. The well-being of the monarchy and the nation are tied together in the worship of God. The king set the example and direction for the nation. As the king worshiped the Lord and maintained the temple as the center of Israel's worship, so the nation generally responded to his leadership. Zeal for the Lord would lead the king to destroy the high places, the competing shrines of idolatry scattered throughout the land. By purging the land, he enforced the worship of God alone. This in turn would lead to the blessings of continued peace, prosperity, and security in the land.[15]

But what about the rest of the nations? The Abrahamic covenant envisions blessings on all peoples as mediated by Abraham and his descendants. Here too the Davidic covenant positions the Davidic king as the mediator of this blessing to all. This is already implied in 2 Samuel 7:10-11 (cf. 1 Chron. 17:9-10) in the promise to pacify the enemies of Israel, which can come in the form of punishing judgment (as in David's crushing military campaigns) or under a peaceful hegemony (as in Solomon's rule). Ultimately, it is the latter in which the promise will prevail.

The function of the king as the mediator of covenant blessing to all the nations is set forth in Psalm 72.[16] The king is righ-

167

teous, just, and wise, and Israel enjoys covenant blessings. There is peace, prosperity, justice, and full possession of the Promised Land. The king is also seen to rule over the entire earth, over all the peoples of the earth (vv. 8-11), with the result that the blessings of peace and prosperity extend throughout the earth. The blessing on Israel comes as the people bless the king (v. 15). Likewise, the nations are blessed as they "bless themselves by him."

This is the language of the Abrahamic covenant. The descendants of Abraham have been restructured politically so that the function of mediating blessing rests chiefly with the king. Whereas God had said, "I will bless you," the *you* must now be seen in a political structure with the king at the top, receiving the blessing and mediating it to the rest of the people. And whereas God had said that He would bless all nations "in you" (Gen. 12:3) and "in your descendants" (Gen. 22:18), the "you" and the "descendants" must likewise no longer be taken in a uniform sense of all the descendants generally, but in a monarchical sense, meaning first of all the king and then the nation in submission to him. It is through him and his rule that the Abrahamic covenant promise to bless all nations will be fulfilled.

***The Davidic Covenant and the Mosaic Covenant.*** The Davidic covenant was given under the dispensation of the Mosaic covenant. As a grant covenant tied to the future fulfillment of the grant covenant given to the patriarchs, its ultimate fulfillment looks beyond the Mosaic dispensation. However, the experience of the blessings of the Davidic covenant during the time of the Mosaic dispensation was conditioned by the Mosaic covenant. There was even a form of the Davidic covenant which was conditional and which correlates with the conditional nature of the Mosaic covenant itself.[17]

As we have noted, the Davidic blessing is both a form of Abrahamic blessing and the mediation of Abrahamic blessing. Under the Mosaic dispensation, the Abrahamic blessing is offered in terms of the specific blessings of the Mosaic covenant. Consequently, during that dispensation, the Davidic king is blessed and brings blessing to others precisely in terms of the Mosaic blessings spelled out in Deuteronomy 28.

The Mosaic covenant, however, can also bring God's curse

into the experience of the people. Under that dispensation, the mediation of the Davidic king can also bring God's curse. This can happen in two ways. First, by his own disloyalty and faithlessness, the king may provoke God's curse on the nation. Note the Lord's warning to Solomon.

> But if you or your sons shall indeed turn away from following Me, and shall not keep My commandments and My statutes which I have set before you and shall go and serve other gods and worship them, then I will cut off Israel from the land which I have given them, and the house which I have consecrated for My name, I will cast out of My sight. So Israel will become a proverb and a byword among all the peoples. And this house will become a heap of ruins; everyone who passes by will be astonished and hiss and say, "Why has the Lord done thus to this land and to this house?" And they will say, "Because they forsook the Lord their God, who brought their fathers out of the land of Egypt, and adopted other gods and worshiped them and served them, therefore the Lord has brought all this adversity on them" (1 Kings 9:6-9).

We see here that idolatry and disobedience on the part of the king would bring the ultimate curse of the Mosaic covenant — expulsion from the land. We also see the implication that the people would follow the example of the king in covenant faithlessness, thus showing the king's power to influence the religious worship of the nation as a whole.

The other way in which the king might mediate the curse of the Mosaic covenant would be as an instrument of the Lord to chasten and punish those in Israel who broke the covenant. Ruling justly and in righteousness meant carrying out the requirements of the law including its punishments for transgression.

***The Davidic Covenant and the New Covenant.*** A new covenant was prophesied to replace the Mosaic covenant in order to bring the Abrahamic blessing fully and permanently into the experience of the descendants of Abraham. The new covenant would do this by the grant of another blessing, the renewal and sanctification of the human heart by the indwelling Holy Spirit, along with resurrection from the dead and everlasting life. To this renewed, sanctified, and resurrected people, the promise of blessing would be fulfilled forever.

The Davidic covenant was also given to bring the Abrahamic covenant blessing into everlasting fulfillment. Consequently, the Davidic and new covenants must come together in this task. In the Davidic covenant, the blessing which comes upon the king *is* the Abrahamic blessing. In the Mosaic dispensation, it came upon him *as* the Mosaic covenant blessing. In a future dispensation, blessing would come upon the king as new covenant blessing. That new covenant blessing would be the fulfillment of the promised blessing to Abraham. This included many of the things envisioned by the Mosaic covenant—peace, prosperity, and security in the land of promise. But it also included the promise of resurrection life with a new heart. Consequently, the fulfillment of the Davidic covenant will take place in a king who embodies the new covenant promise of a new heart and an immortal life mediated by the indwelling Spirit of God.

The prophets who predicted the new covenant often spoke of the fulfillment of the covenant to David in the reign of a future king. This king is repeatedly characterized by righteousness, justice, and faithfulness. He is fully indwelt by the Spirit of God, ruling forever with godlike wisdom and power (see Isa. 9:6-7; 11:1-10; Jer. 23:5-6; 33:14-26). Whereas under the Mosaic dispensation the king of Israel had certainly been indwelt by God's Spirit (1 Sam. 16:13), that blessing was not necessarily permanent (1 Sam. 16:14; cf. Ps. 51:11), did not result in the complete renewal of the heart leading to full obedience as envisioned in the promises of the new covenant, nor did it render him immortal. The king who was prophesied by the prophets of the new covenant greatly surpasses in character, power, and length of reign both David and Solomon, the greatest of Israel's former kings.

We have also seen that the Davidic covenant constituted the king as a mediator of covenant blessing to the rest of Israel as well as a mediator of blessing to all the nations. Since the new covenant is the form in which Abrahamic covenant blessing will be fulfilled, then according to the structure of the Davidic covenant, new covenant blessing will be mediated by the Davidic king. This would mean that even the blessings of resurrection, renewal, and sanctification by the indwelling Holy Spirit will in some way be mediated through the king.

We can see this implied in the new covenant scenario of Ezekiel 37, where the promises are fulfilled with David (i.e., the Davidic king) ruling over the people and God dwelling in their midst forever. We also note how in the predictions of the rule of this king, the Scripture often moves from the king's character of righteousness to the righteousness that characterizes the kingdom (Isa. 11:1-10; Jer. 23:5-6). But the evidence is stronger in texts such as Isaiah 49:5-8 and 55:3. The servant, predicted in oracles from Isaiah 41–53, is sometimes the nation Israel but sometimes a person within Israel, a person who represents and acts on behalf of the nation. That person in Isaiah 52:13 is a future king of Israel, the Messiah of God.[18] In Isaiah 49:8, this servant will be given "for a covenant of the people, to restore the land, to make them inherit the desolate heritages." In other words, this servant will function as God's covenant, bringing the promises to fulfillment. How he does that seems to be implied in 49:5 — he will "bring Jacob back to Him, in order that Israel might be gathered to Him." He brings Israel to God for the fulfillment of covenant blessing. The new covenant is God's work of grace bringing Israel back to Himself for the full reception of covenant blessings. This future king, who will be given in an act of atonement for the sins of the nation (Isa. 53), will be used by God to mediate the blessing which renews and restores his people.

But as the covenant promises envision blessing upon all people, the future Davidic king likewise will mediate the new covenant blessing to all nations. In Isaiah 49:6, we read:

It is too small a thing that You should be My Servant
To raise up the tribes of Jacob, and to restore the preserved ones of Israel;
I will also make You a light of the nations
So that My salvation may reach to the end of the earth.

This accords with other prophecies that through the future Davidic king, blessing would come to the Gentiles (Isa. 11:10; 55:3-4). As the king is the one in whom all will be blessed, he is the one through whom peace will come upon all peoples. Consequently, he is the one through whom renewal, resurrection, and sanctification by the indwelling Spirit of God will be given not just to Israel but to all peoples.

## Summary

The history of the covenants prior to Jesus Christ is the story of the divine promise to bless all life on earth — all nations and the people that compose them. It is the story of the divine plan of redemption, of reconciliation, which holds forth the hope of the accomplishment of that purpose which was revealed in the creation: an earth filled with life, filled especially with human beings living in peace, prosperity, and full fellowship with God.

It is necessarily a story of redemption because the blessings of God set forth in the covenants stand in contrast to fundamental judgments against sin — warnings and pronouncements of misery, insecurity, destruction, and death.

The covenant with Abraham is foundational, for it picks up the promise of the Noahic covenant (made with all life) and directly addresses human existence. It offers God's blessing upon human life both individually and in its collective national identities. The story of the Bible, from Abraham on, is the story of God's relationship with human beings as set forth in this covenant and developed from it as its features are expanded and detailed in subsequent revelation.

Blessing (in contrast to deserved judgments of misery, death, and destruction) was decreed by divine initiative as a grant to Abraham, who in turn received it by faith and experienced many of its aspects in his personal and family life as he walked with the Lord in obedience to His commandments. The covenant designated Abraham a mediator of God's blessing to all peoples and nations on earth. All who blessed Abraham, believing the promise of blessing God granted to him, would likewise be blessed by God.

Blessing and mediation of blessing passed to Abraham's descendants as they were chosen by God to inherit the covenant. A new dispensation for blessing was instituted by the Mosaic covenant, which constituted the descendants of Abraham, Isaac, and Jacob as a nation, taking the divine name for Jacob — Israel. The law of the Mosaic covenant challenged the generations of Israel to trust in God alone and obey His commandments. Those who were of the faith of the patriarchs sought to worship God according to its commandments. They were the true heirs of the patriarchal grant and mediated its blessing (in the specific dispensational form of the Mosaic blessing) to the rest of the nation and to other peoples as well. When the Israel of faith constituted only a small remnant of physical Israel, the curses of the Mosaic covenant, judgments of misery, destruction, exile, and death threatened the nation. But the remnant of faith held to the hope of inheriting divine blessing in an eschatological age.

During the Mosaic dispensation, the role of mediating blessing was politically restructured as a function of the Davidic king. A covenant was made with David to bless him and his son(s) with rulership over Israel and the rest of the nations, an intimate and blessed relationship with God, and the mediation (even priestly mediation) of *blessing* to Israel and to all peoples and nations. In the Mosaic dispensation, this grant manifested itself to varying degrees in the reigns of those Davidic kings who trusted in the Lord according to the Mosaic covenant.

But as the history of Israel's faithlessness and apostasy finally led to national destruction and exile, the prophets looked to a new dispensation in which a new covenant would replace the Mosaic covenant and bring the Abrahamic grant into everlasting fulfillment. In this new covenant, God would grant the blessing of new reconstituted hearts, filled with His Spirit, fully trusting and obeying Him, having God's will written directly into their very lives. He would eliminate the problem of sin so that the grant of blessing would be received fully, completely, and eternally. He would grant full forgiveness of sins and resurrection from the dead to life immortal. All the promises of blessing for personal and national life in communion with God, with peace and prosperity, would be fulfilled forever.

The new covenant blessing would be exemplified in the life of a Davidic king under whose rule and through whose mediation the blessings would come to the Israel of faith—that remnant of physical Israel which trusts in God—and to all those of the nations who trust in God through this king and thus come to constitute those nations who are blessed forever "in Him."

# Chapter Six
# The Fulfillment of the Biblical Covenants Through Jesus Christ

In the New Testament the name Jesus is most often accompanied by the title Christ. In the preaching of the early church, Christ was so often used in conjunction with Jesus or as a substitute for the name Jesus, that many Gentiles mistook it for part of His name.[1] That confusion continues even today.

Actually, the word Christ is an English transliteration of the Greek noun *christos,* which means *the Anointed One.* It is related to the verb *chrio* meaning *to anoint.* Both priests and kings were anointed in the Old Testament, so either one could be called a *christos,* an anointed one. Most often, however, the title was reserved for the king. In the Septuagint (the Greek translation of the Old Testament which was most popular in the early church) *christos* translates the Aramaic *meshicha* and Hebrew *mashiach* from which we get the English word Messiah. Thus we see that both English words Messiah and Christ are ultimately derived from the same source. They should be viewed as synonyms, both meaning *the anointed one,* the king.[2]

The title, Christ, clearly means king in the Gospels. In Matthew 2:2, 4, the titles *King of the Jews* and *Christ* are used in parallel. In Mark 15:32, the title Christ is defined to mean, "the

King of Israel." The genealogy of Jesus in Matthew 1 is introduced as "the genealogy of Jesus Christ, the son of David, the son of Abraham." The genealogy then carefully traces not only His descent from Abraham, but also from David through Solomon and the line of Davidic kings.

All of this brings us to this observation, that the most well known fact of the New Testament proclamation of Jesus, namely that He is the Christ, is a proclamation that He is the Davidic king, the King of Israel. This means that the primary mode for understanding Jesus and His ministry lies in the grant covenant to David. And since, as we have seen, the fulfillment of the Davidic covenant is the means for bringing to fulfillment all of the great covenant promises of God, the consideration of Jesus' Davidic kingship will reveal Him to be the fulfillment of the biblical covenants.

## Jesus and the Fulfillment of the Davidic Covenant

*The New Testament Presentation of Jesus, the Covenant King.* In Luke 1:32-35, the Angel Gabriel makes this prediction to Mary about the child that she will bear:

> He will be great, and will be called the Son of the Most High; and the Lord God will give Him the throne of His father David; and He will reign over the house of Jacob forever, and His kingdom will have no end. . . . The Holy Spirit will come upon you, and the power of the Most High will overshadow you; and for that reason the holy offspring shall be called the Son of God.

The prediction concerns the transference of the Davidic grant to Jesus. Both aspects of Davidic promise are present here, the establishment of the Davidic house through the establishment of the kingdom and throne of this descendant of David forever and the intimate relationship between God and this descendant so that He will be God's Son.

Zacharias, the father of John the Baptist, prophesies that Jesus is the "horn of salvation" which God *"has raised up . . . in the house of David His servant."* This recalls the Davidic covenant promises in Psalm 89:17, 24 and Psalm 132:17 re-

175

garding the horn of David as well as the promise about "raising up" a descendant in 2 Samuel 7:12. The anointing of Jesus, by which He is revealed to be the Christ, the Davidic king, took place at His baptism by the Prophet John in the Jordan River.[3] The Holy Spirit came upon Him[4] and the divine testimony declared from heaven, "Thou art My *beloved Son*, in Thee I am well pleased" (cf. Matt. 3:17; Mark 1:11; Luke 3:22). Through the language of Psalm 2:7, the heavenly voice affirmed Jesus in the relationship with God which belonged to the Davidic king—*sonship* (cf. 2 Sam. 7:14; 1 Chron. 17:13; and Heb. 1:5, which connects Ps. 2 with 2 Sam. 7 and 1 Chron. 17) and abiding *loving-kindness* (2 Sam. 7:15; Ps. 89:2, 24, 28).

Having been anointed by the Holy Spirit, Jesus proceeds to a ministry which essentially fulfills the role of the Servant predicted by Isaiah. His activity demonstrates His power to grant blessings of peace, prosperity, and well-being, blessings of the kingdom predicted for the son of David. The people acknowledge Him as son of David (see Matt. 12:23; 21:9) and He is declared to be greater than either David or Solomon (Matt. 12:42; 22:42-45).

As the Servant of God, He fulfills the chastening predicted of the Davidic house (a prediction which was also part of the Davidic covenant): "I will correct him with the rod of men and with the strokes of men" (2 Sam. 7:14). (This of course was not for His own personal sin, but He substitutes Himself for the judgment on the sins of the house of David.) We see this in the language used of the crucifixion in Matthew 27:29-30 where Gentile soldiers saluted Him as "King of the Jews" and "took the reed [rod] and began to beat Him." His crucifixion is due to His claim to be the Christ, the Son of God (Matt. 26:63-65), and the terms of Davidic promise are hurled as insults to Him as He dies:

He is the King of Israel; let Him now come down from the cross, and we shall believe in Him. He trusts in God; let Him deliver Him now, if He takes pleasure in Him; for He said, "I am the Son of God" (Matt. 27:42-43).

Most messianic claims terminated with the death of the claimant. Jesus, however, rose from the dead, and that fact, His resurrection, along with His ascension into heaven and His post-ascension activity, renewed and affirmed the faith of many that He was and is indeed the prophesied king, the ultimate fulfillment of the promises to David.

Beginning in Acts 2, Jesus' apostles began to preach that His resurrection was the fulfillment of the covenant promise to "raise up" David's descendant. The promise to raise up a descendant, in 2 Samuel 7:12, is connected with the promise to establish His kingdom or, putting it another way, to establish His throne. Peter argues in Acts 2:22-36 that David predicted in Psalm 16 that this descendant would be raised up from the dead, incorruptible, and *in this way,* He would be seated upon His throne (Acts 2:30-31). He then argues that this enthronement has taken place upon the entrance of Jesus into heaven, in keeping with the language of Psalm 110:1 that describes the seating of David's son at God's right hand. Peter declares (Acts 2:36) that Jesus has been made Lord over Israel (Ps. 110:1 uses the title Lord of the enthroned king) and Christ (the anointed king) by virtue of the fact that He has acted (or been allowed to act) from that heavenly position on behalf of His people to bless them with the gift of the Holy Spirit.

Paul gives a similar argument in Acts 13. He observes, "From the *offspring* of this man [David] according to promise God has brought to Israel a Savior, Jesus" (v. 23). The promise to which he refers is 2 Samuel 7:12, "I will raise up your *descendant [offspring]*[5] after you, who will come forth from you, and I will establish His kingdom." He then goes on to proclaim the good news that God has fulfilled "the promise made to the fathers" (v. 32) in that He "raised up Jesus" (v. 33). The verb "raised up" is the same as in 2 Samuel 7:12, " I will raise up your descendant," indicating that the raising up of Jesus was precisely the fulfillment of *that* promise to the fathers, the one to which Paul also alluded in verse 23. But this *raising up,* in Jesus' case, was not just human descent but also resurrection from the dead (v. 30: "But God raised Him from the dead"). He then argues (vv. 34-37) that *this kind of raising up* was predicted by Psalm 16 and Isaiah 55:3. Being raised up in this sense, the blessings of David have been established with Him (Acts 2:33-34), a position which is also coordinate with His having the title Son of God (v. 33).[6]

The raising up of Jesus son of David from the dead, His title *Son of God,* His enthronement at the right hand of God, and

His activity of blessing Jews and all other peoples who bless Him, who trust in Him, are all aspects of the Davidic promise. The New Testament repeatedly proclaims these as presently fulfilled. Paul even speaks of this as the Gospel.

> The Gospel of God, which He promised beforehand through His prophets in the holy Scriptures, concerning His Son, who was born of the seed of David according to the flesh, who was declared with power to be the Son of God by the resurrection [being raised up] from the dead, according to the Spirit of holiness, Jesus Christ our Lord (Rom. 1:1-4).

> Remember Jesus Christ, risen [raised up] from the dead, descendant of David, according to my gospel (2 Tim. 2:8).

Enthronement at the right hand of God, the position promised to the Davidic king in Psalm 110:1, is ascribed to Jesus in many New Testament texts. It is, of course, proclaimed in Acts 2:33-36. Acts 5:31 states that "He [Jesus] is the one whom God exalted to His right hand as a Prince and a Savior." Stephen testified at his martyrdom that he saw Jesus "standing at the right hand of God" (7:55-56). Paul writes that "Christ Jesus . . . who is at the right hand of God . . . intercedes for us" (Rom. 8:34). Ephesians 1:20-22 and Colossians 3:1 also see Christ seated at the right hand of God, with the latter passage stressing the fact that all things are presently in subjection to Him.[7] Christ's position at the right hand of God is referred to repeatedly in Hebrews (Heb. 1:3, 13; 8:1; 10:12; 12:2), and once in 1 Peter 3:22, where Peter joins Paul in stressing the present subjection of authorities and powers to Him.

The description of Christ as "seated at the right hand of God" in Colossians 3:1 appears in context with the phrase "kingdom of His [God's] beloved Son" (1:13), a phrase that combines three features of Davidic promise—kingdom, abiding loving-kindness, and sonship—and applies them all to Jesus' present position and activity. We also find in the context, descriptions of Jesus as "firstborn of all creation" and "firstborn from the dead" (1:15, 18). The title "firstborn" recalls His covenant position as "Son" of God and also the preeminence of His kingdom over all rule and authority on earth as seen in the language in Psalm 89:27: "I also shall make Him My firstborn, the highest of the kings of the earth." As we have seen, New Testament theology portrays the "raising up" of Jesus to the Davidic kingship as taking place in His resurrection from the dead. Consequently, Colossians 1:18 declares Him to be the ruler,[8] "the *firstborn from the dead* [uniting Sonship with the manner in which He was "raised up"], so that He might come to have the first place in everything." Having "the first place in everything" corresponds to being "the highest of the kings of the earth" in Psalm 89:27. Revelation 1:5 is even more explicit in applying Psalm 89:27 to Jesus' present position by describing Him as "the firstborn of the dead, and the ruler of the kings of the earth."

The description of the Davidic king as having the greatest *name* and the *highest* authority is applied to Jesus in several texts as well. Philippians 2:9-10 says that, "God highly exalted Him, and bestowed on Him the name which is above every name, that at the name of Jesus every knee should bow, of those who are in heaven, and on earth, and under the earth, and that every tongue should confess that Jesus Christ is Lord, to the glory of God the Father." Both Acts 2:33 and 5:31 speak of His *exaltation* to His present position, and Paul in Ephesians 1:21 describes His position as "*far above* all rule and authority and power and dominion, and every name that is named, not only in this age but also in the one to come." The language of exaltation here is the same as that used in Psalm 89:27, "the *highest* of the kings." And it is conceptually related to the descriptions of Solomon found in 1 Chronicles 29:25: "And the Lord highly exalted Solomon in the sight of all Israel, and bestowed on him royal majesty which had not been on any king before him in Israel"; and in 2 Chronicles 1:1: "and the Lord his God was with him and exalted him greatly."

In keeping with the covenant relationship between the son of David and the house of the Lord, Jesus predicted that He would build the temple of God. However, this prediction is also tied to His prophecy that the temple then existing would be destroyed. Paul presents Jesus in Ephesians 2 as the enthroned and exalted Lord who is building the house of God by uniting Jews and Gentiles together for the dwelling of God by the Spirit.

We have traced in some detail the fact that the New Testa-

ment presents Jesus' present position and activity as a fulfillment of promises of the Davidic covenant. This has been necessary because earlier forms of dispensationalism tended to
deny it. They were concerned to underscore the future fulfillment of the political and earthly aspects of the Davidic promise
as that promise interfaces with the political and earthly promises of the other covenants. We need to note that the New
Testament does indicate that the political aspects of Jesus' Davidic kingship will be fulfilled in the future. But earlier
dispensationalists tended to miss the fact that in biblical theology, *the Davidic nature of Christ's present activity guarantees
the fulfillment of all of the Davidic promise in the future,
including the national and political dimensions of that
promise.*

We can see this in Acts 1–3. When the disciples ask Jesus,
"Lord, is it at this time that You are restoring the kingdom to
Israel?" they show that they expected Him to fulfill the political
and national role predicted for the son of David. They could
hardly have misunderstood His teaching since they asked their
question after receiving forty days of instruction by the resurrected Jesus on "the things concerning the kingdom of God"
(Acts 1:3, 6). His answer, "It is not for you to know the times or
the epochs which the Father has fixed by His own authority" (v.
7), assures their expectation while warning that the time is
unrevealed.

Peter argues in Acts 3:21 that "heaven must receive [Him]
until the period of restoration of all things, about which God
spoke by the mouth of His holy apostles from ancient time." At
that time, God will "send Jesus, the Christ appointed for you
[Israel, cf. 12, 20]." Although the King is in heaven now, the
revelation of Jesus at His coming will bring with it a revelation
of the kingdom on the earth (2 Tim. 4:1). Paul speaks of all
Israel being saved (Rom. 11:26). Hebrews 2:5 speaks of the
subjection of the world to come. Jesus predicted that "when
the Son of Man comes in His glory [a reference to His apocalyptic coming described in Matt. 24] . . . then He will sit on His
glorious throne. And all the nations will be gathered before
Him; and He will separate them from one another, as the shepherd separates the sheep from the goats." To some He will say,
"Come you who are blessed of My Father, inherit the kingdom
prepared for you from the foundation of the world."[9]

In the Book of Revelation, the present-future Davidic activity of Jesus is quite apparent. Jesus is now "the firstborn of the dead, and the ruler of the kings of the earth" (1:5; cf. Ps. 89:27); He has already received authority over the nations (2:26-27); He has the "key of David" (3:7); He has "sat down with the Father on His throne"; and He writes to the churches *as* "the root and the offspring of David, the bright morning star" (22:16). This is the one who is "coming with the clouds" (1:7); the one who "*will* rule them [the nations] with a rod of iron" (19:15); the one who is "coming quickly" (22:12, 20), who is called upon by the church to "come" (22:17, 20).

## Answering Some Objections

The New Testament presents Jesus as the heir of the Davidic covenant. Furthermore, it teaches that certain blessings of the Davidic covenant have already been granted to Jesus, while other blessings await His return.

In controversies between covenantalists and dispensationalists, however, objections have been raised against both present and future fulfillments of the Davidic promise. Some dispensationalists object to interpreting Christ's past and present relationship with the Father as well as His present session in terms of the Davidic covenant. They believe that Davidic covenant blessings will only and completely be fulfilled at Christ's return when He rules over Israel and all the nations.[10]

Some covenantalists object to the belief that there will be a future fulfillment of national-political aspects of the Davidic covenant when Christ returns to earth. They believe that the Davidic promise is completely fulfilled in Jesus' present session.

Support for these views seems to come from a reliance on part of the biblical evidence to the exclusion of the whole. A number of false dichotomies are created in this way: fulfillment must be either present or future, either complete or not at all, either material or spiritual, either earthly or heavenly. When the whole of Old and New Testament Scripture is taken into account, presumed antitheses become stages in the progress of revelation—not polar opposites but partial accounts in the unfolding history of redemption.

This chapter has already demonstrated the correctness of a present-future progression in the fulfillment of the Davidic covenant. The next chapter will add further support to this view by studying the progressive stages of the kingdom of God. However, it may prove helpful to respond to some typical objections raised against the notion of Jesus' present Davidic position and activity. This will add to the more general response presented above and will serve to summarize the data in a perhaps more convenient form.

**Objection 1.** *The throne Jesus received at His ascension was not the throne promised to David.* This objection assumes that the throne of David and of his descendant as promised in the Davidic covenant should be understood solely as a national-political office geographically located in Israel, or more specifically, in Jerusalem. Geographical location is particularly crucial to this interpretation. Christ's present location *in heaven* appears to be an obvious contradiction to any claim that He occupies a Davidic throne. David ruled on the earth, in Jerusalem, as did the line of kings descended from him. How can one say that Christ's present throne is a fulfillment of Davidic promise?

First of all, the objection fails to observe the fact that *every New Testament description of the present throne of Jesus is drawn from Davidic covenant promises.* Repeatedly, the New Testament declares that He is enthroned at the right hand of God in fulfillment of the promise given in Psalm 110:1. This is a Davidic promise; it is the son of David who fulfills it. In Acts 2:30-36, the resurrection, ascension, and seating of Christ in heaven at the right hand of God (Ps. 110:1) are presented in light of the prediction "that God had sworn to him [David] with an oath to seat one of his descendants upon his throne" (Acts 2:30). No other throne is discussed in this text except the Davidic throne.

New Testament descriptions of this enthronement at the right hand of God are often filled with other Davidic features such as being exalted above all other kings, all rule, and all authority. Having all his enemies subjected to him or in some texts waiting to have all things subjected to him are both descriptions drawn from Davidic promises. The title Son of God also appears quite often in these texts and is explicitly linked to the Davidic promise of divine Sonship.

Hebrews 1 is a good example of what we are talking about. The title Son, introduced in 1:2, and ascribed to one enthroned "at the right hand of the Majesty on high" in 1:3, is subsequently identified in 1:5 by the promise made in 2 Samuel 7:14, "I will be a Father to Him, and He shall be a Son to Me." His exaltation over all is seen in His appointment as heir of all things (Heb. 1:2), His upholding all things (v. 3), His superiority to angels (v. 4), and His more excellent name (v. 4). His title "firstborn" (v. 6) adds another Davidic designation. The description of this Son's throne in 1:8 ("Thy throne, O God, is forever and ever") is drawn from a Davidic psalm speaking of a Davidic king.

His present kingship is further elaborated in Hebrews in terms of its Melchizedekian priestly office and function, another Davidic covenant promise (the oath sworn to David and revealed in Psalm 110:4). This priestly office is brought together with the already defined Davidic sonship to describe again His present throne—the "throne of grace" (Heb. 4:16), occupied by our "great high priest . . . Jesus the Son of God" (4:14, cf. 5:5-6).

One verse which is sometimes cited as an exception to the Davidic descriptions of Jesus' present throne is Revelation 3:21, "He who overcomes, I will grant to him to sit down with Me on My throne, as I also overcame and sat down with My Father on His throne." It is alleged that this verse teaches that Jesus is not sitting on the Davidic throne but the divine throne. This interpretation fails to note the frequent references to Jesus' Davidic position and activity in the immediate context. Revelation 1:5 describes Jesus' present position in Davidic covenant language drawn from Psalm 89:27. Furthermore, Jesus identifies Himself as the Son of God (Rev. 2:18 ) who *has received* authority from His father to rule the nations (2:26-27). He *has* the key of David (3:7) and will build the house of God (3:12). The statement in 5:5 that "the Root of David, has overcome" provides an identity reference for the "I" in 3:21 who "overcame and sat down with My Father on His throne." It is the "Root of David" who is sitting on the Father's throne. But the fact that it is said to be the Father's throne, far from presenting a problem to our interpretation, actually affirms it. For this is one of the ways in which the Old Testament spoke of the throne inherited by the Davidic king; it is in fact the throne of the Lord.[11] Even His reference to the throne as belonging to "My Father" is a covenantal expression (1 Chron. 17:13-14; Ps. 89:26).

Even the fact that Christ's present seating *in heaven* is at the right hand of God is in accord with the Davidic pattern of kingship. Throughout the Psalms, David is spoken of as the one who is at God's right hand.[12] In Psalm 139:8, 10, he contemplates how he would be received should he ascend into heaven. He says, "Even there Thy hand will lead me, and Thy right hand will lay hold of me." This is David speaking of his relationship with the Lord which has been established by covenant. Reception into heaven at the right hand of God is a *Davidic* blessing. And this is what the New Testament declares to have been granted to Jesus, Son of David.

The second problem with the objection is that *it fails to comprehend the relationship between God's heavenly rule over Israel and the rule of His chosen king.* It misses the fact that in Old Testament theology, the throne of God, that is the kingship of God, is covenantally oriented to Israel. To be sure, God is said to be sovereign over all things. He always was and always will be. In that sense we can speak of the heavenly throne of God as His eternal sovereignty over all things. But we must also note that in Old Testament theology, God establishes Himself in a special way as King over Israel. In keeping with His covenant promise to Abraham, He created a nation out of his descendants with Himself as *their* king, formalized in the Mosaic covenant. When human kingship was instituted, it did not replace God's special kingship over Israel, but functioned under it. This is why Chronicles speaks of the throne which Solomon inherits as the throne of the Lord. *The human, earthly throne is a manifestation of the heavenly throne and rule over Israel.*[13]

In Acts 2, Peter declares the enthronement of Jesus in heaven as having great implications for Israel. He is not primarily speaking of Jesus' deity, although that in itself has great implications. He is not speaking of Jesus' divine eternal sovereignty. Rather the point he is making is that this resurrected, immortal son of David has been made Christ and Lord on the divine throne *over Israel.* Because of the covenant orientation of the heavenly throne to Israel, Jesus' enthronement there makes Him the Christ, the anointed king of Israel. And because God, the King of Israel, had covenanted to David that his descendant would rule Israel and all the nations, this installation of Jesus (the son of David whom God has raised up from the dead) in heaven by the divine King of Israel portends an imminent descent to the Jerusalem throne.

**Objection 2.** *Jesus' present activity is best understood as divine sovereignty, not Davidic kingship.* Once again, this objection limits Davidic kingship to merely political functions. Since Christ is not on earth acting as its political ruler, it is assumed that He is not functioning as a Davidic king. All of His present work is characterized as divine activity, including all references to His ruling and reigning.

First of all, we note that *the Bible explains Jesus' present activity in Davidic as well as divine terms.* The divine descriptions of Jesus' activity do not need to be reviewed here since they are not in dispute. But note some of the Davidic characterizations of His present work. Repeatedly through the Book of Acts and the Epistles, it is as the *Christ* (that is Messiah, *the anointed Davidic king of Israel*), seated at the right hand of God (the Davidic position) that He is active today. The miracles that take place in Acts are ascribed to Jesus *Christ* (cf. Acts 3:6, "Jesus Christ the Nazarene"). The Gospel which we receive, and which brings salvation, is the good news about the Davidic Messiah (Rom. 1:1-4; 2 Tim. 2:8). When we receive it, we are transferred into the kingdom of God's beloved Son, a description in covenantal language. In Ephesians, Christ acts from His position at the right hand of the Father, with all His enemies subjected to Him, to build the house of God. He does this by giving the Holy Spirit — an activity which John the Baptist predicted and which the Apostles confirmed would be and is performed by the Christ. In Hebrews, Jesus mediates for us as our Melchizedekian priest, the priestly office and function covenanted to David (and David's descendant). In the Book of Revelation, He instructs the churches *as the Davidic king:*

> I, Jesus, have sent My angel to testify to you these things for the churches. I am the root and the offspring of David, the bright morning star (Rev. 22:16).

Secondly, *the objection fails to understand the divine-human unity of Christ's person, as well as how that unity fulfills the converging prophecies of divine and messianic rule in the eschatological kingdom of God.* Undoubtedly, the reason why Christ is able to forgive sins and give the Holy Spirit is because He is God by nature. But it is the Person of Christ, the God-Man, who acts. His human volition is active along with the divine in the unity of His personal decision. Added to this is the fact that His humanity is not generic; He is a descendant of David who has been anointed, enthroned, and given "all authority in heaven and *on earth*" (Matt. 28:18). When He acts, He acts as the divine *and Davidic king.*

In the next chapter, we will see that some of the prophets predicted an eschatological kingdom in which God would rule on earth while others predicted the everlasting rule of a future descendant of David. The rule in both lines of prophecy is the same: same activities, same results. We now see, however, that these prophecies come together in one person, whom we know as Jesus, who is both God and a descendant of David. The prophecies regarding God's rule and the Davidic king's rule are simultaneously fulfilled by the conjunction of divine and human volitions in the singular unity of Jesus' personal action. One cannot exclude His human volition from this activity. This is why in the language of Scripture, actions which can only take place by divine power are ascribed to Jesus of Nazareth, the Christ.

*Objection 3. To speak of the present fulfillment of Davidic promises by Christ in heaven is a spiritual interpretation of earthly, political promises.* This objection only has appeal if Davidic promises are reduced to merely the political activities of the Son of David on earth. It is then assumed that the claim of present Davidic fulfillment hermeneutically transforms these future earthly activities into transcendent spiritual realities.

Nothing could be further from the truth. First of all, the Bible itself describes the present position and activity of Christ in terms of the promises covenanted to David. These truths are discerned through a historical-literary interpretation of Scripture. We are not following a "spiritual interpretation" when we read and understand the title *Christ* to mean the anointed Davidic King and interpret the Scriptures as saying that Jesus presently is and acts as the Christ. We are not following a "spiritual interpretation" when we see the covenantal promise of a Father-Son relationship presently fulfilled in the person of Jesus.

186

Nor are we following a "spiritual interpretation" when we read Peter's proclamation that Jesus has been raised up in accordance with the promise to seat one of David's descendants upon his throne and then hear him say that Jesus has been seated at the right hand of God and made Lord and Christ. No "spiritual interpretation" is at work when we understand Hebrews to say that Jesus has received the office of Melchizedekian priest, the office which God covenanted by oath to David. No "spiritual interpretation" is at work when we interpret the Scripture as saying that Jesus is now the highest of the kings of the earth, that He has been established forever in God's kingdom, that the Father's loving-kindness abides with Him forever, and that He is indeed building a house for the dwelling place of God. These and many other aspects of Christ's present Davidic ministry as seen in the preceding pages come from a grammatical, historical, and literary study of New Testament teaching.

This raises questions, however, about the hermeneutic of those who claim the Bible does not teach these things. As noted in the chapters on hermeneutics, we inevitably come to Scripture with a preunderstanding formed by our tradition. The real test of whether Scripture or tradition is our fundamental authority lies in our willingness to test those preunderstandings by further study of the Scripture, examining its teachings again in a literary-historical manner. If the interpretations advanced in this chapter are correct, they will be verified and further developed if necessary in such a manner. Those who take a contrary view need to enter into the same process of study. Hopefully this will contribute to a better understanding of Scripture by us all.

## Jesus and the Fulfillment of the Abrahamic Covenant

In Luke 1:46-55, we find Mary's song of praise in response to the news that her Son would fulfill the covenant promise to David. She concludes with this praise:

He has given *help* to *Israel His servant*,
In remembrance of His mercy,
As He spoke to our fathers,
To *Abraham* and his *offspring* forever.

187

This language recalls the first of the series of Servant oracles found in the Book of Isaiah (41:8-10).

But you, *Israel, My servant,*
Jacob whom I have chosen,
*Descendant [offspring, seed] of Abraham*, My friend.
You whom I have taken from the ends of the earth,
And called from its remotest parts,
And said to you, "You are My servant,
I have chosen you and not rejected you.
Do not fear, for I am with you;
Do not anxiously look about you, for I am your God.
I will strengthen you, *surely I will help you,*
Surely, I will uphold you with My righteous right hand."[14]

Mary's song reveals her belief that the one whom she would bear to fulfill the promises to David would also fulfill the promises made to Abraham. In her mind the fulfillment of the Davidic covenant was the means by which the Abrahamic promise would be accomplished. And it does not seem to be a coincidence that she states the Abrahamic promise in the language of Isaiah's first Servant oracle, for as the series of oracles progresses, the Servant is eventually identified as an individual within Israel who serves Israel and through whom Israel's service to God is accomplished (Isa. 49:5-6).

Zacharias' prophecy in Luke 1:68-79 continues this theme by proclaiming "the Lord God of Israel . . . has raised up a horn of salvation for us in the house of David His servant . . . *to remember His holy covenant, the oath which He swore to Abraham our father.*" This will lead, he says, to Israel serving God "in holiness and righteousness all our days," a description which recalls the covenant promise that they would be His people and He would be their God.

Peter's second sermon, Acts 3:12-26, proclaims Jesus as the Servant of the God of Abraham, Isaac, and Jacob who has been sent to Israel to turn them back to God (vv. 13, 26). The reference to Isaiah 49:5-6 (where the Servant brings Israel back to God) is unmistakable. Furthermore, he declares Him to be the mediator of the blessing promised in the Abrahamic covenant.

It is you who are the sons of the prophets, and of the covenant which God made with your fathers, saying to

Abraham, "And in your seed all the families of the earth shall *be blessed.*" For you first, God raised up His Servant, and sent Him *to bless you* by turning every one of you from your wicked ways" (Acts 3:25-26).

Here the repentance which the Servant of God would effect in Israel is seen to be an aspect of the blessing which God promised to Abraham. This is in fact tied to the promise of the new covenant which we will examine subsequently. But note verses 20-21 of this sermon. Peter looks forward to the future coming of Christ at which all features of the promised blessing will be confirmed. He states that "heaven must receive [him] until the period of restoration of all things, about which God spoke by the mouth of His holy prophets from ancient time." This must include the national and territorial aspects of the Abrahamic covenant, since the prophets frequently spoke of the *restoration* of those blessings.

Peter's sermon confirms that blessings of the Abrahamic covenant are mediated by the Christ.[15] As the Davidic covenant is fulfilled with Him, so the blessings of the Abrahamic covenant are fulfilled with respect to its various recipients. However, the fulfillment will occur in stages which are tied to the history of the Christ. Certain blessings are now available. Other blessings await the time of His return.

The teaching in Luke and Acts that the Christ, the anointed king, is the one who mediates the blessings of the Abrahamic covenant agrees completely with our study of the Davidic covenant in the Old Testament, especially Psalm 72. Furthermore, this Old Testament background helps to interpret Paul's remarks in Galatians 3 about Christ fulfilling the promises to Abraham. He says in Galatians 3:16, "Now the promises were spoken to Abraham and to his seed. He does not say, 'And to seeds,' as referring to many, but rather to one, 'And to your seed,' that is, Christ." Paul is not saying that Christ is the only individual who will be blessed, for in verse 14, he had already said, "in Christ Jesus the blessing of Abraham . . . [comes] to the Gentiles." And in verse 29, he speaks of Jews and Gentiles who "belong to Christ" and are consequently "Abraham's seed, heirs according to promise."

*Seed* is a collective noun in both Greek and English. While its singular form can refer to a single seed, it often means many seeds of the same kind. For example, we might say that a farmer buys a sack of seed (meaning several seeds of the same kind) and then that he sows his seed in his field (meaning again that he has planted all the seeds). Also we note the organic, reproductive nature of seed. Out of one seed sown in the ground can come many seeds. Consequently we see a relationship between the singular form and the plural meaning of seed.

Paul appears to be arguing that the Davidic covenant has structured the seed of Abraham in such a way that the blessing of the covenant first of all envisions the King, a single individual, and then through Him all other covenant recipients. Thus he says that the promises refer "to one . . . that is, *Christ.*" Christ, the anointed king, receives the blessing and mediates it to His subjects. The subjects have "clothed" themselves "with Christ" by virtue of baptism (v. 27) so that they are "all one in Christ Jesus" (v. 28). In this way they are all together "Abraham's offspring [seed], heirs according to promise" (v. 29).

From the standpoint of the New Testament, the promises of Abraham are being and will be fulfilled through the Christ, who is proclaimed as Jesus. The language of the covenant promise, "I will bless you . . . and in you [or "in your seed," cf. Gen. 22:18] all families of the earth will be blessed" (Gen. 12:2-3), has come to mean that God blesses Christ, the seed of Abraham, the seed of David, and all those of Abraham and of the nations of the earth who are *in Him.*

It is in this regard that we should understand the Pauline doctrine of blessing *in Christ.* It is a covenantal term combining the Abrahamic and Davidic covenants, in which the latter functions as the means for the fulfillment of the former. We will see that the phrase also has reference to the new covenant, since as revealed in the Old Testament, the new covenant is the form in which Abrahamic covenant blessing will be everlastingly enjoyed.

Before leaving the Abrahamic covenant, however, we need to note two other important aspects of its fulfillment which the New Testament presents to us: (1) that the blessing includes Gentiles as well as Jews; and (2) that both Jews and Gentiles must receive the blessing by faith in Christ.

### Blessing upon the Gentiles

Paul's teaching on the Abrahamic covenant focuses particularly upon the promise to bless "all nations." In Galatians 3:8, he

190

says, "And the Scripture, foreseeing that God would justify the Gentiles by faith, preached the Gospel beforehand to Abraham, saying, 'All the nations shall be blessed in you.' " Paul understands this promise of blessing the Gentiles as presently being fulfilled through Christ. He writes in verse 14, "in Christ Jesus the blessing of Abraham [comes] to the Gentiles."

It is important to note that the blessing which Paul has in mind in Galatians 3 is the reception of the Holy Spirit (see 3:2, 5; 4:6 ) and the gift of righteousness (3:21-22). These are in fact new covenant blessings, but Paul presents them as blessings of the Abrahamic covenant. Again, this shows that the new covenant is the form in which the Abrahamic covenant will be fulfilled. It is also important to note that Paul, just like Peter, sees the Abrahamic blessing mediated in stages which are tied to the history of Christ. The stages distinguish not only between degrees of blessing but also between different kinds of blessing. Thus Peter spoke of the restoration of all things predicted by the prophets at the future coming of Christ. This certainly includes the national promises to Israel, since those promises are included in "all things predicted by the prophets." Paul likewise spoke of the salvation of all Israel at the coming of Christ (Rom. 11:26), based on the fact that "from the standpoint of God's choice, they are beloved for the sake of the fathers; for the gifts and the calling of God are irrevocable" (vv. 28-29). His language here recalls the words of Moses in Deuteronomy that after all the curses of the Mosaic covenant, the Lord would restore national and territorial blessings to Israel because He would not "forget the covenant with your fathers which He swore to them"; and "Because He loved your fathers, therefore He chose their descendants after them . . . to give you . . . [this] land for an inheritance" (Deut. 4:31, 37-38).

With the future national blessing tied to the return of Christ, there are in the present time certain blessings being given to Jews and Gentiles equally. These blessings are being given in fulfillment of the promise to bless "you" (Jews) and to bless "all nations" (Acts 3:25-26; Gal. 3:8, 14). In conjunction with the promise to bless all nations "in you," Gentiles who were "strangers to the covenants of promise" (Eph. 2:12) have been reconciled "in Christ" and blessed along with Jews. The blessing is being given equally without any distinctions of race, class, or gender (Gal. 3:28).

191

## The Reception of the Blessing by Faith

Much of what the New Testament has to say about the Abrahamic covenant has to do with how and to whom its blessings are given. John the Baptist warned the Jews that physical descent alone was not sufficient to guarantee reception of the covenant blessings. Rather he predicted a coming judgment on all who did not repent (Matt. 3:9; Luke 3:8). Jesus also warned His listeners that not all the descendants of Abraham, Isaac, and Jacob would inherit the kingdom of God (Matt. 8:11; Luke 13:28), which is to say that not all physical descendents of Abraham share in the future fulfillment of covenant promises.

In John 8:39-58, Jesus rebuked His hearers, physical descendants of Abraham, for not being *true* children of Abraham, that is, for not replicating in their lives the faith and works of Abraham. They were, he said, children of the devil, seeking to do the deeds of the devil.

Paul argues that "it is those who are of faith that are sons of Abraham" (Gal. 3:7). He observes that in Genesis 15:6, Abraham received the promise by faith: "He believed in the Lord; and He [the Lord] reckoned it to him [Abraham] as righteousness." Paul sees faith as the means of receiving the grant covenant of Abraham. Such reception is appropriate to the gracious nature and intention of the promise.

> For the promise to Abraham or to his descendants that he would be heir of the world was not through the Law, but through the righteousness of faith. . . . For this reason it is by faith, that it might be in accordance with grace, in order that the promise may be certain to all the descendants, not to those who are of the Law only, but to those who are also of the faith of Abraham, who is the father of us all (Rom. 4:13, 16).[16]

Again, he says (in Gal. 3:9), "those who are of faith are blessed with Abraham, the believer." This necessarily presupposes a distinction within Israel: those who are of the faith of Abraham and consequently receive the blessings of the Abrahamic covenant and those who are not of Abraham's faith and who consequently forfeit the possibility of inheriting his blessing. In Romans 9:6-8, he argues:

> For they are not all Israel who are . . . from Israel; neither are all the children Abraham's descendants [seed], but: "through Isaac your descendants [seed] will be named." That is, it is not the children of the flesh who are children of God, but the children of the promise are regarded as descendants [seed].[17]

Here, the children of the promise are those physical descendants whom God has chosen (see Rom. 9:11, 16, 18; 11:5). They are also seen as those who believe. Those who are rejected are rejected "for their unbelief" (11:20). But, "if they do not continue in their unbelief, [they] will be grafted in" (v. 23). Those Jews who fail to attain the covenantal blessing do so because "they did not pursue it by faith, but as though it were by works. They stumbled over the stumbling-stone, just as it is written, 'Behold, I lay in Zion a stone of stumbling and a rock of offense, and he who believes in Him will not be disappointed' " (9:32-33).

Gentiles who believe in Jesus Christ receive the blessings of Abraham consistent with the promise to bless all nations in him. Paul argues in Romans 4:9-12 that Abraham received the promise by faith before he was circumcised. This is a sign that Gentiles would be blessed through this covenant by faith. In Galatians 3:8, Paul calls the promise to bless the nations the Gospel which is to be received by faith. "So then those who are of faith are blessed with Abraham, the believer." It is "in Christ Jesus" that "the blessing of Abraham" comes "to the Gentiles . . . through faith."

The blessing which Jews and Gentiles receive through faith is shared equally by both groups without distinction of race, gender, or social class (Gal. 3:28; Eph. 2:14-16; 3:6). As for the specific content of that blessing, we must turn to the new covenant.

## Summary

In His present and future Davidic ministry, Jesus receives and mediates the blessings of the Abrahamic covenant. In Him and through Him that covenant is and will be fulfilled. His mediation of the blessing extends to all peoples, to Jews and Gentiles who trust in Him. But He mediates it in stages, with the national and political blessings awaiting the dispensation of His return.

## Jesus and the Mosaic Covenant

We have seen that the Mosaic covenant was an arrangement in which Israel and Judah could experience the blessing of the Abrahamic covenant (or conversely the Lord's curse) in their daily national life. As God's response to the people, the blessings or curses were the fulfillment of the covenant. Consequently, the Mosaic covenant was being continuously fulfilled in the day-to-day history of Israel, for they were ever under God's blessing or curse.

The promises of a new covenant, however, looked to a time when the Mosaic covenant would be replaced. It would come to an end and be replaced by the new covenant.

The New Testament teaches that Jesus Christ brought the Mosaic covenant to its final fulfillment. In Matthew 5:17-18, Jesus taught:

> Do not think that I came to abolish the Law or the Prophets; I did not come to abolish, but to fulfill. For truly I say to you, until heaven and earth pass away, not the smallest letter or stroke shall pass away from the Law, until all is accomplished.

The term *Law* is used here as a reference to Scripture itself. When it is used along with *Prophets* it refers to the Pentateuch, the first five books of the Old Testament, commonly referred to as the Torah, or Law. The second use of law, in verse 18, refers to the Old Testament Scripture as a whole. It is important to note that Jesus is not referring to divine commandments alone when He speaks of *law* here. The broad use covers those commandments *as they appear within the covenants to which they belong.* That broad use also covers the patterns of God's dealings with Israel presented in the historical narratives of Old Testament Scripture. Jesus includes all of this when He says that He did not come to abolish but to fulfill.

The operative word is *fulfill.* Some have suggested that this means that He came to uphold and proclaim the Law much like other teachers of Scripture. The use of the word *fulfill* in Matthew's Gospel, however, seems to lead to a different understanding. Jesus fulfilled the Scripture by replicating in His own life the patterns of God's historical relations with Israel and by accomplishing in His own history the predicted events of prophecy.[18]

When it comes to the covenants presented or predicted in the Old Testament, He accomplishes them as well. We have already seen how He is presented as the fulfillment of the Davidic and Abrahamic covenants, a fulfillment that takes place in His ongoing work. When it comes to the Mosaic covenant, however, the New Testament presents that covenant as completely fulfilled in the death of Jesus Christ. The specific terms of that covenant were not to be arbitrarily set aside (abolished). The covenant was legally binding down to the smallest letter or stroke until heaven and earth (the witness of the covenant in Deut. 4; 30) passed away.[19] But Jesus introduces another *until,* "until all is accomplished." The accomplishing of the covenants, the prophecies, and the patterns of Scripture take place in the history of His ministry—some during the time of His birth, childhood, and adult pre-ascension ministry, some in His death, resurrection, and ascension, some in His present session, and the rest in His future return and everlasting reign. It is in this "accomplishment" of the covenants, the prophecies and the patterns of Scripture, that the Mosaic covenant as such is said to be fulfilled and replaced by a new covenant which abides forever.

Hebrews 8–10 speaks of this covenantal change. Much of what it has to say concerns the rationale, the basis, and the implications of the establishment of the new covenant. The Mosaic covenant is referred to as "obsolete," "growing old," and "ready to disappear." Certain ceremonial features of that covenant are especially singled out as having been replaced.

Using the language of Deuteronomy 30, Paul says in Romans 10:1-10, that "Christ is the end of the law" (v. 4). The word *law* here refers to the stipulations of the Mosaic covenant, for it was those covenant stipulations as a whole which were in view in Deuteronomy 30. The same is true for his statement in Ephesians 2:14-15, that Christ "broke down the barrier of the dividing wall [a structural feature of the temple which separated Gentiles from Jews] by *abolishing in His flesh . . . the Law of commandments contained in ordinances.*" The word *Law* here refers to the stipulations section of the Mosaic covenant which was often referred to as "the commandments, the statutes, and the judgments [ordinances]" (Deut. 6:1-2, 17; 7:11; 8:11; 11:1; 12:1; 28:1, 15; 30:10, 16). The stipulations were perhaps the most striking and vital feature of the Mosaic covenant, such that a reference to this portion of the covenant was a reference to the covenant as a whole.

This observation becomes even clearer in Romans 7:1-6 where Paul compares *the law* to a marriage covenant. Certainly, in this passage, the law means the Mosaic covenant itself. Paul speaks of our relationship to the law (Mosaic covenant) ending in the death of Jesus Christ just as a marriage partner's obligation to the marriage covenant ends in the death of the other partner (vv. 3-4). It is possible for that marriage partner to enter into a new marriage covenant, and likewise Paul using the language of the prophecies of the new covenant, speaks of our being "released from the law" (freed from the Mosaic covenant) and "serving in the newness of the Spirit" (brought into the new covenant).

The end of the Mosaic covenant is also proclaimed in Galatians 3–4, where Paul speaks of the church's present reception of the Holy Spirit (3:2, 5; 4:6), a new covenant provision. Throughout the section he refers to the Mosaic covenant by the term *law* and to the Abrahamic covenant by the term *promise.* The appearance of the term *covenant* in 3:15, 17 helps to clarify that covenants are indeed in view, as does also the historical reference to the law being formally instituted (v. 19) 430 years after the promise (v. 17). Finally, in Galatians 4:24, Paul explicitly states that he is speaking of *two covenants,* one of which was made on Mount Sinai. He makes several observations about these covenants:

1. The Abrahamic covenant takes precedence over the Mosaic covenant.

2. The Mosaic covenant did not set aside the Abrahamic covenant (3:17).

3. The Abrahamic covenant is received by faith.

4. The blessings of the Mosaic covenant are received by obedience to its stipulations (v.12).

5. The Mosaic covenant was instituted because of sin (v. 19).

6. The Mosaic covenant was temporary, being in effect "until the seed should come to whom the promise had been made" (v. 19).

This last point receives extended attention from 3:19 through 4:31. Jesus Christ is the "seed" (3:16) whose coming marks the end of the Mosaic covenant. Paul repeats this point in three ways.

First, he says that we are no longer under the Mosaic covenant (the law) now that faith in Jesus Christ has come (vv. 22-25). Faith existed before the incarnation since, as Paul argues, Abraham was a believer and the Abrahamic promise has always been received by faith (3:6-9, 14). But when God the Son, the Redeemer, became incarnate as Jesus of Nazareth, faith in God focused itself specifically upon Jesus. The law (Mosaic covenant) functioned like a "tutor to lead us to Christ" (3:24), "But now that faith has come [that is faith in Jesus Christ, since Jesus Christ has now come] we are no longer under a tutor" (3:25). Since the "tutor" is the Mosaic covenant, Paul is saying we are no longer under that covenant.

Secondly, he speaks of the Mosaic covenant as a steward in charge of children "until the date set by the father," until they reach the age of inheritance (4:1-2). The implication is that when the age of adulthood is reached, the stewardship of the steward comes to an end. The coming of Jesus has done that for us with respect to the Mosaic covenant. Now that Jesus has come, has redeemed us and given us blessing of a new covenant (v. 6, the promised Holy Spirit), we are no longer under the stewardship of the Mosaic covenant (v. 7, cf. vv. 1-3).

Finally, Paul argues with an allegory in 4:21-31. Using the story of Sarah and Hagar, her slave, Paul teaches that new covenant Christians are children of the Abrahamic promise. As Hagar was "cast out" along with her son, so the Mosaic covenant has been set aside. Those who attempt to relate to God through the terms of that covenant have missed the new covenant relationship which God has established through faith in Jesus Christ, a relationship that bestows the blessing of Abraham apart from the Mosaic covenant.

In Galatians 3:10-13, Paul explains how the death of Christ fulfilled and thus terminated the Mosaic covenant. "Christ redeemed us from the curse of the Law, having become a curse for us—for it is written, 'Cursed is every one who hangs on a tree.'" Christ took the curse of the Mosaic covenant upon Himself so as to completely satisfy God's demands. This would not have happened, however, if He was Himself a sinner, needing atonement for His own sins. But as Paul says in 2 Corinthians 5:21, "He made Him who knew no sin to be sin on our behalf, that we might become the righteousness of God in Him." He was completely obedient to the stipulations of the Mosaic covenant. This is why those who are *in Christ* are counted righteous (cf. Deut. 6:25; 1 Cor. 1:30) and find the curse of God completely satisfied for them.

The sinless mediation of Christ which fulfilled and ended the Mosaic covenant and opened the new dispensation of the new covenant is a major teaching in the letter to the Hebrews. Hebrews states that He is a high priest who is without sin. Consequently, He is able to intercede completely on behalf of His people.

> For it was fitting that we should have such a high priest, holy, innocent, undefiled, separated from sinners and exalted above the heavens; who does not need daily, like those high priests, to offer up sacrifices, first for His own sins, and then for the sins of the people, because this He did once for all when He offered up Himself (7:26-27).

Hebrews argues that this priestly act was a mediatorial function of His Melchizedekian priesthood, which belongs to Him as the Christ, the Son of David. He offered the one sacrifice of Himself which fulfilled the sacrificial system of the Mosaic covenant, and "sat down at the right hand of God," as Lord (Ps. 110:1) of Israel and the nations (Heb. 10:1-18; see esp. v. 12). Having fulfilled the Mosaic covenant, He has made possible the establishment of a new covenant in its place.

Romans 7:1-6 views the death of Christ as the death of a covenant partner which therefore marks the end of a bilateral covenant. Paul does not explain how Christ is to be seen as a covenant partner. The fact that He is the Christ, the king of Israel, would suggest that His death is representative of the nation. That thought is connected to His role as the Servant of God, who is both Israel and a representative of Israel ministering on behalf of Israel and the nations. He is also God (Rom. 9:5), the covenant maker, thus His death is more significant than that of any previous Davidic king. And when we add the fact that His death was a covenant satisfaction for the transgressions of God's people, fulfilling the curse of the covenant, the termination of the Mosaic covenant is seen to be complete.

Before leaving the matter of Jesus' fulfillment of the Mosaic covenant, we should point out that the termination of that covenant does not mean that God's people are left in a state of lawlessness. Certainly Abraham was not in a state of lawlessness 430 years before the *law* (Mosaic covenant) was given. The Lord Himself commanded him, "Walk before Me, and be blameless" (Gen. 17:1), and later He said of him, "I have chosen him, in order that he may command his children and his household after him to keep the way of the Lord by doing righteousness and justice" (Gen. 18:19). The termination of the Mosaic covenant was in view of the establishment of a new covenant in which God would write *His law* into the hearts of His people (Jer. 31:33) and cause them to walk in His ways (Ezek. 36:27). So, although Paul teaches that Christ is the end of the law (Rom. 10:4; that is, law in the form of the Mosaic covenant), he also says that believers are "not . . . without the law of God but under the law of Christ" (1 Cor. 9:21; cf. Gal. 6:2; this is law in the form of the new covenant). He also speaks of this new covenant law as the "law of the Spirit" (Rom. 8:2), since the Spirit is the characteristic feature of the new covenant. James refers to it as the "royal law" (James 2:8, 12) connecting it again to the Christ, the anointed king.

The progressive dispensationalism of New Testament theology is not antinomian.[20] For while it teaches that Mosaic covenant law has ended dispensationally, it also teaches that it has been replaced by new covenant law, and it presents this dispensational change as integral to God's plan of redemption which affirms and fulfills the divine demand for righteousness and holiness even as it saves and eternally blesses the redeemed.

## Jesus and the New Covenant

Our study of the history of the covenants shows them to be the structure by which the history of redemption is carried out. That history unfolds in a progression of divine dispensations. The grant covenants to the patriarchs which promised blessing for all were given dispensational expression in the Mosaic covenant. The Davidic grant provided for a mediator in and through whom the patriarchal grants would be finally fulfilled. That mediator would oversee the dispensational transition from the Mosaic to a new covenant for the everlasting fulfillment of the promises of blessing. That mediator is Jesus, the Christ, who brought the temporary dispensation of the Mosaic covenant to a close and who, in His own history of fulfilling the Davidic promise, inaugurated the new covenant and directs the history of its fulfillment to its everlasting consummation.

## Jesus, the Mediator of the New Covenant

On the night before He was crucified, Jesus gathered with His disciples in the upper room of a Jerusalem home to celebrate the Passover. It is recorded in Luke 22:20, that He took the cup before sharing it with the disciples and gave it this significance: "This cup which is poured out for you is the new covenant in My blood." Matthew 26:28, relating the same incident, reports Him as saying, "this is My blood of the covenant, which is to be shed on behalf of many for forgiveness of sins." In light of the numerous citations and allusions to Old Testament Scripture in both Luke's and Matthew's account of this event, it is only proper to trace Jesus' remarks about the new covenant for the forgiveness of sins to that promise in Jeremiah 31:31-34 which begins: "I will make a new covenant with the house of Israel and with the house of Judah"; and ends with the words: "I will forgive their iniquity and their sin I will remember no more."

Paul places the New Testament church under this very same new covenant arrangement when he identifies the church's practice of the Lord's Supper as a sharing of the bread and of the cup which Jesus instituted that night before the crucifixion. He repeats Christ's words as found in Luke 22:20: "This cup is the new covenant in My blood" (1 Cor. 11:25). He speaks of the church as drinking this cup (vv. 26-29) in obedience to Jesus' commandment given on that night (vv. 23, 25), and he explains this activity as their proclamation of Christ's death (v. 26) and as their own participation in His blood (10:16).

In 2 Corinthians 3:6, Paul identifies himself and his fellow ministers as "servants of a new covenant." This is not some indefinite new covenant but that one which was predicted by Jeremiah and Ezekiel. We know this because Paul identifies the key features of this new covenant as those which Jeremiah and Ezekiel predicted when they prophesied the future new covenant.

Jeremiah: " 'But this is the covenant which I will make with the house of Israel after those days,' declares the Lord, 'I will put My law within them, and on their heart I will write it' " (Jer. 31:33).

Paul: "You are a letter of Christ . . . written not with ink, but with the Spirit of the living God, not on tablets of stone, but on tablets of human hearts" (2 Cor. 3:3).

Ezekiel: "I will put My Spirit within you and cause you to walk in My statutes, and you will be careful to observe My ordinances" (Ezek. 36:27). "And I will put My Spirit within you, and you will come to life . . ." (Ezek. 37:14).

Paul: "[We are] servants of a New Covenant . . . of the Spirit; for . . . the Spirit gives life" (2 Cor. 3:6).

Furthermore, Paul goes on to contrast this new covenant ministry with the ministry of "the old covenant" (2 Cor. 3:14) which was associated with Moses (2 Cor. 3:7, 13, 15), the same "old covenant" against which Jeremiah and Ezekiel prophesied a coming new covenant (Jer. 31:32). The letter to the Hebrews culminates this testimony by quoting Jeremiah 31:31-34 in full (Heb. 8:6-13) and proclaiming Christ to be "the mediator of a new covenant . . . for the redemption of the transgressions that were committed under the first covenant" (Heb. 9:15). It goes on to say that Christ's death is the atonement for all sins in accordance with the promise revealed in Jeremiah 31:33-34.

He, having offered one sacrifice for sins for all time, sat down at the right hand of God. . . . For by one offering He has perfected for all time those who are sanctified. And the Holy Spirit also bears witness to us; for after saying,
"This is the covenant that I will make with them
After those days, says the Lord:
I will put My laws upon their heart,
And upon their mind I will write them,"
He then says,
"And their sins and their lawless deeds
I will remember no more" (Heb. 10:12-17).

The letter goes on to trace the line of faith from the saints of the Old Testament to believers in Jesus today, concluding with a picture of the City of God in which the "church of the first-born" and "the spirits of righteous men made perfect [a reference to Old Testament saints, see Heb. 11:40 where "they" refers to the preceding list of saints]" are joined together with "Jesus the mediator of a new covenant" (Heb. 12:22-24).

It is indisputable that the New Testament views the new covenant predicted by Jeremiah and Ezekiel as established in the death of Jesus Christ with some of its promised blessings now being granted to Jews and Gentiles who are believers in Jesus. These are not blessings which are *like* those predicted by Jeremiah and Ezekiel. They are *the very same* blessings which those prophets predicted. For the new covenant which is presently in effect through Jesus Christ is not one which is *like* that predicted by Jeremiah and Ezekiel, but it is *that very same* covenant which they prophesied which is in effect today. There are features promised in that covenant whose fulfillment has been delayed until the return of Christ (such as the national and territorial promises in Jer. 31:31, 36 and Ezek. 36:28 and 37:14). But these are features that go back to the Abrahamic covenant itself, and yet the New Testament speaks of the present blessings of the Abrahamic covenant. The present, inaugurated form of the new covenant is in fact the dispensational form in which the Abrahamic blessings are present today.

## The Forgiveness of Sins

We have seen that the New Testament interprets Jesus' death as the foundational sacrifice which has inaugurated the new covenant. Jesus Himself explained the forgiveness of sins which comes through His death as a blessing of the new covenant. He commanded His disciples, "that repentance for forgiveness of sins should be proclaimed in His name to all the nations — beginning from Jerusalem" (Luke 24:47). After Jesus' ascension, on the Day of Pentecost, Peter began to preach in Jerusalem, "Repent, and let each of you be baptized in the name of Jesus Christ for the forgiveness of your sins" (Acts 2:38). Paul also preached in the synagogues, "therefore let it be known to you, brethren, that through Him forgiveness of sins is proclaimed to you, and through Him everyone who believes is freed from all things, from which you could not be freed through the Law of Moses" (Acts 13:38-39).

The New Testament doctrine of the forgiveness of sins, expounded in the Pauline and General Epistles, has its basis here. From the words of Jesus the night before the crucifixion, we can see the entire New Testament teaching on forgiveness as an extended exposition of the blessing of the new covenant, which is in turn a revelation of the specific meaning of the more generally stated Abrahamic promise: "I will *bless you.*" When Paul recounts the *blessings* which God has bestowed upon us in Christ (Eph. 1:1-14) he states that "In Him we have redemption through His blood, the forgiveness of our trespasses, according to the riches of His grace, which He lavished upon us." This is a blessing that is not only given to Jews according to the patriarchal promise, "I will bless you," but also to Gentiles according to the patriarchal promise "I will bless all nations in you." Consequently, Paul says that Gentiles who were "dead in . . . trespasses and sins," who were "strangers to the covenants of promise, having no hope and without God in the world," now "have been brought near by the blood of Christ" (Eph. 2:1, 12-13). The Gospel itself, which goes "to the Jew first and also to the Greek" (Rom. 1:16), is a proclamation "that Christ died for our sins according to the Scriptures" (1 Cor. 15:3), a proclamation which the church, Jews and Gentiles united in Christ (12:13), also makes when it partakes of the cup of remembrance (11:26), that cup of which Jesus said, "This cup is the *new covenant* in My blood; do this . . . in remembrance of Me" (11:24).

## The Promise of the Holy Spirit, the New Heart, and Resurrection from the Dead

Perhaps the most striking feature of the new covenant as prophesied by the Old Testament prophets was the promise of the indwelling Holy Spirit and the renewal of the human heart. When Paul identifies himself and his associates as ministers of a new covenant in 2 Corinthians 3:6, it is this activity of the Holy Spirit that he especially identifies. As he continues in his letter, he contrasts this new covenant ministry which he calls "the ministry of the Spirit" (3:8) with the ministry of the Mosaic covenant which he calls "the ministry of death, in letters engraved on stones" (3:7) or "the ministry of condemnation" (3:9). He speaks of how the ministry of the old covenant was confronted by a veil of hardness over the hearts and minds of the people (3:14-15). But the Spirit of the Lord takes away the veil of hardness and effectively transforms people into the image of the Lord (3:16-18). Paul's language is practically the same as that of Ezekiel who spoke of the Lord renewing hardened hearts by the Holy Spirit.

The theme of veiled hearts is carried into chapter 4 where the problem is diagnosed as a satanic blindness (4:3-4). Most significantly, the message of new covenant blessing is called the Gospel in these verses. In the new covenant ministry (note the continuation of "this ministry" in 4:1, looking back to the new covenant ministry of 3:6ff), God is removing the blindness of human hearts and minds by causing the light of the Gospel to shine "in our hearts to give the light of the knowledge of the glory of God in the face of Christ." The knowledge of God was also one of the promises of the new covenant (Jer. 31:34). The light of glory "in the face of Christ" is set in contrast with the fading glory of Moses (2 Cor. 3:13), once again emphasizing the difference in these covenants. Paul continues to speak of the internal renewal under the new covenant ministry (4:16) which will lead to the resurrection of the dead (5:1-5). Again the theme is consistent with Ezekiel 36–37 where we have renewal of the heart and resurrection from the dead, both accomplished by the indwelling Holy Spirit. The themes are continued further as Paul speaks in 2 Corinthians of those in Christ as *new creatures* (5:17), joined together as "the temple of God" just as it is written in Ezekiel 37:27 – "I will dwell in them and walk among them; And I will be their God, and they shall be My people."

Paul uses the term "new covenant" only once in 2 Corinthians, and yet he unmistakably carries the language and concepts of new covenant blessing through the argument of his letter. When we read at the end (13:14), "and the fellowship [*koinonia*] of the Holy Spirit, be with you all," we must understand this phrase in the way that Paul did in his letter – a sharing in the new covenant ministry of the Holy Spirit. So important is this concept of new covenant pneumatology that we are inclined to look for it elsewhere in Paul's writings, even in the absence of a specific reference to new covenant.

Paul's letter to the Romans is a case in point. Nowhere does the term *new covenant* appear. Yet the language of New Covenant blessing accompanied by contrasts drawn between that blessing and conditions under the Mosaic covenant leads us to see Paul's self-conception as a minister of the new covenant (so defined in 2 Cor. 3:6) as standing behind and interpreting his remarks in this letter. It would be impossible to treat the theme in detail, but a few items can be mentioned. In Romans 2, Paul contrasts Jews who are circumcised in the flesh and who possess and teach "the Law" with "a Jew who is one inwardly; and circumcision . . . which is of the heart, by the Spirit, not by the letter" (2:29). The language of Spirit and letter is the same as in 2 Corinthians 3:6, where Paul identified such a ministry of the Spirit as a blessing of the new covenant. Paul also brings in for display, "Gentiles who do not have the Law . . . [who] show the work of the Law written on their hearts" (Rom. 2:14-15). Romans 7:1-6 speaks of a covenantal change in which "we have been released from the Law . . . so that we serve in newness of the Spirit and not in oldness of the letter" (v. 6). The condition under "the Law" is contrasted with "now" (8:1), when God through "the law of the Spirit of life in Christ Jesus has set you free from the law of sin and death," doing "what the Law [Mosaic covenant] could not do" (8:2-3). This ministry of the Holy Spirit will eventually lead to the resurrection of their bodies, a blessing which is also part of the new covenant promise (recall again Ezek. 36–37).

> But if the Spirit of Him who raised Jesus from the dead dwells in you, He who raised Christ Jesus from the dead will also give life to your mortal bodies through His Spirit who indwells you (Rom. 8:11, cf. 18-25).

Romans 11:26-27 quotes Isaiah 59:20-21, a new covenant prediction, with a view toward the future salvation of all Israel, a reference to the nation as a whole. Romans 12:2 commends the reader to "the renewing of your mind"; and 15:13 gives the blessing of joy and peace, abounding "in hope by the power of the Holy Spirit."

Two further themes associated with Paul's teaching on new covenant renewal and indwelling of the Holy Spirit require closer attention. One is the teaching that this ministry takes place in Christ, and the other is the fact that there is yet a future fullness to new covenant blessing. While the new covenant has unmistakably been inaugurated, it is only a beginning. Not all that was predicted about renewal by the Holy Spirit (including resurrection from the dead) has yet occurred. The new covenant has been inaugurated, but complete fulfillment awaits the return of Christ.

### New Covenant Blessing in Christ

We have noted earlier in this chapter that the Davidic king functions as a mediator of covenant blessing. We have also seen that the gift of the Holy Spirit is prominent among the blessings of the new covenant. But is it possible that a Davidic king could mediate this gift of the Holy Spirit? Throughout Old Testament history, it was God who gave the Spirit. Giving the Spirit recalls creation. God who "breathed into" dust to form Adam is the one who promises to put His Spirit into His people, raising them back from the dust and re-creating their hearts, minds, and wills.

Divine authority and Davidic mediation come together when God becomes incarnate as Jesus. As the *human*, Davidic king, He is the primary recipient of the new covenant blessing. This means that not only would He receive the Spirit, in accordance with His kingship, but that the Spirit would abide with Him and preserve Him in holiness and immortality forever. Accordingly, the Scripture testifies that at His baptism, the Spirit came *and remained* upon Him (John 1:32; cf. Matt. 3:16; Luke 3:22). He was "full" of the Holy Spirit and led by the Spirit (Luke 4:1; Matt. 4:1). He ministered in the power of the Spirit (Luke 4:14, 18-19; Matt. 12:18-21, 28), and He was raised from the dead, immortal, by the Spirit (Rom. 1:4; 2 Tim. 1:10; Heb. 7:16; 1 Peter 3:18).

As the *divine*, Davidic king, He is the one who gives the Spirit to His people, re-creating their hearts, and binding them in submission to Himself. It was said of Him that He would baptize people with the Holy Spirit (Matt. 3:11; Mark 1:8; Luke 3:16; John 1:33), a testimony which He began to fulfill on the Pentecost following His ascension (Acts 1:5, 8; 2:2-4, 33, 38-39).

This function of giving the Spirit is especially treated in John's Gospel where Jesus invites the thirsty to come to Him, drink, and become a source of living water (John 7:37). The language is partly that of Isaiah 55:1-3, a new covenant text, where those who are thirsty are invited to the waters and given "an everlasting covenant . . . according to the faithful mercies shown to David." John explains that Jesus "spoke of the Spirit, whom those who believed in Him were to receive." In other words, Jesus invites people to come to Him to receive the new covenant blessing of the indwelling Holy Spirit.

The invitation of John 7:37-39 to receive the Holy Spirit looks back to the divine revelation given to John the Baptist in John 1:33, "He upon whom you see the Spirit descending and remaining upon Him, this is the one who baptizes in the Holy Spirit." It is connected as well to the discourse with Nicodemus where Jesus stressed the necessity of being "born of the Spirit" to see the kingdom of God. The language of water, Spirit, and wind blowing upon flesh (3:5-8) recalls Ezekiel 36:25-27 and 37:1-14. The theme of Jesus giving the Spirit is carried forward as well to the concluding chapters of the Gospel. On the one hand, Jesus explains that He will petition the Father to send the Holy Spirit (John 14:16), and He promises that the Father will indeed send Him in the name of Jesus (v. 26). On the other hand, Jesus says, "I will send [Him] to you" (15:26), a prediction which He symbolizes after the resurrection by breathing upon them, saying, "receive the Holy Spirit" (20:22). When given, the Spirit will indwell them forever (14:16) and grant them the knowledge of God (14:26; 16:13; cf. the title, "Spirit of truth" in 14:16-17; 15:26), both of which are new covenant promises.

John's teaching about the Holy Spirit does not deny that the Spirit was active prior to the coming of Jesus. However, he is quite clear about a qualitatively new bestowal of the Spirit which was tied historically (or dispensationally) to the ministry of Jesus. We can especially see this in John's interpretation of Jesus' saying about the inner spring of living water: "But this He spoke of the Spirit, whom those who believed in Him were to receive; for the Spirit was not yet given, because Jesus was not yet glorified."

The Acts of the Apostles begins with Jesus' reaffirmation to His disciples to bestow the Spirit upon them (Acts 1:5, 8). Acts

2:1-4 records the event in which the Spirit came (cf. 10:47; 11:15-17). Peter interpreted it as *the action of Christ:* "Therefore having been exalted to the right hand of God, and having received from the Father the promise of the Holy Spirit, He has poured forth this which you both see and hear" (2:33). He invites the people in Jerusalem "to receive the gift of the Holy Spirit" (v. 38), saying "the promise is for you and your children, and for all who are far off, as many as the Lord our God shall call to Himself" (v. 39). Just how far ranging the gift would be became clear in Acts 10:44-47 (cf. 11:15-18), when the Holy Spirit "fell" upon Gentiles who believed in Jesus. At the council in Jerusalem, Peter explained that "God . . . [gave] them the Holy Spirit, just as He also did to us; and He made no distinction between us and them, cleansing their hearts by faith" (15:8-9). The gift of the Holy Spirit and the cleansing of the heart are again the language of new covenant promise. The important point here is that the blessing is given to both Jew and Gentile alike. Furthermore, it is a blessing mediated by the Christ, as Peter goes on to explain, "we are saved *through the grace of the Lord Jesus,* in the same way as they also are" (15:11).

### Future New Covenant Blessing

While the New Testament is clear on the fact that the new covenant has now been inaugurated, that is that blessings belonging to the new covenant are now being dispensed to all those who believe in Jesus (whether Jew or Gentile), it is equally clear that new covenant promises are not yet fully realized. The promises in Jeremiah, Isaiah, and Ezekiel describe a people who have the law written in their hearts, who walk in the way of the Lord, fully under the control of the Holy Spirit. These same promises look to a people who are raised from the dead, enjoying the blessings of an eternal inheritance with God dwelling with them and in them forever.

The New Testament sees the blessings of moral and spiritual perfection along with immortality as blessings to be received in the future, at the coming of Jesus. However, in 2 Corinthians 3:18, Paul describes the present new covenant ministry (3:6) as a process of transformation into that glory which is already fully realized in Christ.

But we all, with unveiled face beholding as in a mirror the glory of the Lord, are being transformed into the same image from glory to glory, just as from the Lord, the Spirit.

Whereas God has put the knowledge of Himself into our hearts (4:6) and we think of ourselves and others in Christ as new creations (5:17); nevertheless, "we have this treasure in earthen vessels" (4:7). We experience the principles of both death and resurrection in a process of daily renewal, looking to the future for our eternal glory (4:10-18), when we will be raised immortal (4:14; 5:1-5). The present gift of the Spirit, which Paul identifies as new covenant blessing (3:3, 6), is the pledge of future new covenant fullness (5:5; cf. Eph. 1:13-14).

Likewise in Romans 8, where Paul says that "the law of the Spirit of life in Christ Jesus has set you free from the law of sin and of death" (v. 2), he nevertheless teaches that full freedom lies in the future. What we have now is "the first fruits of the Spirit" (8:23). And whereas from one standpoint, the present reception of the Spirit has advanced us to the status of full adult heirs (Gal. 4:5-7), from another perspective, we are "waiting eagerly for our adoption as sons, the redemption of our body" (Rom. 8:23; cf. v. 11).

The new covenant promised to remove the heart of rebellion against God and give us hearts fully compliant to His direction. However, in our present experience, we are not fully free from the experience of resistance to God's will. Galatians 5:17 describes the present conflict.

For the flesh sets its desire against the Spirit, and the Spirit against the flesh; for these are in opposition to one another, so that you may not do the things that you please.

We are called to walk by the Spirit, to live by the Spirit, to put to death (daily) the deeds of the flesh, to present ourselves to God for the work of righteousness (Gal. 5:16, 25; Rom. 8:13-14; 6:12-13). This is the condition of living under *inaugurated* new covenant blessings. Only in the future will those blessings be granted in full, and the complete transformation promised by the new covenant will be realized.

That future will arrive when Jesus returns to earth. Paul says in Colossians 3:4, "When Christ . . . is revealed [from heaven], then you also will be revealed with Him in glory." In "the day of Christ," that is, when He returns, we will be perfected (Phil. 1:6), made blameless (1 Cor. 1:8; Jude 24), purified completely just as He is Himself (1 John 3:2-3), raised and transformed bodily in glorious immortality just as He is Himself (Phil. 3:20-21).

The fact that the fullness of new covenant blessing awaits the return of Christ is not surprising since the prophecies of the new covenant envisioned Messiah reigning upon the earth over a transformed people. Included in that vision was the political restoration of Israel in peace with all other nations. Accordingly, Paul the apostle of the new covenant who envisions the fullness of new covenant blessing at the return of Messiah to earth, foresees the national salvation of Israel fulfilled at that time as well.

> Just as it is written, "The Deliverer will come from Zion, He will remove ungodliness from Jacob. And this is My covenant with them, When I take away their sins." . . .From the standpoint of God's choice they are beloved for the sake of the fathers; for the gifts and the calling of God are irrevocable (Rom. 11:26-29).

## Conclusion

The New Testament gives the good news concerning Jesus of Nazareth, a descendant of David, to whom the grant covenant of David has been confirmed. He has been anointed by the Holy Spirit, raised up even from the dead, declared to be Son of God, being made Lord and Christ as He has been enthroned at the right hand of God, becoming the highest of the kings of the earth.

In receiving Davidic blessings, He has become the heir of the blessings promised to Abraham, and He mediates those blessings to others, both from Israel and from the nations, as they are blessed in Him.

In Him, the Mosaic covenant has been fulfilled. The old dispensation has come to an end and a new dispensation has begun as the new covenant has been inaugurated. Jesus Christ has performed a service for Israel and the nations by propitiating the curse of the Mosaic covenant (which extends to God's fundamental curse against sin) in His own death and at the same time providing the sacrificial basis for the new covenant which grants redemption, renewal, and resurrection.

The blessing covenanted to Abraham comes to us in this dispensation as the inaugurated blessing of the new covenant mediated through Jesus the Christ, to whom the Davidic covenant has been and will be confirmed. A remnant of Israel and remnants of the Gentile nations receive this inaugurated blessing equally, without distinction, by faith in God incarnated as Jesus.

The present dispensation is not the end. It looks forward to a future dispensation in which the new covenant will be completely fulfilled and its blessing fully received. All of the grant covenants will be fully realized at that time. The change of dispensation will occur at the descent of Jesus from heaven. New covenant blessing (and thus Abrahamic blessing) will be extended to the national and political dimensions of human existence as He realizes His Davidic prerogative to personally rule the nations. The blessings of the indwelling Spirit and new heart will be completed with resurrection from death and perfection in holiness. The blessing on Him and in Him upon us all will be everlasting, confirming through redemption God's plan of creation.

But more has been revealed as to how this will take place than can be discovered through a study of the covenants. In the next chapter, we turn to the theme of the kingdom of God, which will offer further revelation on the nature of the dispensation to come (including its millennial and eternal aspects) as well as another look at how past and present dispensations lead progressively to it.

# Chapter Seven
# The Kingdom of God in the Old Testament

When God took the descendants of Abraham out of Egypt and covenanted His law to them at Sinai, He made them into a nation. He Himself became their King, and they became His kingdom. Most of what the Old Testament has to say about God being a King speaks of this covenant relationship to Israel and through Israel to the rest of the nations.

We have seen that the Mosaic covenant marked out a new dispensation in God's relationship with the human race. As a result, the kingdom of God refers to something new which came to pass in history. Yet at the same time, this new dispensation was directly rooted in an earlier covenant which God had made with Abraham. And that covenant, in turn, recalled earlier dealings of God with humanity reaching back even to the Creation. The kingdom of God, then, belongs to God's unfolding plan of redemption.

In a certain sense, it might be said that God had always behaved as a King. After bringing Adam and Eve into existence, He gave them a land which He had prepared, and delegated authority to them. God held the power of life and death, of judgment and blessing. He commanded and expected obedience. As they complied, they enjoyed His presence, and He theirs. After their fall in sin, they came under His judgment but held the hope of a future redemption.

After the Lord saved Noah from the judgment that came upon all humanity, He gave him and his descendants the earth, covenanted promises of life and fruitfulness, and commanded His will. Later He bestowed a grant upon Abraham, to bless him and all peoples on the earth. He granted lands, promised blessings, and commanded the steps of patriarchal life.

In all of these actions, He was as He is, *God*. He creates and upholds the existence of all things. Yet, He chose to interact personally and historically with human beings. As the superior in that relationship, the Lord commanded, granted blessing, and punished the insubordinate. The covenant which He made with Abraham was modeled on the form of kingly grants in the ancient Near East. Throughout the entire patriarchal dispensation, God dealt with humanity in a divine yet kingly manner.

However, in His covenant with Abraham, God set up a principle of mediation by which He would relate to the rest of humanity through the descendants of Abraham.[1] The story of the kingdom of God in Scripture is primarily the story of the outworking of this covenant. God will reveal Himself as *Israel's* King. And through Israel, He will manifest His kingly rule over the other nations. It is this set of relationships which will set the direction for divine-human reconciliation.

## God, the King of Israel

*The Lord Is King.* Three songs or psalms attributed to Moses proclaim the Lord's special relationship to Israel as their King. When the nations were given their various boundaries and inheritances, the Lord chose Israel:

> For the Lord's portion is His people;
> Jacob is the allotment of His inheritance (Deut. 32:9).

He chose to be *their* King. He redeemed them by fighting for them against Pharaoh and his army, and He prevailed. The song in Exodus 15 celebrates His victory: "The Lord is a warrior; the Lord is His name" (Ex. 15:3). The Lord is "highly exalted" (15:1). His right hand (His ruling arm) is "majestic in power"

213

(15:6). He stretched forth His (ruling) hand in decree, and the earth responded in obedience (15:12). In "the greatness of [His] excellence" He withstood His adversaries (15:7). The kings of the other nations consequently stand in dismay and terror of Him (15:15-16). But He will take His people to His chosen land where over them, "the Lord shall reign forever and ever" (15:18).

From His decisive victory over Egypt, the Lord took His people to Sinai. Deuteronomy 33:2-5 describes how God came upon them in majesty and glory and entered into covenant with them.

And He was *king* in Jeshurun,
when the heads of the people were gathered,
the tribes of Israel together (v. 5).[2]

This song goes on to speak of God's blessing upon the tribes of Israel. But Deuteronomy 32 warns of punishment should the people turn rebellious. It also warns of revenge against the adversaries of God's people. All of this accords with the treaty the Lord had with them as their King. For they are His people, and it is His land (32:43).

Later, in Israel's history, when God warned His people of impending punishment, it was as their King that He appealed to them. When Isaiah was called as a prophet, he lamented his woe declaring, "My eyes have seen the King, the Lord of hosts" (Isa. 6:5). God warned that He would bring Babylon upon His people. He would do this as "the Lord, your Holy One, the Creator of Israel, your King" (Isa. 43:15). He is the one and only true God, yet He is at the same time, "the King of Israel" (Isa. 44:6).

***The Kingdom of the Lord.*** God's kingship over Israel is specially featured in a group of Psalms known as enthronement psalms. These psalms typically carry the expression, "The Lord reigns."[3] They designate God as the King of Israel. They also speak of the extension of His rule over all nations. They are joined by a number of other psalms that speak of God's kingdom and describe its various features.[4] These descriptions envision a time of God's covenant blessing upon His people. They present us with the most ideal conception of God's kingdom during the Mosaic dispensation.

God, the King, is Most High; He is great and glorious, ruling in splendor, beauty, majesty, and power. He is clothed in darkness and attended by fire. He is righteous and just in all His ways. He is enthroned in heaven over all His works, over all the earth and over all the nations including all the things that idolaters worship. Yet He is also enthroned in Zion. It is His dwelling place; He rules there; He shines forth from there. Heaven and Zion are thus linked together. Their connection is sometimes described as chair and footstool. God's rule proceeds from both.

God judges with justice; He vindicates the righteous, punishes and destroys the wicked. He causes war and violence to cease and establishes peace. He gives life and strength to His people, helping the helpless, and making a home for the lonely. His people, who make up His kingdom, respond with praise, joy, song, and thanksgiving. Their trust is in the Lord with obedience and reverence, but also with great joy.

The kingdom is further described in terms of a people who have been saved and delivered, righteous, prosperous, wise, and secure, filled with gladness and the knowledge of the Lord. The land of Israel is also described as rejoicing with praise and song, blessed with peace, righteousness and fruitfulness.

Israel, the people blessed by God, proclaims the Lord to all the nations. Through them, God's blessing comes to all the nations. He rules them all with justice and righteousness so that the nations and the earth are full of the knowledge of God. The nations are described as praising God with joy and fear, living at peace and filled with the knowledge of God. The earth itself, humbled, melting at His wrath, is described as rejoicing in the Lord who establishes and upholds it forever.

### Messiah, King of Israel

The kingdom of God in the Mosaic dispensation was extended to include a role for human kingship. In the covenant God made with Israel, provision was made for such a king. At the people's request, the Lord would choose a king from among them (Deut. 17:14-15). The king was to exemplify the nation's covenant response to God, loving the Lord with all his heart, trusting in Him alone and walking in His ways. He would be an instrument by which God's kingdom over Israel and over all nations would be established.

***Anticipations of Messiah.*** In biblical theology, the human king of Israel plays an important role in the divine plan for human dominion. At the creation of humankind, God said, "Let them *rule* over the fish of the sea and over the birds of the sky and over the cattle and over all the earth, and over every creeping thing that creeps on the earth" (Gen. 1:26). This was also stated as a command to humankind: "Be fruitful and multiply, and fill the earth, and subdue it; and *rule* over the fish of the sea and over the birds of the sky, and over every living thing that moves on the earth" (Gen. 1:28).

After their sin, this dominion would be exercised under fallen conditions. However, ultimate dominion even over their fallenness is cryptically predicted in the curse on the serpent, the tempter and deceiver: "I will put enmity between you and the woman, and between your seed and her seed; he shall bruise you on the head, and you shall bruise him on the heel" (Gen. 3:15).

Under these conditions, human rulership was restructured hierarchically. We find this first in the Lord's remarks to Adam and Eve, when He said to Eve,"Your desire shall be for your husband, and he shall rule over you" (Gen. 3:16). When the nations of humankind spread across the earth, human dominion took on collective structures, hierarchalized under patriarchs and kings. Eventually this extended to nations' relationships with one another.

The blessing to Abraham envisioned an authority over other nations that would be inherited by the nation descending from him. Isaac clarified this point when he transferred the patriarchal covenant to Jacob (Gen. 27:29).

> May peoples serve you, and nations bow down to you; be master of your brothers, and may your mother's sons bow down to you. Cursed be those who curse you, and blessed be those who bless you.

God's blessing on the nations would be revealed through Jacob's rule over them. This rulership was then specifically transferred by Jacob to Judah (Gen. 49:8-10).

Your father's sons shall bow down to you. Judah is a lion's whelp; from the prey, my son, you have gone up. He couches, he lies down as a lion, and as a lion, who dares rouse him up? The scepter shall not depart from Judah, nor the ruler's staff from between his feet, until Shiloh comes, and to him shall be the obedience of the peoples.

The language of Jacob's blessing upon Judah is repeated in the oracles of Balaam. We have already seen that Balaam speaks of God as Israel's King (Num. 23:21), but he also forsees a human king described in the language of Jacob's blessing upon Judah, one who fulfills the covenant promise of mediating blessing or cursing (Num. 24:9, cf. v. 7).

He couches, he lies down as a lion, and as a lion; who dares rouse him? Blessed is everyone who blesses you, and cursed is everyone who curses you.

This one is further described (Num. 24:17, 19).

I see him, but not now; I behold him, but not near; a star shall come forth from Jacob, and a scepter shall rise from Israel. . . . One from Jacob shall have dominion.

Finally, human kingship makes its first legitimate appearance when Saul is anointed king of all Israel. But Saul was soon rejected by God because of disobedience. David, a descendant of Judah, a "man after God's own heart," was chosen to replace him. David was found to be faithful to God, and God made a covenant with David to establish his house as the royal house of Israel, to raise up his descendant after him and establish his kingdom forever.

**The Messianic Kingdom.** The reigns of David and Solomon typify the ideal of God's earthly kingdom during the Mosaic dispensation. Many of its features are presented throughout the psalms, but an adequate picture can be constructed by examining the royal psalms, psalms which speak directly about the Davidic king, his reign, and his kingdom.[5]

The titles King and Son are used alternately of the Davidic

ruler (see Pss. 2:2, 6-7, 12; 18:50). He is characterized as holy, godly. He hates wickedness (Pss. 101; 45:7). He rules with truth, righteousness, and justice (Pss. 45:4, 6-7; 72:2). He helps the afflicted, the needy and poor (Ps. 72:4, 12-14), saving and delivering them by crushing their oppressors (Ps. 72:4). He is a priest of the order of Melchizedek (Ps. 110:4), mediating prosperity and peace to Israel and to all nations (Ps. 72:6-7, 16).

The kingdom is characterized by righteousness, peace, and prosperity (Ps. 72:3, 6-7, 16). Both God and the Davidic king are blessed (Ps. 72:15, 18-19); God is worshiped and the Davidic king is honored (Ps. 2:11-12).

All nations are envisioned in subjection to God and His Davidic king (Pss. 2; 72:8-11). The Lord has given to His Messiah all nations, in fact, all the earth as an inheritance (Ps. 2:8). They take refuge in Him, and they are blessed (Pss. 2:12; 72:17).

The relationship between God and His human king is the primary subject in these psalms, and it is in the characterization of this relationship that we get the most detailed description of the kingdom. The Davidic king trusts in God (Pss. 18:1-3; 21:7; 28:7; 61:1-4). He proclaims the Lord (Ps. 18:30-31), keeps the ways of the Lord (Ps. 18:21-24), and rejoices in the Lord (Ps. 21:1).

God has anointed His king (Ps. 45:7) and installed him in Zion, the place of God's own rule (Pss. 2:6; 110:2; 132:13-14). He rules at God's right hand (Pss. 18:35; 110:1).[6] God destroys the enemies of His king (Pss. 20:6; 21:8-13; 89:23). He strengthens him for battle (Ps. 18:31-42), subdues peoples under him (Ps. 18:47; 110:1-2, 5-6), and sets him over all the nations (Ps. 89:27). God gives him life (Pss. 18:28; 21:4; 61:6), strength, glory, majesty, and splendor (Ps. 21:5). He grants him loving-kindness (Pss. 18:50; 21:7; 61:7; 89:1-2), blesses him with gladness (Ps. 21:3-6), and includes him within His own greatness (Ps. 18:35), confirming to him all the covenant promises of David (Pss. 89:3-4; 132:10-18).

## Divine and Human Kingship; The Unity of the Kingdom of God

When we compare the descriptions of God's reign in the enthronement psalms with the descriptions of the reign of His Messiah in the royal psalms, we see marked similarity. The two reigns converge toward one descriptive pattern which is the ideal model of God's kingdom in the Mosaic dispensation. Even the greater extension of God's providential rule over creation is brought into the pattern, so that Zion appears as the center of God's universal rule.

The harmony of the two reigns, divine and human, united by covenant, and the revelation of God's greater providential rule are important features of Old Testament kingdom theology. All of these elements are profoundly interconnected, revealing the unity of the kingdom. First of all, God Himself is at the same time God over all and King of the nation Israel. These relationships are not utterly distinct. They intentionally overlap. God's authority and power over the earth and the heavens is employed in His rule over Israel (from the division of the Red Sea waters to seasonal blessings in the land). His rule over Israel mediates His rule over other peoples (in both blessing and curse). Israel, then, becomes the focal point for God's relations with humanity and His providence over the rest of creation.

From this we can also see the interrelationship between heaven and Zion in God's kingdom. The Psalms reference God's rule to both. He is said to be enthroned in both heaven and Zion, exercising from both the same kingly rule. Sometimes the union between heaven and Zion is illustrated as the relationship between a chair and a footstool. Together they support the King and comprise His throne. Even when they are identified separably as thrones of God, they cannot be viewed independent of each other since the same elements of rule are attributed to both. God rules Israel from Zion, and He rules Israel from heaven, with the rule (His blessings and judgments according to His covenant) being the same in both. God rules the cosmos from heaven, but He is also said to rule it from Zion. And from Zion, He rules all peoples on earth.

In Zion we also find the Messiah, the Davidic king. He is said to rule from Zion over Israel and over all the nations with the same descriptive phrases as are applied to God. Although their persons are kept distinct, their activity is nevertheless seen to converge in a unified reign. Messiah's decisions are God's decisions and vice versa, since Messiah has God's word hidden in His heart and God establishes and carries out Messiah's desires and will. Messiah judges and rules with wisdom and righteousness given to Him by God. God's justice is carried out in His decisions. He also carries out God's wrath, punishing wickedness and evil. Obedience to Messiah harmonizes with the people's obedience to God, and the favor of God (covenant blessing) and the favor of Messiah (personally and politically) come together in the people's experience.

The blessings that characterize the kingdom reveal another aspect of the kingdom's unity. The kingdom of God is material and spiritual, sacred and secular at the same time. In biblical grammar, these characteristics collectively describe the same kingdom, with the spiritual features supporting the material. They are not distinguished as if belonging to separate kingdoms (one heavenly and one earthly) unrelated to one another. This is why in the Psalms, the kingdom of God and of His Messiah exhibits spiritual righteousness and material prosperity. It is blessed with the peace of God as well as national and international peace and security. The people enjoy God's forgiveness of sins along with physical and national healing. They grow in knowledge and wisdom but especially in the knowledge of God. Religion and society, temple and palace, God and humanity interrelate in the unified experience of the kingdom of God.

Some dispensationalists have overlooked the unified character of the kingdom of God in the Old Testament, arguing instead for different kingdoms operating in conjunction with one another. They would argue that God's providential rule over the cosmos should be distinguished from the political reality of Israel. Certainly one can differentiate between these two "kingdoms" in respect to time (the former preexists the latter) and duration (the former is unchangeable, the latter varies historically). The fact that the Psalms speak of God reigning in heaven over the cosmos is taken to mean that a heavenly kingdom exists in distinction from kingdoms on earth.

Distinctions of this nature may be helpful in the process of analyzing the complexities of Scripture. One needs to keep in mind the fact that God is as He has always been, sovereign over all He has made. However, the biblical language of kingship is not primarily used in this way. Even in the Scriptures that speak of God reigning in the heavens, implications are close at hand for His relationship to Israel and the nations. Providence and politics, humanity and deity are closely interrelated in the biblical descriptions of the reigns of God and of His Messiah.

This phenomenal unity and harmony of divine and human rule are crucial to the presentation of the kingdom of God found in the Psalms and other Scriptures. This is the phenomena which must be grasped in order to understand the Prophets, Jesus, and His apostles. They will draw upon this model of the kingdom idealized in the reigns of David and Solomon when they in turn describe and depict a kingdom which is yet to come.

There is, however, one important distinction that needs to be clarified in the process of identifying this kingdom of which we speak. The kingdom of God presented to us in the Psalms is an ideal model based on the *blessings* of the Mosaic covenant. This can be confusing, because the Mosaic covenant is the basic kingdom structure which remains constant throughout the Mosaic dispensation. Under the structure of the Mosaic covenant, God's kingly rule over Israel can be revealed in judgment and curse as well as in blessing. But the ideal form of the kingdom, described in the Psalms, is not drawn from these curses. It is *the blessings* of the Mosaic covenant (which are a dispensational revelation of that blessing unconditionally granted to Abraham) which become, in prophetic grammar, the language of the kingdom of God.

Taking this into account, the kingdom of God becomes *an ideal pattern of blessing,* a hope and expectation, which is approximated to varying degrees in Israel's history. It is the ideal pattern of blessing which God set forth in covenant to Israel. In Israel's historical experience, they are most fully revealed to be God's kingdom in the reigns of David and Solomon, and to a lesser extent in those kings who follow their example of faith and obedience. In the reigns of these kings, Israel becomes, to varying degrees, a revelation not only of God's beneficent kingship with respect to her, but of His kindly and blessed reign over all things. Israel is blessed covenantally and mediates that blessing to other nations on earth. God, the King of Israel, shows His rule over the earth and the heavens through His rule in Zion. His vassal king is His instrument, ruling over the works of God. Through this covenantal blessing and mediation God reveals the redemption of His creation, the glory of His divine providence.

Covenant unfaithfulness, however, dims this revelation of a blessed kingdom. Matters may become so bad that Israel does not even know the Lord, much less proclaim Him king and rejoice in His kingship. The time leading up to the establishment of human kingship was one such time of apostasy. Requests for a king like the kings of the other nations were interpreted as rejections of God's kingship (Jud. 8:22-23; 1 Sam. 8:5-7). Abimelech, son of Gideon, made an abortive attempt to establish a monarchy (Jud. 9). He was never recognized by God as His messiah; his "kingdom" is never called the kingdom of God. In the end, God judged both Abimelech and the people who invested him with his office.

The elements which come together under God's blessing in Davidic and Solomonic kingship (and which offer the fullest revelation of the kingdom of God in the Mosaic dispensation), become conflicting and discordant in the reigns of later kings who are faithless and disloyal to God. Solomon's unfaithfulness in the latter part of his reign coupled with the foolishness of his son Rehoboam led to the division of the kingdom. The Davidic king no longer ruled over all Israel, much less over other nations. The tension and strife between Israel, Judah, and the surrounding nations threatened peace and prosperity. As the two nations slipped into ever-increasing idolatry, the curses of the Mosaic covenant brought suffering nationally and individually to the people. When Zion became a center of idolatry, God's *beneficent* reign was no longer revealed there, only the decrees of His wrath. Eventually, God burned the city, razed the temple, and cut off the reign of the house of David.

### The Kingdom of God During the Exile

God's judgment upon Israel and Judah, His termination of experimental reigns in the north and Davidic rule in the south, did not mean the end of the kingdom of God. However, it did mean the temporary end of that kingdom's mediation in Jerusalem (and the permanent end of its dual form in Samaria). In this context, the Book of Daniel presents a new way to speak of God's kingdom. Describing conditions in the Exile, Daniel sees God's kingdom as the interrelationship between heaven and the imperial seat of Gentile power; the conjunction of God's reign and the reign of the chief Gentile king.

In Daniel 2, God reveals to the king of Babylon his place in a succession of earthly empires. In response, the king of Babylon acknowledges, "Your God is a God of gods and a Lord of kings" (2:47). Subsequent judgment on this Babylonian king in Daniel 4 brings him to confess that "the Most High is ruler over the realm of mankind, and [He] bestows it on whom He wishes, and sets over it the lowliest of men" (Dan. 4:17). He acknowledges that God's "kingdom is an everlasting kingdom, and His dominion is from generation to generation" (Dan. 4:3, 34). The chapter ends (Dan. 4:37) with the confession: "Now I Nebuchadnezzar praise, exalt, and honor the King of heaven, for all His works are true and His ways just and He is able to humble those who walk in pride."

God's dealing with Nebuchadnezzar is not simply a manifestation of His divine sovereignty over all things. It is very much like His treatment of the kings of Israel. Along this line, Nebuchadnezzar's son, Belshazzar is judged because even though he knew from his father "that the Most High God is ruler over the realm of mankind, and that He sets over it whomever He wishes," nevertheless, he did not humble himself and glorify God (Dan. 5:21-23). As a result, in a revelation of superior kingship, God stretched forth a hand and wrote a decree on the wall of the Babylonian king's palace announcing the end of his authority, the restructuring of his office, and its bestowal upon others (5:5-6, 24-28).

In Daniel 6, Darius, king of the Medes, is forced to acknowledge that the God of Daniel is "the living God and enduring forever, and His kingdom is one which will not be destroyed, and His dominion will be forever" (6:26).

The irony in this kingdom language, of course, is clear. With Israel in judgment, God established His royal liaison with the ruling Gentile king. Yet in all this, Israel is not forgotten. The faithful remnant of Israel (represented in the person of Daniel and his friends), mediate God's revelation to the Gentile rulers. The time of Gentile domination is revealed to this remnant, and the time is measured in accordance with God's purposes for the land of Israel, after which God will renew His plan for Jerusalem (Dan. 9). Even though Israel is dispersed, the King of Israel shows covenant loyalty to His faithful remnant. His sovereign direction of the nations has this faithful remnant in mind and envisions promises regarding their restoration along with the restoration of kingship to them and through them over the nations.

## The Eschatological Kingdom of God
## in Old Testament Prophecy

The dissolution of the harmony of divine and human kingship in Israel during the Mosaic dispensation is a symptom of the discordance which sin brought generally into divine/human relations. Just as God set forth a plan of redemption to reconcile humankind to Himself, so likewise, Old Testament prophets predict that God will save His kingdom plan which He had set forth by covenant. Furthermore, the restitution of that kingdom would be the means by which the plan of redemption would itself be accomplished. Divine and human rule would converge in a unity never seen before.

*The Eschatological Kingdom in Daniel.* The apocalyptic Book of Daniel underscores the temporary and ironic nature of Israel's exilic experience by predicting a *kingdom of God* which is *coming in the future.*[7] At that time, "the God of heaven will set up a kingdom which will never be destroyed, and . . . will not be left for another people; it will crush and put an end to all these kingdoms, but it will itself endure forever" (Dan. 2:44). In the dream given to Nebuchadnezzar, this *coming kingdom* is pictured as a stone which falls from heaven, crushing the kingdoms on which it falls, and becoming a great mountain which fills the whole world (Dan. 2:34-35). The mountain is a reference to Zion, which appears repeatedly in biblical imagery as the greatest of the mountains, especially in prophecies about the coming eschatological kingdom.

In Daniel 7, Daniel envisions a time after the succession of Gentile kingdoms when "One like a Son of Man" will come on the clouds of heaven before the Ancient of Days to receive "dominion, glory and a kingdom, that all the peoples, nations, and men of every language might serve Him. *His dominion is an everlasting dominion which will not pass away; and His kingdom is one which will not be destroyed*" (7:13-14). This description of the coming kingdom is similar to the descriptions of God's present kingdom which we find in Daniel 4–6. However, the coming kingdom will be especially manifested on the earth in replacement of, not just in conjunction with, existing Gentile political structures. A human king will exercise his authority *in replacement* of the sovereignty given to Gentile kings.

The description of the coming kingdom appears again in Daniel 7:27: "Then the sovereignty, the dominion, and the greatness of all the kingdoms under the whole heaven will be given to the people of the saints of the Highest One; His kingdom will be an everlasting kingdom, and all the dominions will serve and obey Him." The kingdom that is coming is a mediation of the rule and authority which God was already manifesting over the nations, but it would be exercised politically and socially by "the people of the saints of the Most High" (the same as were being persecuted by the nations) through a king whom God would choose from among them.

The dreams and visions recorded in Daniel foresee this kingdom *coming in a time of catastrophic judgment* upon Gentile kingdoms. The judgment envisioned parallels the judgment which had already fallen upon Judah and her king, bringing death, destruction, and exile. In contrast to the begrudging acknowledgment of God forced out of Nebuchadnezzar in the early chapters of the book, Daniel's later visions foresee a future imperial ruler who arrogantly blasphemes God, persecutes the saints, and perpetrates war and suffering upon the earth. His portrait reappears in successive visions from Daniel 7–12. Daniel is told that in "a time of distress such as never occurred since there was a nation until that time . . . your people, everyone who is found written in the book, will be rescued" (Dan. 12:1). Daniel 7:9-11, 26, foresees the Ancient of Days pronouncing judgment and destroying this powerful ruler (cf. Dan. 2:34-35, 45), giving sovereignty to the Son of Man and to the saints of the Most High. They will "receive the kingdom and possess the kingdom forever, for all ages to come" (Dan. 7:18). Sin will be atoned for. Transgression will be finished. It will be a time of everlasting righteousness (Dan. 9:24).

***The Eschatological Kingdom in the Old Testament Prophets.*** The Old Testament prophets also predict the coming eschatological kingdom. Its general features are remarkably consistent throughout the predictions, one prophet emphasizing one aspect, another some other detail, but all together converging in a harmonious pattern. The features of divine and Davidic kingship will once again be brought together in close relationship. The same future kingdom is sometimes described from the standpoint of God's kingly rule in one passage and from the perspective of the reign of His Messiah in another.

*The Coming Rule of God.* Several passages speak of a future kingdom on earth in which God will rule the nations. This is not simply the assertion of His everlasting sovereignty, but the revelation of His kingship in a future worldwide kingdom directed by God from Zion.

Both in Isaiah 2:2-4 and Micah 4:1-8 we are given descriptions of the worldwide kingdom which God will set up "in the last days." The word of the Lord will go forth from Jerusalem. The nations will submit to Him and to His law. "The Lord will reign over them in Mount Zion . . . forever" (Micah 4:7). The nations will know the Lord. War will be done away, and there will be worldwide peace and prosperity.

In Isaiah 43:15 and 44:6, the Lord identifies Himself to Israel as her king and appeals to her to return to Him that He may grant them the blessings promised to the fathers. As part of this general context, Isaiah 40:10 proclaims:

Behold, the Lord God *will come* with might, with His arm *ruling* for Him. Behold, His reward is with Him, and His recompense before Him. Like a shepherd He will tend His flock, in His arm He will gather the lambs, and carry them in His bosom; He will gently lead the nursing ewes.

Likewise, in Malachi 1:11, 14, the Lord declares that He is a great king and that in every place He will be worshiped.

The *coming* of the Lord to rule as King is described as a Day of the Lord. The Day of the Lord is a repetitive theme in the Prophets. It was the term invoked to describe God's judgment of destruction upon Israel and Judah at the hands of Assyria and Babylon (Amos 5:18-20; 8:8-9; Isa. 13:1-22; Ezek. 7:1-27). However, it is also used by postexilic prophets to refer to a judgment which was yet to come (Mal. 3:1-6; 4:1-6).[8] It would be a day when God would come in judgment and punishment on sin, a day of wrath, sorrow, darkness, despair, and death. He will punish the wicked, purging evil from the earth. But those who trust in Him will be delivered. Both Israel and the nations will be tried, tested, and judged in the Day of the Lord.

The Day of the Lord is the transition into the Lord's eschatological reign on the earth. In Zechariah 14:9, God comes in the Day of the Lord to take up His rulership as King. In Zechariah

14:16-17, we see that He will reign as King in Jerusalem. Those of the nations that survive the Day of the Lord must come to worship Him in Zion. The possibility of rebellion exists, but the Lord will subjugate the nations.

Isaiah 24–25 also gives us a prediction of the coming Day of the Lord, the day of judgment and wrath. As a consequence of this judgment, "the Lord of hosts will reign on Mount Zion and in Jerusalem, and His glory will be before His elders" (Isa. 24:23). A further description of His kingdom is given in Isaiah 25:6-9. Unlike Zechariah 14, however, the description is one of peace, blessing, and joy both for Israel and all the nations, more like the description given in Isaiah 2. But there is this added feature. God will give immortality to redeemed humanity:

> And on this mountain [Mount Zion], He will swallow up the covering which is over all peoples, even the veil which is stretched over all nations. He will swallow up death for all time, and the Lord God will wipe tears away from all faces, and He will remove the reproach of His people from all the earth; and it will be said in that day, "Behold, this is our God for whom we have waited that He might save us. This is the Lord for whom we have waited; let us rejoice and be glad in His salvation" (Isa. 25:7-9).

Predictions in Isaiah 65 and 66 of a new creation, the new heavens and new earth, are also part of this theme of the coming kingdom. Many of the features of the eschatological kingdom are repeated in these prophecies (note especially the literary repetition between Isa. 65:25 and 11:6-9). It is a time of joy, peace, prosperity, long life (though not exactly the immortality of Isa. 25; cf. 65:20 and 25:7-8), the fulfillment of blessing on Israel in her inheritance on the earth.

*The Coming Rule of Messiah.* Like the kingdom of God manifested in the days of David and Solomon, the coming eschatological kingdom will be ruled by a Davidic king. In Amos 9:11, the Lord predicts a time when He will raise up "the fallen booth of David, and wall up its breaches . . . raise up its ruins, and rebuild it as in the days of old." Isaiah 11:1 pictures the house of David as a tree that has been cut down. Yet the prophet predicts a time when "a shoot will spring from the stem of

Jesse, and a branch from his roots will bear fruit." Isaiah 9:7 prophecies the reoccupation of the throne of David. Micah 5 speaks of a future king being born in Bethlehem. And Ezekiel 37:24-28 predicts the future reign of David (that is, a Davidic king), corresponding to the fulfillment of all covenant blessings.

The kingdom over which this future Davidic king reigns is described in the same way as that eschatological kingdom over which God is expected to rule. It is a kingdom of righteousness and justice (Isa. 9:7; 11:4; Jer. 23:5; 33:15). Peace will be everlastingly secured for both Israel and the nations (Amos 9:13-15; Isa. 9:6-7; 11:6-9; Micah 5:5; Jer. 23:6; 33:16; Ezek. 34:25-29; 37:26; Zech. 9:10), as the dominion of the king extends over all nations (Amos 9:12; Isa. 11:11-12; Micah 5:4; Zech. 9:10). There will be no more war (Zech. 9:10). The earth will be fruitful and prosperous (Amos 9:13-15; Isa. 11:6-9; Ezek. 34:25-29).

Like God coming in the Day of the Lord, but consistent with His function of mediating blessing and curse, this Davidic king is described as decreeing judgment and punishing wickedness. "He will strike the earth with the rod of His mouth, and with the breath of His lips He will slay the wicked" (Isa. 11:4). Through His judgment on wickedness, the peace and prosperity of the kingdom comes (Isa. 11:6-10).

Ezekiel 37:24-28 draws both notions of rulership together in one setting. The Davidic king will reign over Israel and the sanctuary of the Lord will be established in their midst. God will dwell with them, sanctifying them, and His Messiah will rule.

*Summary.* The Old Testament prophets, including the apocalyptic visions of Daniel, predict that God will establish a worldwide kingdom on the earth centered at Jerusalem in which He and His Messiah, a descendant of David, will rule Israel and all nations. This kingdom is envisioned as taking place at a time which remained future to the prophets, a time which is sometimes referred to as "the last days." (The word *eschatology* comes from the Greek word *eschatos* which means *last;* our phrase *eschatological kingdom* means that kingdom which is expected to come in "the last days.")

The structural features of this eschatological kingdom bear

an intentional resemblance to the kingdom of God idealized in the Psalms, the highly blessed reigns of David and Solomon. The descriptions of that kingdom form a type or model which are carried over and fulfilled to an even greater degree in the prophetic kingdom which is to come. That typology focuses on a Davidic king who embodies the characteristics of both David and Solomon, but who exceeds both of them in power, authority, and character. Through His rule, God's rule over Israel and all nations will be revealed, though to a greater extent than was the case in the Davidic-Solomonic model. However, in the eschatological kingdom, the relationship between God and the Davidic king will be everlastingly stable. But even more than this, just as the Psalms celebrated God's own personal rule in Zion, so the prophets describe the eschatological kingdom as a personal revelation of God. He is envisioned as coming personally, taking position in Zion, and ruling the earth, Israel, and all the nations.

The coming of the Lord to establish this eschatological kingdom is a visitation of judgment upon the nations of humankind. The prophets refer to this judgment as the Day of the Lord. It is a judgment upon human sin, both individual and corporate (social and political), and it extends to both Israel and the Gentile nations. Daniel's visions of the kingdom's apocalyptic entry are similar. The visions in the latter half of Daniel foresee a time of great distress and trouble under a powerful evil ruler. God's destruction of this king and his kingdom is decisive and sure (the key illustration being the judgment of Belshazzar, given in Dan. 5). He will replace them with the eschatological kingdom of "the Son of Man" and "the saints of the Most High."

Drawing upon the prophecies and the typology which those prophecies form with the Psalms, we can identify various characteristics of the eschatological kingdom. The Davidic ruler is cast as a world ruler, ruling not only Israel but all nations. In him, the house of David is restored and established forever. He is powerful, filled with God's Spirit, benevolent, and wise. But the most often mentioned trait of his character is righteousness. He rules with justice.

The kingdom itself is a worldwide political and religious structure. It will be constituted on earth, centered in Jerusalem, and extending not just over (a reestablished) Israel but

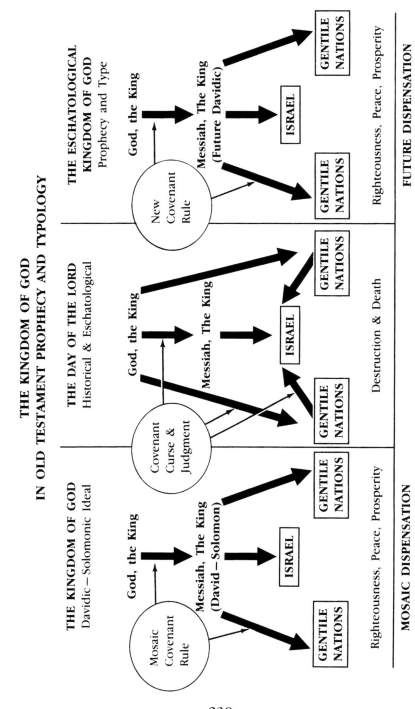

also over all nations. It is most often described in terms of its righteousness and justice. It is a kingdom of peace and security, marked by the absence of war. It is a time of prosperity. Some descriptions view it in terms of long life; others see it as a time of immortality, the elimination of death and sorrow. Consequently, it is marked by joy and gladness. Sin and evil are eradicated in some descriptions; in others they are suppressed. This coordinates with different views of peoples on earth. Some texts envision the subjugation of unruly subjects, others see all peoples rejoicing in the knowledge of and worship of God.

# Chapter Eight
# The Kingdom of God in the New Testament

T he New Testament writings carry forward the theme of the eschatological kingdom. What makes them different from Old Testament writings is that they present us with the story of that kingdom's fulfillment. The story focuses upon Jesus of Nazareth. The opening pages of each of the four Gospels declare Him to be the Christ, the anointed King. *He* is *that* son of David of whom the prophets were speaking when they predicted the eschatological King. His actual appearance in history marks the *imminent fulfillment* of the eschatological kingdom. Without the King, the kingdom lay completely in the future. Once the king appears, the future is at hand.

## The Eschatological Kingdom in the Person and Message of Jesus

*Early Testimony to Jesus the King.* The Gospels report several early testimonies to Jesus as the Christ. What kind of a kingdom did they envision for this Christ? How was their conception of His messiahship related to Old Testament prophecy?

Luke tells us that prior to her conception, Mary received a revelation from the angel Gabriel about the child she would bear: "He will be great, and will be called the Son of the Most High; and the Lord God will give Him the throne of His father David; and He will reign over the house of Jacob forever; and His kingdom will have no end" (Luke 1:32-33). The kingdom predicted in this announcement is entirely consistent with the one expected by the prophets.

Luke also presents a series of psalms and prophecies occasioned by the births of John the Baptist and of Jesus which speak of the covenant promises concerning Israel and all the nations being fulfilled. Matthew introduces Jesus' messiahship by giving His genealogy through the royal house of David, Gabriel's announcement to Joseph, and the testimony of the star.

The star is significant not only because of its literary connection to Balaam's prophecy ("A star shall come forth from Jacob, and a scepter shall rise from Israel"; Num. 24:17), but because it is interpreted by the Magi as indicating the birth of the "King of the Jews" (Matt. 2:2) in a very real and political sense. Matthew places significance on the fact that these Gentiles "fell down and worshiped Him" (Matt. 2:11). The prophets had predicted that Messiah would rule the Gentiles, and Daniel had said that all peoples would serve (or worship) the Son of Man (Dan. 7:14). Herod interpreted the news in light of messianic prophecy and felt politically threatened by Jesus. Every indication points to the fact that the kingship discussed in Matthew 2 in reference to Jesus is precisely that which was set forth, described, and anticipated by the Old Testament prophets.

A highpoint in the early identification of Jesus as the Christ, and one which appears in each of the Gospels, is Jesus' baptism in the Jordan River. Here we have the testimony of the Prophet John, the voice of God the Father from heaven, and the descending Holy Spirit. The preaching of John the Baptist had focused on a call to repentance due to the proximity of the Christ and the nearness of the kingdom (Matt. 3:1-12; Mark 1:2-8; Luke 3:1-18; John 1:6-28). John denied being himself the Christ and spoke of one who was coming. That one, then, is presented as Jesus. When Jesus was baptized by John, God spoke from heaven affirming Jesus in the language of the Davidic covenant: "My beloved Son, in whom I am well pleased" (Matt. 3:17; Mark 1:11; Luke 3:22). The Spirit of God also came upon Him (Matt. 3:16; Mark 1:10; Luke 3:22). John testified that the whole event verified to him that Jesus was truly the Christ (John 1:29-34).

John's understanding of the kingdom, which he preached as near (Matt. 3:2), was consistent with the teaching of Old Testament prophecy. Like the earlier prophets, he expected the kingdom to come in a revelation of judgment and wrath. Consequently, he preached repentance, alerting his hearers that "the axe is already laid at the root of the trees; every tree therefore that does not bear good fruit is cut down and thrown into the fire" (Matt. 3:10). He warned that the Christ (who was coming after him) would "baptize . . . with . . . fire. . . . His winnowing fork is in His hand, and He will thoroughly clear His threshing floor; and He will gather His wheat into the barn, but He will burn up the chaff with unquenchable fire" (Matt. 3:11-12).

In this prophecy, John was employing literary features from Malachi's prediction of the coming Day of the Lord: " 'For behold, the day is coming, burning like a furnace; and all the arrogant and every evildoer will be chaff; and the day that is coming will set them ablaze,' says the Lord of hosts, 'so that it will leave them neither root nor branch' " (Mal. 4:1). We recall that the prophets believed that the coming Messiah would strike the earth and punish the wicked. Similarly, John forsees the Christ as the One who will execute the judgment of the Day of the Lord.[1]

In summary, the early testimonies to Jesus identify Him as the Christ of the eschatological kingdom. The kingdom itself is understood in the terms of Old Testament prophecy. Its coming would be marked by judgment, a Day of the Lord. Its extent would be worldwide, with Gentiles submitting themselves to the Christ. It would be a political and spiritually enlivened kingdom in which the promises of blessing to all peoples, including Israel's national promises, are secured. And all of this would take place through a king who would fulfill the promises to David in both political power and intimacy with God—Jesus of Nazareth.

### *Jesus' Proclamation of the Coming Eschatological Kingdom.*
Like the Old Testament prophets and John the Baptist, Jesus also predicted the coming kingdom of God. Like John, but unlike the prophets, Jesus proclaimed the kingdom as being *near* (Matt. 4:17; 10:7; Mark 1:15; Luke 10:9). This was "good news." But it called

for repentance in light of the judgment that would precede the kingdom's arrival. (The nearness of the kingdom made the judgment imminent.) Jesus taught His disciples to pray for the coming of the kingdom (Matt. 6:10; Luke 11:2). They were to seek it more than food, clothing, and shelter (Matt. 6:33; Luke 12:31). This future sense of the kingdom is also seen in Matthew 13:47-50; 16:28; 20:21; 26:29; and Luke 13:29.

*Centrality of the Kingdom Theme.* The kingdom of God was not merely one of Jesus's themes. It was the overall topic of all His preaching, as can be seen in the way Matthew and Mark summarize His preaching ministry: "The time is fulfilled, and the kingdom of God is at hand; repent and believe the Gospel" (Mark 1:15, cf. Matt. 4:17). Both writers place these words at the beginning of their accounts functioning as a summary statement for the whole of His preaching and teaching.[2]

The kingdom of God was the guiding theme of all His ministry, as we can see in another summary comment by Matthew:

And Jesus was going about in all Galilee, teaching in their synagogues, and proclaiming the gospel of the kingdom, and healing every kind of disease and every kind of sickness among the people. And the news about Him went out into all Syria; and they brought to Him all who were ill, taken with various diseases and pains, demoniacs, epileptics, paralytics; and He healed them. And great multitudes followed Him from Galilee and Decapolis and Jerusalem and Judea and from beyond the Jordan (Matt. 4:23-25).

The works which Jesus performed, specifically in these verses, healing and exorcism, were part of His ministry proclaiming the good news of the coming kingdom. They in turn contribute to an understanding of what that kingdom would be like, an understanding which accords very well with the expectations of the Old Testament prophecies.

The centrality of the kingdom theme for Jesus is also seen in His constant reference to Himself as the *Son of Man.* We have already noted that "Son of Man" was a title applied by Daniel to the one who would rule the eschatological kingdom (Dan. 7:13). Jesus clearly uses it in this sense.

In Matthew 16:13, Jesus asked His disciples the question, "Who do people say that *the Son of Man* is?" He was speaking about Himself, as the parallel passages ("Who do people say that I am?" Mark 8:27; Luke 9:18) and His follow-up question in Matthew 16:15 ("But who do you say that I am?") indicate. Peter answers for the disciples, "Thou art the Christ, the Son of the living God" (Matt. 16:16). In other words, Peter understands this title to refer to *Messiah* rather than just a human being (see Ps. 8:4) or even a prophet (cf. Matt. 16:14 with Dan. 8:17 and Ezek. 2:1–3:27). Jesus affirms Peter's interpretation as a revelation from the Father (Matt. 16:17), and then elaborates the messianic meaning of *Son of Man* with the following remark: "For the Son of Man is going to come in the glory of His Father with His angels; and will then recompense every man according to his deeds" (Matt. 16:27). This coming in glory is rephrased in the next verse as "coming in His kingdom." The language affirms Daniel's apocalyptic view of the coming eschatological kingdom of the Son of Man, with the additional point that the judgment which Daniel envisioned as coming from the Ancient of Days is actually administered by the Christ, the Son of Man (consistent with Messiah's mediation of blessing and curse).[3]

Other "Son of Man" sayings by Jesus affirm His belief in a coming kingdom consistent with the prophecies of Daniel, and they demonstrate that He thought of Himself as the central figure. They also reaffirm the Old Testament expectation that judgment will mark the kingdom's coming (see Matt. 13:41-43; 19:28; 24:1–25:46 [Mark 13:1-37; Luke 21:5-36]).

*A Worldwide Political Kingdom.* Jesus believed that as the Messiah, He Himself would come in glory, judge the nations of humankind, and assert His own political rule over them (Matt. 25:31-46).

> But when the *Son of Man* comes in His glory, and all the angels with Him, then He will sit on His glorious throne. And *all the nations* will be gathered before Him; and He will separate them from one another, as the shepherd separates the sheep from the goats; and He will put the sheep on His right, and the goats on the left. Then the King will say to those on His right, "Come you who are blessed of My Father, inherit the *kingdom* prepared for you from the foundation of the world." . . . Then He will also say to those on His left, "Depart from Me, accursed ones, into

the eternal fire which has been prepared for the devil and his angels." . . . And these will go away into eternal punishment, but the righteous into eternal life.

At His trial, in answer to the high priest's inquiry as to whether He was the Christ, the Son of God, Jesus said that He was and claimed that Daniel 7:13 and Psalm 110:1 would be fulfilled for Him (Matt. 26:63-64; Mark 14:62; Luke 22:67-70). He taught that He would go away to receive the kingdom, but that He would return to reign over it (Luke 19:11-15). His kingdom would be the fulfillment of the grant to David (and consequently, the fulfillment of prophecies that the Davidic house would be reestablished). He would rule over Israel and all the nations forever (Matt. 25:31, 34, 46; Luke 1:33). He would be enthroned with all His enemies in subjection to Him (Matt. 26:64).

The focus on Israel's national promises is also seen in His sending of the disciples specifically "to the lost sheep of the house of Israel," telling them to "preach, saying, 'The kingdom of heaven is at hand'" (Matt. 10:6-7). In Acts 1:6, after forty days of instruction by the resurrected Jesus on the kingdom of God (Acts 1:3), the disciples ask Him if He would be "restoring the kingdom *to* Israel" at that time. The national hope of Israel appears in their question as a given. The question has to do only with the time of fulfillment.

This passage in Acts, standing as it does at the close of Jesus' preascension ministry, is a most significant testimony to the continuity of Jesus' teaching with that of the Old Testament prophets. The notion of a political, earthly kingdom has not dropped out or been resignified.[4]

It would seem that most of Jesus' teachings take the political nature of the kingdom for granted. He is more concerned to warn His hearers of the judgment that precedes this coming kingdom. However, even His pronouncements of judgment underscore the political nature of the kingdom.

In the Parable of the Vineyard (Matt. 21:33-46), Jesus rebuked the Jewish political rulers of His day for opposing Him. He presented Himself as the true heir to the throne of Israel. They are only servants, keeping shop for their master. Their opposition to Him is like the opposition David received in Psalm 118:22. In spite of resistance, David became "the chief cornerstone" of the kingdom. Using the stone metaphor, Jesus then conflates Isaiah 8:14 and Daniel 2:44 to predict the destruction of the Jewish political rulers of His day. The Daniel reference is particularly important because it speaks of the establishment of the eschatological kingdom. Jesus cast the Jewish rulers of His day in the part of those Gentile rulers who would be crushed by the establishment of God's kingdom.

In this context, Jesus says, "Therefore I say to you, the kingdom of God will be taken away from you, and be given to a nation producing the fruit of it" (Matt. 21:43). His judgment applies to themselves their earlier response to His parable, that the vineyard should be rented out "to other vine-growers who will pay him the proceeds at the proper seasons." In the context of Old Testament prophecy, this "nation," the "other vine-growers," would be the remnant of faith, the eschatological nation made up of those who endure the refining fire of the Day of the Lord — those of Israel who are delivered rather than purged out (cf. Micah 2:12-13; 4:6-8; Zeph. 3:12-20; Mal. 3:16-17).

In fact, Jesus had already appointed His own apostles to ruling positions in the coming kingdom. They would take the places of those who were ruling at that time.

> Truly I say to you, that you who have followed Me, in the regeneration when the Son of Man will sit on His glorious throne, you also shall sit upon twelve thrones, judging the twelve tribes of Israel (Matt. 19:28).

In summary, we see that Jesus affirmed the tradition of Old Testament prophecy and apocalypticism and proclaimed a coming worldwide political kingdom in which He as Messiah of the house of David would rule Israel and all the nations. We see Him making preparations for the administration of that coming kingdom by promising His disciples ruling positions along with Him, while announcing the exclusion of authorities then present.

*Coming in Judgment.* In the Olivet Discourse, the extended eschatological sermon of Matthew 24:1–25:46 (cf. Mark 13:1-37; Luke 21:5-36), Jesus responded to His disciples' questions about His "coming and the end of the age" (24:3). He explained that His coming would take place at a time of trouble and distress, of great evil and persecution. In describing the time, He uses the themes, features, and literary citations from Old Testament prophecies of the coming Day of the Lord. But He also made explicit reference to Daniel's visions of a coming time of great stress marked by the activity of one perpetrating an abomination of desolation (Matt. 24:15; Mark 13:14; cf. Luke 21:20).[5] In this way, Jesus integrated the prophets' notion of a coming Day of the Lord with Daniel's vision of a coming time of trouble. The result was a synthetic prediction of evil and judgment which forms the context of His coming.[6] The coming itself is presented in Matthew 24:30 (cf. Mark 13:26; Luke 21:27) by a citation of Daniel 7:13, and is completed in Matthew 25:31 where the Son of Man reigns as King in the kingdom of God on earth.

In Matthew's Gospel, a number of illustrations and parables associated with the Olivet Discourse (Matt. 24:37–25:30) repeat the warning to be ready for the judgment which takes place at the coming Son of Man. Many of Jesus' other parables, recorded elsewhere in the Gospels, reiterate the same warning, the frequent repetition showing how prevelant it was in Jesus' teaching. And it is picked up in the summary of His message recorded early in Matthew and Mark in Jesus' call for repentance in light of the coming kingdom of God.

*At an Unknown Time.* We should note Jesus' remarks about the *time* of this coming kingdom. He told His hearers the kingdom was near: "The time is fulfilled, and the kingdom of God is at hand [near]" (Mark 1:15). The fact that the Christ was there, having already been born in Bethlehem and living at that time in history, made the kingdom near. Without the King, the kingdom remained a distant hope; but with the King present, with history having become His own personal history, then for the first time, the eschatological kingdom became a present possibility.

As to the precise time when it would come, Jesus claimed not to know. In the Olivet Discourse, Jesus responded to the question, "When will these things be?"—the "things" being the destructive judgments that would signal His coming and the coming of the kingdom (Matt. 24:3). Jesus answered this question by saying, "But of that day and hour no one knows, not even the angels of heaven, nor the Son, but the Father alone" (24:36). This was then followed up by several sayings and parables to the effect that people should be ready since no one but the Father knows when the kingdom will make its apocalyptic entry.

In Luke 19:11 we read that on one occasion, as Jesus neared Jerusalem, many people "supposed that the kingdom of God was going to appear immediately." In their minds, the combination of *Christ* and *Jerusalem* meant *kingdom.* They did not understand that He came to do the ministry of the Servant (Isa. 49; 53) first, and that after His resurrection from the dead, He would ascend to the position where Daniel envisioned Him—in heaven, ready to descend in the glory and judgment of the coming kingdom. At the present time, however, He was performing the ministry of the Servant, calling Israel back to God (Isa. 49:5) as just witnessed in Luke 19:9-10 by His ministry to Zaccheus: "Today, salvation has come to this house, because he, too, is a son of Abraham. For the Son of Man has come to seek and to save that which was lost."

So "He went on to tell a parable" to correct their misunderstanding about the time of the coming kingdom. The parable is about "a certain nobleman" who "went to a distant country to receive a kingdom for himself, and then return" (Luke 19:12). The parable teaches that Jesus would not walk right into Jerusalem and establish the eschatological kingdom. Rather He would go away first. He would receive the kingdom in "a far country." And then He would return in judgment to execute His reign. Nothing, however, is said as to how long His departure would last or when after His departure He would return.

Jesus confirmed this teaching in Acts 1:6-7. At that point He had been resurrected from the dead and was preparing to ascend into heaven. The disciples asked Him, "Lord, is it at this time You are restoring the kingdom to Israel?" He responded with, "It is not for you to know times or epochs which the Father has fixed by His own authority." This then became the official view of the church as seen in Peter's teaching in Acts 3:21: "heaven must receive [Jesus, the Christ] until the period of restoration of all things, about which God spoke by the mouth of His holy prophets from ancient time." Only God knows when that time will be, it remains in the future at a time of God's own choosing.

*Physical and Material Aspects of the Kingdom.* In Old Testament theology, there is no thought of a future kingdom metaphysically separate from the earth. And there is nothing in the teaching of Jesus to indicate a radical departure from the tradition which preceded Him. The fact that He expected a political kingdom on earth sufficiently reveals the physical nature of the kingdom which He taught. His ministry activities also confirm this. They demonstrate the kind of kingdom He expected as He preached "the kingdom is near," or in some instances, "has come upon you."

Jesus, the King, truly was and is physically human. Many of the Gospel testimonies to His Davidic kingship appear in narratives about His birth. As He preached *the good news about the kingdom,* He healed people from physical infirmities, healing "every kind of disease and every kind of sickness among the people. . . . They brought to Him all who were ill, taken with various diseases and pains, demoniacs, epileptics, paralytics; and He healed them" (Matt. 4:23-24).[7]

The Gospels are filled with stories about physical healings, more than could be recalled here. Physical healing was a *blessing,* listed among the blessings of the Mosaic covenant, a manifestation of the promise made to Abraham to *bless* humankind. It was also a sign of the blessed life of the kingdom, quite in keeping with Old Testament expectation. Furthermore, the fact that *Jesus* healed people was a sign of *His kingship,* for as we have seen, the Davidic covenant made the king the mediator of the blessings of God. When John's disciples asked Jesus if He was the coming one, that is, if He were the King, He answered, "The blind receive sight and the lame walk, the lepers are cleansed and the deaf hear, and the dead are raised up, and the poor have the gospel preached to them" (Matt. 11:5).

The ultimate physical healing was bodily resurrection from the dead. Jesus is recorded as raising three individuals who had died (Luke 7:14-15; 8:49-56; John 11:43-44; but also note Matt. 27:52-53), but in His own resurrection He revealed the future of immortal life (2 Tim. 1:10). Consequently, the New Testament refers to Him as the "first fruits" from the dead.

The bodily nature of His resurrection life is emphasized in the Gospels with the record of His disciples touching (even embracing) Him (Matt. 28:9; Luke 24:39; John 20:17), speaking with Him (Matt. 28:10; Luke 24:13-35; John 20:14-17; 26-29), being taught and commissioned by Him (Matt. 28:16-20; Luke 24:13-35, 44-53; John 21:15-23; Acts 1:1-11), eating with Him (Luke 24:41-43; John 21:1-14; Acts 10:40-41), and walking along the road with Him (Luke 24:13-35).

What happened to Him in His bodily form is a revelation of human life in the coming kingdom of God, a life free from the curse of sin and death. In an image which recalls Isaiah 25:6-9, He predicted that many would come from east, west, north, and south and join Abraham, Isaac, and Jacob and all the prophets at a great banquet in the kingdom of God (Luke 13:28-29). Just before the cross Jesus promised His disciples that He would eat and drink the Passover meal again with them in the kingdom (Luke 22:16, 18).

Corresponding to the resurrection is the renewal of the earth. Many kingdom prophecies speak of the fruitfulness of the earth along with peace and harmony in the animal world. They anticipated a "new creation" of joy and gladness. Jesus affirmed these expectations. As he preached the coming kingdom of God, he performed miracles over nature. He "rebuked the winds and the sea" so that they became "perfectly calm" (Matt. 8:26; Mark 4:39; Luke 8:22-24). Twice, he "blessed" a small amount of food, and it multiplied to feed a large crowd (Matt. 14:19-21; 15:34-38; Mark 6:41-44; 8:5-9; Luke 9:16-17; John 6:9-14). He filled the nets of fishermen (John 21:5-6) and he "walked" through a storm at sea without harm (Matt. 14:24-33).

These activities function as illustrations of his message about the coming kingdom. Together with physical healings, they both portray the nature of kingdom life and affirm the messianic ruling authority of Jesus.

*A Spiritual Kingdom.* The kingdom which Jesus proclaimed was as much a spiritual as a physical kingdom. This is not a contradiction because the adjective *spiritual* does not imply a change in the metaphysical status of God's subjects. It refers to the presence of God with His creation in which He renews and blesses it.

The spirituality of the kingdom is seen first of all in the fact that it is the kingdom *of God.* As much as the kingdom is a political kingdom, it is a kingdom in which *God* rules and reigns over the nations. It is a *coming of God's* rule described in the same way as the Old Testament prophets spoke of God's coming reign. Accordingly, Jesus taught His disciples to seek "His [the Father's] kingdom" (Matt. 6:33; Luke 12:31), and to pray, "Our Father . . . Thy kingdom come" (Matt. 6:9-10; Luke 11:2).

But undoubtedly the most striking revelation about God's presence in the kingdom was the very person of Jesus the Messiah.

Whereas we saw that in Old Testament prophecy, the reigns of God and Messiah were expected to come together in the closest harmonious rule, the New Testament directly proclaims the Messiah to be God incarnate! Paul writes, "From them [the people of Israel] is traced the human ancestry of Christ, who is God over all, forever praised! Amen" (Rom. 9:5; NIV). John proclaims Jesus as the Word, who was God and who became flesh (John 1:1, 14). Thomas worshiped Him as "my Lord and My God" (John 20:28). Paul wrote that "all the fulness of deity" dwelt in Him (Col. 2:9), and referred to Him as "our great God and Savior, Christ Jesus" (Titus 2:13; cf. 2 Peter 1:1).

Jesus Himself continually spoke of God as His Father, and God the Father designated Jesus publicly as His Son. We have already discussed the covenant nature of this terminology; most important for understanding Jesus' messiahship. But the intimacy of Father and Son revealed in Jesus transcends the divine-Davidic relationship even as it includes it. It points the way to understanding how the truth of Jesus' deity relates to the deity of the Father.

In John 5:20-26, Jesus reveals a Father-Son relationship much greater than what was revealed in David or Solomon.

For the Father loves the Son, and shows Him all things that He Himself is doing; and greater works than these will He show Him, that you may marvel. For just as the Father raises the dead and gives them life, even so the Son also gives life to whom He wishes. . . . [The Father] has given all judgment to the Son, in order that all may honor the Son, even as they honor the Father. . . . For just as the Father has life in Himself, even so He gave to the Son also to have life in Himself.

The writer to the Hebrews declares that the Son "is the radiance of [God's] glory and the exact representation of His nature, and upholds all things by the word of His power (Heb. 1:3). Father and Son know one another uniquely (Matt. 11:27; Luke 10:22); their persons interpenetrate one another, so that anyone who sees the Son, sees the Father (John 14:9-11).

Consequently, in this Messiah, in this son of David become Son of God by covenant, is revealed an eternal, preexisting, and ever-continuing divine sonship—the Word who "was in the beginning with God," who "was God," that is, "the only begotten God" (John 1:1-2, 18). Divine sonship and Davidic covenant sonship are brought together in the one person of Jesus. As a consequence, the term *Son of God* comes to be used in an expanded sense in the New Testament. The traditional meaning refers to the Davidic king, but the newly revealed (although eternally preexistent) divine sonship comes into its referent. The term expands in its meaning in a complimentary (incarnational) manner.[8]

This also happens to the term *Lord*. We have already seen how Peter in Acts 2:36 declares Jesus to be Lord and Christ, using the term *Lord* to designate Jesus as the recipient of Davidic authority.[9] But the title *Lord* ascribed to Jesus also picks up a reference to God through Peter's citation of Joel 2:32 (Acts 2:21)—"Everyone who calls on the name of the Lord shall be saved"—and his appeal that people be baptized in the name of Jesus (Acts 2:38) in order to be saved (Acts 2:40). Paul later describes his baptism as "calling on His [Jesus'] name" (Acts 22:16). The One who has been enthroned with Davidic covenant authority as Lord is in fact the Lord who saves. The lordship is now unified and the action one. Salvation comes to those who *"call upon* the name of our *Lord Jesus Christ"* (1 Cor. 1:2; cf. Rom. 10:13; 2 Tim. 2:22). For the one who was "in the form of God" (the divine Lord) took the "form of a bond-servant" (the Servant Messiah) and made atonement for our sins, after which he was "highly exalted" with "the name which is above every name"so that all will "confess that Jesus Christ is *Lord,* to the glory of God the Father" (Phil. 2:6-11).[10]

With the Messiah as God incarnate, the kingdom could hardly be called a purely political kingdom. Rather, this will be the kingdom in which He bestows new covenant blessings, including the forgiveness of sins and the giving of the Holy Spirit to indwell and renew human hearts. Already Jesus was at work forgiving sins just as He was healing diseases (Matt. 9:2-6; Mark 2:5-10; Luke 5:20-24; 7:47-49). He gave His life to inaugurate the new covenant, providing the sacrificial basis for the atonement and redemption which He proclaimed. He revised and reinterpreted the Passover as a new covenant meal focused on His sacrificial death, predicting that He would partake of it again with His disciples in the kingdom of God (Matt. 26:26-29; Mark 14:22-25; Luke 22:15-20). He overcame the devil and sin (Matt. 4:1-11; 16:23; Mark 1:12-13; 8:33; Luke 4:1-13). He cast out demons, proclaiming such exorcisms as kingdom power (Matt. 12:22-28).

Jesus taught that the kingdom would be inhabited by people "born of the Spirit," telling Nicodemus that "unless one is born again, he cannot see the kingdom of God" (John 3:3, 5-8). This is the new covenant blessing of the Spirit of God in human hearts, as in Ezekiel 36–37 and Isaiah 59:21 where the remnant that becomes the nation is indwelt, renewed, and resurrected by the Holy Spirit. Jesus taught that the Spirit of God, given by God the Father, would be mediated through Him, God the Son – Son of God, Messiah (John 7:37-39; 14:16-17; 16:7).

The kingdom which Jesus preached was thus a kingdom of holiness and righteousness as much as it was a worldwide political kingdom. There is no contradiction or tension between these notions. They are just as compatible in the teaching of Jesus as they were in the predictions of the Old Testament prophets.

*The Sermon on the Mount and Kingdom Righteousness.* The righteousness of the kingdom is the theme of the Sermon on the Mount in Matthew 5–7. While we cannot provide a detailed exposition in these pages, we can note a few structural features which emphasize the theme. The Beatitudes proclaim the kingdom of heaven as a time of comfort, mercy, gentleness, peace, and purity of heart. It will be a kingdom on earth (5:5). The citizens of that kingdom will be "sons of God," and they will see God. The reason for this is the gift of God's righteousness.

Righteousness receives special emphasis in these Beatitudes. Structurally, it is the theme of the fourth and eighth blessings, concluding two cycles of four blessings each. In the fourth blessing (5:6), the righteousness is a gift from God: "Blessed are those who hunger and thirst for righteousness, for they shall be satisfied." In this sermon about the *eschatological* kingdom, the anticipated righteousness would appear to be the righteousness of new covenant blessing, in which God would write His law directly into the hearts of His people.

In the eighth blessing (5:10), Jesus promises the kingdom to those "who have been persecuted for the sake of righteousness." The repetition of the theme of righteousness underscores its importance for the sermon which follows. The ninth and final Beatitude, is poetically parallel to the eighth, repeating the same thought about blessing upon those who are persecuted. However, the word *righteousness* is replaced by *the person of Jesus,* emphasizing a connection between Himself and the righteousness that would be given. This connection is further stressed in 5:17, where Jesus claims that He came to fulfill the Law and the Prophets. The righteousness of the kingdom is already present in Himself.

The eschatological righteousness exceeds the righteousness of the old dispensation. Consequently, it surpasses that exhibited by the scribes and Pharisees, teachers and practitioners of the Mosaic law (5:20). From 5:20 through 5:48, Jesus expounds the superlative quality of eschatological righteousness by making comparisons to the way the law of the old covenant might be applied in specific situations of His own day. In 6:1-34, Jesus describes the eschatological righteousness as the quality of one's private life before God. This quality eliminates hypocrisy, the pretense of righteousness before others.

Finally, the sermon closes by admonishing the hearers "to seek first His *kingdom,* and His *righteousness*" (6:33). He promises that "everyone who asks receives; and he who seeks finds; and to him who knocks it shall be opened" (7:8). The Father will "give what is good to those who ask Him" (7:11). In Luke's version of this discourse, that good gift is the Holy Spirit (Luke 11:13), the agent of new covenant righteousness.

However, one needs to seek the righteousness by entering the right gate (Matt. 7:13-14), by going to the teacher who truly exhibits this righteousness (7:15-23), and more explicitly, by believing and acting upon the teaching of Jesus. He is the rock that preserves one's life through judgment (7:24-27). The concluding appeal is similar to the invitation that we find in Matthew 11:28-30.

Come to Me, all who are weary and heavy-laden, and I will give you rest. Take My yoke upon you, and learn from Me, for I am gentle and humble in heart; and you shall find rest for your souls. For My yoke is easy, and My load is light.

*Summary.* The kingdom of God was the constant theme of Jesus' ministry. He reiterated the basic features of this coming kingdom as commonly proclaimed by the Old Testament prophets, and He made special use of themes and images from Daniel's apocalyptic visions. The kingdom will come in a crisis of judgment in a Day of the Lord, a time of great distress on all peoples. But the kingdom will be established as a worldwide political rule over all nations. Israel will be blessed nationally, and through her King, the Davidic Christ, blessings will flow to all peoples.

Life in that kingdom will be blessed—no disease, no demonic oppression. Death itself will be eliminated—the dead will be raised and granted everlasting life. The earth will be blessed with peace and fruitfulness. It will be a life of joy and gladness, marked by the elimination of sin and wickedness. The people will be forgiven, their sins having been atoned for. They will be born of the Spirit and filled with righteousness. The mercy, comfort, and peace of God will abide with them. They will see God and dwell with Him forever.

The difference between Jesus and the prophets regarding the future coming kingdom lies not in the basic understanding of its nature and reality, but in the revelation of the Messiah. Jesus proclaimed Himself and was proclaimed by others to be the Messiah. Furthermore, the testimony about Him points to this startling fact: He, the Messiah, the chosen heir of David, is also God incarnate. The harmony of Divine and Davidic rule, in the prophetic vision of the kingdom, is now seen to be the single, personal action of God incarnate as Son of David. Now, a more profound harmony has come into revelation—the harmony of the triune God—Father, Son, and Holy Spirit.

The crisis of judgment through which the kingdom will come into its worldwide political dominion, is revealed to be the apocalyptic coming of Jesus. He is the Lord of the Day of the Lord, and He it is who will judge and rule the nations. The time of the kingdom's apocalyptic entry is known only to the Father.

The Son will act at the Father's will to bring the kingdom to pass. All authority is given to the Son. He will establish the kingdom and grant its blessings.

Both physical and spiritual blessings are given by Jesus. He makes atonement and forgives sins. He will give the Spirit, and He will raise the dead. He will bring peace to the earth and make it fruitful. He will give both joy and gladness. He, as both God and Davidic King, will shepherd His peoples with peace, security, and joy forever.

***The Kingdom As Present in Jesus.*** Whereas Jesus advances the tradition of the Old Testament prophets by predicting the coming of the eschatological kingdom with Himself as Messiah, there are some occasions in the Gospels when He speaks of the kingdom as being *present* in His own day. In these sayings, the kingdom is present in the sense that He Himself, the King of that kingdom, is present among them, displaying in Himself and in His activity the characteristics of the eschatological kingdom.

Three passages address this matter specifically. First, in Matthew 11, Jesus identifies Himself to John the Baptist's disciples as the Coming One by recounting His ministry activities. These activities are phenomena belonging to Messiah's eschatological reign. They were already present in Jesus' ministry at that time, affording a basis for speaking of the *presence* of the kingdom. After speaking with John's disciples, Jesus addressed the crowd about John's importance and the coming kingdom. He says, "He who is least in the kingdom of heaven is greater than he [John]" (Matt. 11:11; Luke 7:28). In that statement, the kingdom of heaven is a future reality. However, in the next verse (Matt. 11:12; cf. Luke 16:16), Jesus says, "And from the days of John the Baptist until now the kingdom of heaven suffers violence, and violent men take it by force." Although a difficult verse to translate, it seems to make the kingdom a *present* object of opposition. That opposition had come to focus upon Jesus, the central referent of the kingdom for both John and Jesus.

In Matthew 12:22-30 (cf. Luke 11:14-23), some Pharisees accuse Jesus of exorcising a demon by the authority of Beelzebub. Jesus rebuts their accusation by pointing out the illogic of Satan being divided against himself. Then He says, "But if I cast out demons by the Spirit of God, then *the kingdom of God has come upon you*" (Matt. 12:28). The kingdom of God is present (it *has* come) by virtue of the fact that He is exorcising demons by the power of the Holy Spirit. This activity causes the crowd to surmise His identity as the Son of David (Matt. 12:23). The fact that the King Himself is there, acting in the power of the Spirit, forms a basis for speaking of the presence of the eschatological kingdom.

In Luke 17:20-21, Jesus is questioned by some Pharisees "as to when the kingdom of God was coming." Jesus' answer begins with the claim, "The kingdom of God is not coming with signs to be observed." This comment seems odd in light of His teaching later in the same Gospel about the signs that precede the coming of the kingdom of God (Luke 21:7-31). Even in Luke 17, Jesus went on to speak of how the coming of the Son of Man would take place (17:24, 30). However, His response to the Pharisees becomes clear in verse 21. He tells the Pharisees, "Nor will they say, 'Look, here it is!' or, 'There it is!' For behold, the kingdom of God is in your midst." He directs their attention away from anything "over there" or "over here" to Himself.[11] He is in their midst, the very King of the kingdom. There is no greater sign of the kingdom than Himself, for in fact all other signs point to Him. Since they reject Him, no other signs will help them. But for our purposes, we note that His presence at that very time was the occasion for speaking of the kingdom being *present.*

In summary, the Gospel's present Jesus speaking of the kingdom being present in His own day by virtue of the fact that He Himself, the Christ, is present ministering by the power of the Holy Spirit, manifesting in His works characteristics belonging to the eschatological kingdom of God. He forgives sins, drives away disease, demons, and death. He pacifies the weather and multiplies food. He brings His hearers to repentance and leads them to the knowledge of and worship of God.

A theology which intends to be biblical must incorporate this presence of the kingdom in the precross ministry of Jesus into its understanding of the eschatological kingdom. For the first time in the history of prophecies about the eschatological kingdom, that kingdom was spoken of as being *present,* an assertion which was justified on the basis of the king's presence and activity. There is not the slightest indication that this assertion

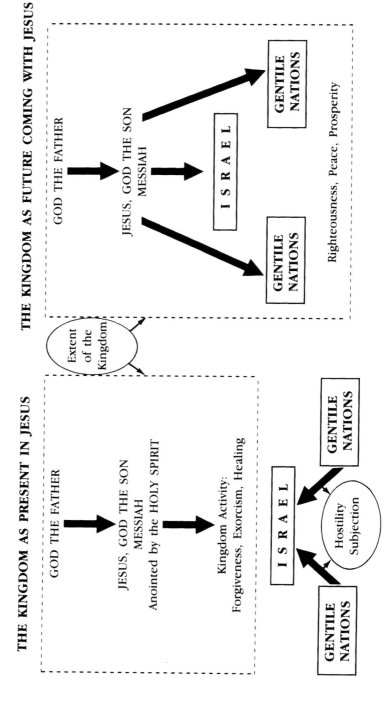

THE *PRESENT* AND *FUTURE* ESCHATOLOGICAL KINGDOM
AS TAUGHT BY JESUS

THE KINGDOM AS FUTURE COMING WITH JESUS

GOD THE FATHER

JESUS, GOD THE SON
MESSIAH

GENTILE
NATIONS

I S R A E L

GENTILE
NATIONS

Righteousness, Peace, Prosperity

Extent
of the
Kingdom

THE KINGDOM AS PRESENT IN JESUS

GOD THE FATHER

JESUS, GOD THE SON
MESSIAH
Anointed by the HOLY SPIRIT

Kingdom Activity:
Forgiveness, Exorcism, Healing

GENTILE
NATIONS

I S R A E L

Hostility
Subjection

GENTILE
NATIONS

contradicted Jesus' teaching about the kingdom's *future* coming. In actual fact, it provided stronger support for that teaching. For if the kingdom could be seen in Jesus, if He indeed demonstrated the power and authority of that kingdom, then there was even more reason to believe that a future coming of Jesus in glory would in fact bring the kingdom in all its glory.

The difference between the kingdom's presence in Jesus at the time of His pre-cross ministry and the kingdom's future presence is not only a difference between His service of suffering and His future glory, but also the difference between the kingdom being *in Jesus* and the kingdom being *universally established*. The kingdom was revealed in and through Jesus' activity. It was quite dynamic, being seen in displays of His power. However, He did not at that time *institute* the kingdom as an abiding structure for the world. It was only after the cross that He inaugurated certain aspects of the kingdom in an institutional sense. Scripture speaks of these features as a deposit (Eph. 1:13-14), an initial structure which awaits completion at His glorious coming in the Day of the Lord. His teachings on the future coming of the kingdom look forward to the full institutional establishment of the kingdom.

**A Presence of the Kingdom Prior to Christ's Return.** Much of Jesus' teaching was given in the form of parables. Since the kingdom of God was the major topic of His preaching, it is not surprising that many of the parables concern this subject and its related themes. We cannot undertake a major study of parables in these pages. Rather, we want to note Jesus' teachings on *mysteries of the kingdom* which appear to give new revelation about the kingdom beyond that which we have seen so far. Included in the new revelation was the prediction of a form or stage of the kingdom's presence prior to its full and apocalyptic establishment. This new stage does not appear to be the presence of the kingdom in Jesus' own Person as was discussed earlier (although the epistles will link these concepts together). While it is not altogether clear in the parables that this newly revealed presence of the kingdom will *follow* the cross, it is clear that it is a stage which *precedes* the apocalyptic coming of the kingdom.

A helpful collection of parables bearing on this subject is given in Matthew 13. Jesus explains why He teaches in parables.

> To you it has been granted to know the mysteries of the kingdom of heaven, but to them it has not been granted. . . . But blessed are your eyes, because they see; and your ears, because they hear. For truly I say to you, that many prophets and righteous men desired to see what you see, and did not see it; and to hear what you hear, and did not hear it (Matt. 13:11, 16-17).

Mark tells us that although Jesus taught in parables, "He was explaining everything privately to His own disciples" (Mark 4:34). The Parable of the Sower (Matt. 13:3-9, 18-23) speaks to this matter as well. Only some (i.e., His disciples) receive "the word of the kingdom" (13:19) fruitfully.

A most important parable, and one which stands at the beginning of the collection in Matthew 13 (after the introductory Parable of the Sower), is the Parable of the Wheat and the Tares (13:24-30). Jesus explains the parable to His disciples (13:36-43): the Son of Man will plant "sons of the kingdom" in the world where they will coexist with "sons of the evil one" until "the end of the age."

> The Son of Man will send forth His angels, and they will gather *out of His kingdom* all stumbling blocks, and those who commit lawlessness, and will cast them into the furnace of fire; in that place there shall be weeping and gnashing of teeth. Then the righteous will shine forth as the sun *in the kingdom* of their Father. He who has ears, let him hear.

The coming of the Son of Man at the conclusion of this passage is consistent with Jesus' teaching elsewhere about the Son of Man coming in an apocalyptic manner, executing judgment and instituting the kingdom of God. What is different, however, is the phrase, "they will gather *out of His kingdom* all stumbling blocks." This would appear to identify a situation *before* the coming of the Son of Man as *His kingdom*. Both those who belong to Him and those who will be condemned are present in that form of the kingdom. After His coming, only the saved will be present in the kingdom. Both conditions, before and after His coming are called "kingdom." Since the kingdom phase prior to this coming is the only new teaching in this parable, it would appear to be the "mystery of the kingdom of heaven" which the parable gives us. It is not a separate kingdom from that which follows, but a phase, a *mystery form* of the same kingdom.

The Parables of the Mustard Seed (13:31-32) and the Leaven and Meal (13:33), speak of an organic development of the kingdom from a small beginning to the full kingdom reality. The mustard seed parable even uses an illustration from Daniel 4:12, where it describes an imperial kingdom. These parables should not be pressed for implications about the rate of kingdom growth. They do not imply a smooth mathematical progression. They do not rule out apparent "set backs." Neither do they contradict the teaching of the wheat and tares. Evil will be present prior to the coming of the Son of Man. But these parables add this to the teaching of the former parable: the beginning of the kingdom phase which precedes the apocalypse will be small, but it is organically related to that kingdom which is to come. It is the eschatological kingdom in an initial form. It will grow and develop during the dispensation before the Son of Man's coming. In the consummation, the eschatological kingdom will be revealed in all its fullness, as predicted by the prophets and developed by Jesus.

The Parables of the Treasure and Field (13:44), and the Merchant and Pearl (13:45-46) have literary similarities that join them together. They seem to speak of two kinds of people who come to possess the kingdom during the dispensation preceding the apocalypse. Some people, like the person in the field, are unaware of the kingdom. But when they encounter it, they recognize that it is worth everything they have to possess it. Others, like the merchant, are in fact looking for the kingdom. When they encounter it, they likewise recognize that it is worth everything they have. Both of these would be counted as "sons of the kingdom" in the wheat and tares parable.

The Parable of the Householder (13:51-52) forms an important conclusion to this collection. Like the introductory Parable of the Sower it speaks of revelation about the kingdom. Concerning their "understanding" of His teaching, He says:

Therefore, every scribe who has become a disciple of the kingdom of heaven is like a head of a household, who brings forth out of his treasure things new and old.

The new treasure corresponds to the new knowledge which He has given them concerning "the kingdom of heaven." These are "the mysteries of the kingdom of heaven." The old treasure would be the already revealed prophecies about the kingdom. Both the new and the old are in the possession of the householder. The new does not replace the old. The old does not exclude the new. They are not two separate treasures. The new truths complement the old truths to make up one "treasure," the kingdom of heaven.

To summarize, in these parables, Jesus appears to be predicting a form of the kingdom which will precede its expected apocalyptic arrival. This is a different form of the kingdom from His own presence in the world (which He had identified as a presence of the kingdom). Rather, it consists of the presence of "sons of the kingdom" (that is, people who truly belong to the eschatological kingdom) in the world prior to the coming of the Son of Man. The Son of Man Himself will put them into the world in an initial "sowing" which appears small. But its reality is that of the eschatological kingdom, and it will grow and develop in the world even in the presence of evil until the time of the coming of the Son of Man.

## THE ESCHATOLOGICAL KINGDOM OF GOD
## AS TAUGHT BY JESUS

| The Kingdom Present in the Person of the King | The Kingdom in Mystery Form King in Heaven Kingdom Citizens on Earth | A Day of the Lord | The Kingdom In Its Fullness |

# The Eschatological Kingdom in the Life and Hope of the Church

The testimony of the church from its earliest days to the present is that Jesus is the Christ. He was invested with the royal authority of the eschatological kingdom of God upon His ascension into heaven. He was seated at the right hand of God, the position appropriate for the Davidic King. He waits upon the Father for the day of His return when He will personally and everlastingly rule the peoples of earth, bringing to fulfillment the blessings of the covenants of promise.

The church's testimony to Jesus is based on the relationship which Jesus established with her from His ascended position in heaven. He had already provided the atonement which made possible a new covenant in all of its blessings. His resurrection from the dead revealed and confirmed these blessings in Himself— the firstfruits from the dead. However, a few days after His ascension into heaven, on Israel's Day of Pentecost, Jesus (acting from heaven) gave His disciples a "down payment" on the new covenant blessings of the kingdom, the gift of the Holy Spirit. This action constituted His disciples a community of the eschatological kingdom of God, under the rule and blessing of Jesus the Messiah. All who come to faith in Jesus are likewise blessed by the gift of the Spirit and join this kingdom community, which has come to be known as the church.

Jesus had predicted that His disciples would be "baptized by the Spirit"; He predicted that He Himself would send the Spirit to them after He returned to the Father. He predicted that anyone who believed in Him would be born of the Spirit, a condition necessary for seeing the kingdom of God (John 3:3). After forty days of final instructions about the kingdom of God (Acts 1:3), including its restoration to Israel politically and nationally (the timing of which would not yet be revealed, Acts 1:6), the disciples were commanded to wait in Jerusalem "for what the Father had promised" and what He had also taught them to expect.

> For John baptized with water, but you shall be baptized with the Holy Spirit not many days from now. . . . You shall receive power when the Holy Spirit has come upon you; and you shall be My witnesses both in Jerusalem, and in all Judea and Samaria, and even to the remotest part of the earth (Acts 1:5, 8).

When the Spirit came upon the disciples, they saw it as a messianic act by Jesus, indicating that He had indeed been received by the Father in heaven, had been granted messianic (kingdom) authority, and had begun to act on that authority:

> Therefore having been exalted to the right hand of God, and having received from the Father the promise of the Holy Spirit, He has poured forth this which you both see and hear. . . . Therefore let all the house of Israel know for certain that God has made Him both Lord and Christ—this Jesus whom you crucified. . . . Repent, and let each of you be baptized in the name of Jesus Christ for the forgiveness of your sins; and you shall receive the gift of the Holy Spirit (Acts 2:33, 36, 38).

The earliest community of believers were all Jews. They viewed themselves as the remnant of faith who would inherit the kingdom when Jesus descended from heaven as the apocalyptic Son of Man. As they proceeded to carry out His command to proclaim to all peoples, including Samaritans and Gentiles, the good news of the kingdom of God (Acts 8:12; 28:23, 28-31), they saw many of these peoples come to faith in Jesus. They also witnessed the fact that Jesus bestowed upon these Samaritan and Gentile believers the same blessing of the Holy Spirit as He had given to them (Acts 8:14-17; 10:44-48; 11:15-18). They interpreted this action as God "taking from among the Gentiles a people for His name" (Acts 15:14). Such activity was seen to be part and parcel of the plan of the eschatological kingdom, as predicted in passages like Isaiah 49:6 and Amos 9:11-12 (see Acts 13:46-48; 15:14-18). Together the believers constituted a microcosm of the coming kingdom in which all peoples, Jews and Gentiles, would be subject to the rule of the Christ and blessed by Him.

The nature of Christ's blessing during this time of ascension, and the equality of its bestowal upon Jews and Gentiles (as well as both genders and all social classes), brought into history the reality known as *the church*. As they lived in hope of the coming of Jesus, both Jewish and Gentile believers would meet together regularly to worship the Lord and encourage one another in the faith. Their assembly was united by their one faith in one God and one messianic Lord and the fellowship of one Spirit.

For even as the body is one . . . so also is Christ. For by one Spirit we were all baptized into one body, whether Jews or Greeks, whether slaves or free, and we were all made to drink of one Spirit. . . . Now, you are Christ's body . . . the church (1 Cor. 12:12-13, 27-28).

For all of you who were baptized into Christ have clothed yourselves with Christ. There is neither Jew nor Greek, there is neither slave nor free man, there is neither male for female; for you are all one in Christ Jesus (Gal. 3:27-28).

And He [the Father] put all things in subjection under His [Jesus'] feet, and gave Him as head over all things to the church, which is His body, the fulness of Him who fills all in all. . . . There is one body and one Spirit, just as also you were called in one hope of your calling; one Lord, one faith, one baptism, one God and Father of all who is over all and through all and in all (Eph. 1:22-23; 4:4-6).

**The Church as a Present Revelation of the Kingdom.** Much has already been said about the New Testament witness to the present messianic authority of Jesus. Repeatedly, He is portrayed as enthroned at the right hand of God in fulfillment of promises that belong to God's covenant with David. His enthronement and present authority is *messianic*. It is as the *Christ* that He is presently active. We have seen that the New Testament proclaims this Christ to be God. But He is God incarnate, and *incarnate* not as generic humanity but as the son of David. In this time of His ascension, He has not become, nor does He act as God disincarnate. In the language of the New Testament, all of His activities, including all of His relations with the church, are ascribed to *Jesus* (His human name) *Christ* (His royal title of Davidic kingship).

In Paul's letter to the church at Colossae, that is to "the saints and faithful brethren *in Christ* at Colossae," he described the believers as having been delivered "from the domain of darkness, and transferred . . . to *the kingdom* of His [the Father's] beloved Son" (Col. 1:13). We have already noted that this kingdom language belongs to the Davidic covenant. It is the messianic kingdom that the members of the Colossian church have been transferred to. Furthermore, the context indicates that Paul is speaking of their *present* relationship to the kingdom. He is not speaking proleptically of their future transference to that kingdom, as if their present identity in Christ could be described as being under "the domain of darkness."[12]

Paul's prayer in Colossians 1:9-12, assumes the saints' present status as members of the eschatological kingdom, for he prays that God will presently give them blessings belonging to that kingdom: the knowledge of God, the fruit of righteousness, and obedience to the Christ (1:9-10). In Colossians 3, Paul speaks of the church's present identification with Christ's death, resurrection, and ascension. They are to identify themselves in their present behavior with the resurrected Messiah who is at God's right hand (3:1-2). What follows is a list of exhortations directing them to righteousness. The sanctification to which the church is called is the present rule or reign of the Messiah in the church (3:15). It anticipates the future coming of Christ at which time we will be "revealed with Him in glory" (3:4).

The identity of the church as a present reality of the coming eschatological kingdom receives further explanation in Ephesians. The church expects an inheritance in the coming "kingdom of Christ and God" (5:5). Its hope is fixed on "the riches of the glory of His inheritance in the saints" (1:18). But the church's present reality is due to the fact that "after listening to the message of truth, the gospel of your salvation — having also believed, you were sealed in Him [Christ] with the Holy Spirit of promise" (1:13). The Holy Spirit has been given as a "pledge of our inheritance, with a view to the redemption of God's own possession" (1:14).

A pledge or down payment is a partial payment in advance of a future payment in full. The down payment guarantees the future just as much as it itself is a part of that future reality. Accordingly, the work which the Holy Spirit does in the church, and by which the church is constituted in its reality as the church, is a partial revelation in the present of that kingdom which is coming in the future. Since its reality belongs to the kingdom, and since it exists in the present, consequently the church must be understood as a present form of the eschatological kingdom, a *presence* which *guarantees* the *future* coming of that kingdom in all its fullness.

This view of the church is further developed in Ephesians 1:15–2:22. Paul prays the church may know their hope, "the riches of the glory of His inheritance [i.e., the kingdom, cf. Eph. 5:5] in the saints" and "the surpassing greatness of His power toward us who believe" (1:18-19). That power is then explicated in 1:20–2:22 in a description of the present activity of the Messiah building the church. We have already noted how this entire passage is framed in the language of Davidic covenant promise. The Messiah has been raised up, seated (enthroned) at the right hand of God, all things, specifically all rule and authority, have been subjected to Him, and He is building the house of God.

The house of God which Messiah is building far excels that which was built by Solomon, for Jesus is building a "living" house (cf. 1 Peter 2:5). Redeemed humanity will itself be the dwelling place of God. This was, of course, foreseen in the promise of the new covenant that God's Spirit would dwell in His people. Paul sees that promise fulfilled in the living temple, the church (2 Cor. 6:16 quoting Ezek. 37:27). Ephesians 2 offers an expanded explanation of these ideas.

God, working in and through Messiah, makes people alive (2:1-5).[13] We share in the power which was revealed in and through the Messiah Himself. We were "made . . . alive together with Christ . . . and raised . . . up with Him, and seated . . . with Him . . . in Christ Jesus" (2:5-6). The Messiah Himself is reconciling Jews and Gentiles who are thus made alive in Him. He establishes peace between these formerly hostile peoples as they are united to Him in His atonement (2:15-17; cf. Col. 3:15). The establishment of peace is exactly what the prophets expected the Messiah to do; it is one of the most prominent features of the eschatological kingdom next to righteousness. This peace is established through a new covenant (Eph. 2:14-15, 22). In keeping with the Abrahamic promise to "bless all peoples in you," believing Gentiles along with believing Jews are blessed with the new covenant blessing of spiritual renewal. This is the key action which brings into existence the redeemed peoples of the eschatological kingdom, all living in peace, filled with the knowledge of God.[14] The "new man" is this eschatological humanity.

The "making" of "the two [Jews and Gentiles in Christ] into "one new man" (2:15) is then elaborated in 2:18-22 with a change of metaphor. The new humanity is the temple of God which Jesus is constructing. Messiah is not only the temple builder, but also high priest, cornerstone, and the temple itself (2:18-22), a conjunction of images due to the convergence of several lines of prophecy using different metaphors but all relating to the temple. The "temple" itself is constituted as a temple by being "a dwelling of God in the Spirit" (2:22). Both Jews and Gentiles in Christ have "access in one Spirit to the Father" (2:18).

This brings us back to Ephesians 1:13-14. The Spirit is the "pledge," the down payment on our future inheritance, which is "the kingdom of Christ and God" (Eph. 5:5). He creates in us at the present time a reality that belongs to that future kingdom, thus bringing the eschatological kingdom into present existence. All of this is elaborated in 1:15–2:22 in language picturing the Messiah enthroned and engaged in kingdom activity. This activity is the present reality of uniting Jews and Gentiles through the kingdom down payment into a kingdom reality!

The changes introduced by Christ in the relationship of Jews and Gentiles to God are significant enough that Paul identifies them as a new dispensation (Eph. 3:4-9). The previous dispensation revealed the kingdom of God under the Mosaic covenant. The inauguration of the new covenant under the eschatological Messiah has brought realities belonging to the eschatological kingdom into present existence. Here is where the church finds its identity. *All of the language describing the church in the New Testament is either directly drawn from or is compatible with the genres of covenant promise and the Messianic kingdom.*

The present dispensation is not the full and complete revelation of the eschatological kingdom. It is a progressive stage in the revelation of that kingdom. The changes that accompany the final revelation of the eschatological kingdom are significant enough to constitute another and final dispensational change in God's relationship with humanity (Eph. 1:10). Present kingdom blessings are but a "down payment." In the future dispensation, "payment" will be received in full. The blessing of the Spirit is presently given in mortal conditions, then in resurrection immortality (Rom. 8:10-11; 2 Cor. 4:7–5:9). We are not yet glorified, not yet perfected. Present blessings of spiritual re-

# THE ESCHATOLOGICAL KINGDOM PRESENT IN THE CHURCH

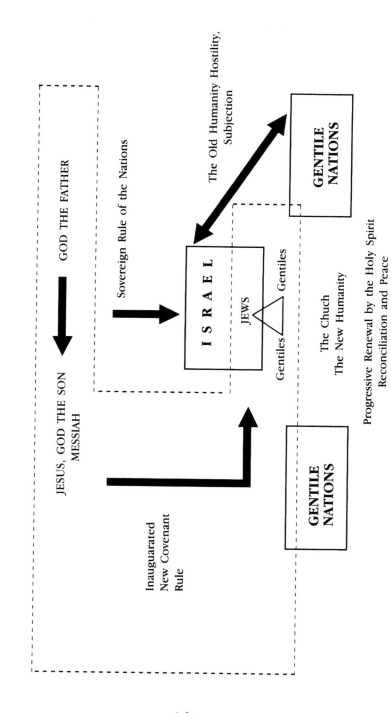

newal are given progressively (2 Cor. 3:18) in dispersion conditions with the Christ absent. In the future, when Christ is revealed, kingdom blessings will be given in full.

Being a dispensation of the kingdom, the church corresponds to that mystery form of the kingdom which Jesus revealed in the parables of Matthew 13. It is a community of citizens of the kingdom prior to the coming of the Son of Man. It is a new revelation of God, a mystery of the kingdom. But it is a mystery *of the kingdom.* Although new in the progress of revelation, it is not wholly different, not a secondary, parallel plan of God. As illustrated in the Parable of the Householder (Matt. 13:52), this new revelation complements the revelation previously given, adding new treasures to one household, the new and the old sitting side by side in complementary fashion.

**The Hope of the Church, the Future Eschatological Kingdom.** The hope of the church is centered on the return of Christ Jesus. In 1 Thessalonians 1:10, Paul described the church as waiting "for His Son from heaven, whom He raised from the dead, that is Jesus, who delivers us from the wrath to come." He wrote that grace instructs us to be "looking for the blessed hope and the appearing of the glory of our great God and Savior, Christ Jesus" (Titus 2:13). Again he says, "we eagerly wait for a Savior [to come from heaven], the Lord Jesus Christ" (Phil. 3:20). Peter writes, "fix your hope completely on the grace to be brought to you at the revelation of Jesus Christ" (1 Peter 1:13). The last book in our present New Testament, "The Revelation of Jesus Christ," is a work which envisions and proclaims His coming, with bracketing announcements at the beginning ("Behold, He is coming with the clouds"; 1:7) and the end ("Behold, I am coming quickly. . . . Yes, I am coming quickly"; 22:12, 20 – set amidst a rising chorus of "Come, Lord Jesus," cf. 1 Cor. 16:22).

*The Day of the Lord.* What the church expects to happen at the coming of Jesus correlates generally with Old Testament predictions regarding the coming of the kingdom. It will be a Day of the Lord, a time of wrath and judgment against sin and evil (1 Thes. 5:1-9; 2 Peter 2:9; 3:7-12; Rev. 6:17; 16:14). It is "the Day of our Lord Jesus Christ" (1 Cor. 1:8); which takes place at His "revelation" from heaven (1 Cor. 1:7). The Old Testament literary descriptions of God coming in wrath in the

Day of the Lord are combined with the new understanding of Messiah as taught by Jesus. The notion that the judgment has been entrusted to and will be executed by the Son of God (Messiah) who comes on the clouds of heaven as the Son of Man is carried over in the teaching of the apostles. We see this in the way certain sayings of Jesus mark New Testament descriptions of the Day of the Lord — such as the illustration that the day is coming like a thief (1 Thes. 5:2; 2 Peter 3:10; Rev. 16:14-15). But primarily we see this in the way the coming of God in the Day of the Lord is presented as the coming of Jesus.

> The Lord Jesus shall be revealed from heaven with His mighty angels in flaming fire, dealing out retribution to those who do not know God and to those who do not obey the gospel of our Lord Jesus. And these will pay the penalty of eternal destruction away from the presence of the Lord and from the glory of His power, when He comes to be glorified in His saints on that day, and to be marveled at among all who have believed (2 Thes. 1:7-10).

The judgment that Jesus brings begins first with "the household of God" (1 Peter 4:17; cf. 1 Cor. 4:5; James 5:7-9; 1 John 2:28) in order to reveal what is true and lasting. Accordingly, Paul says that the Day of the Lord will reveal each one's work. Some will suffer loss even though they are saved (1 Cor. 3:13-15). The judgment then proceeds to unbelievers.

However, the passages that relate believers to the Day of the Lord mostly speak of deliverance, a theme which is also consistent with the Old Testament. The abiding of God and His love in us gives us confidence for the day of judgment (1 John 4:17). Paul likewise speaks of confidence that "He who began a good work in you will perfect it until the day of Christ Jesus" (Phil. 1:6). To the Corinthians, he writes, "our Lord Jesus Christ . . . shall also confirm you to the end, blameless in the day of our Lord Jesus Christ" (1 Cor. 1:7-8). Believers will rejoice in the culmination of each other's spiritual growth and progress as the Lord completes their salvation in the day of His coming (Phil. 1:10; 2:16; 2 Cor. 1:14).

Deliverance in the Day of the Lord is a special theme of 1 Thessalonians. At His return, Jesus "delivers us from the wrath to come" (1:10). Paul teaches the church that the Day of the Lord will not "overtake you like a thief" (5:4). This is further explained in 5:9, "For God has not destined us for wrath, but for obtaining salvation through our Lord Jesus Christ." In the context, this deliverance would seem to be the blessing of resurrection and translation into immortality which Christ will grant His own at His coming (1 Thes. 4:13-18), an event which is called the Rapture (from the verb *rapere*, "caught up," in 1 Thes. 4:17). This deliverance, or rapture, would appear to coincide with the inception or coming of the Day of the Lord, since that is the focus in 1 Thessalonians 5:2-4.[15]

The theme of deliverance at the return of Christ is sounded elsewhere in the New Testament. Believers expect to be saved, resurrected, awarded the crown of life, transformed into the image of Christ, and glorified in His glory (John 14:1-3; Col. 3:4; Phil. 3:20-21; 2 Tim. 4:8; 1 Peter 1:7; 4:13; 1 John 3:2).

*A Future Kingdom.* With the coming of Christ comes the eschatological kingdom in its future manifestation. In Revelation 19:11-16, the coming of Jesus is envisioned in a conflation of multiple images drawn mostly from the Old Testament, including several messianic descriptions. Included is "He *will rule* them [the nations] with a rod of iron" (19:15).

Repeatedly, in the grammar of the New Testament, the kingdom is mentioned in the future tense, as something which will come and be inherited in the future. Believers will "enter" it at a future time (Acts 14:22; 2 Peter 1:11). James speaks of those who are "heirs of the kingdom which He promised to those who love Him" (James 2:5). Paul speaks of those who "will not" inherit the kingdom (1 Cor. 6:9-10; Gal. 5:21; Eph. 5:5). The Thessalonian church is described as suffering for the kingdom of God (2 Thes. 1:5), expecting "relief . . . when the Lord Jesus shall be revealed from heaven . . . to be glorified in His saints on that day" (1:7, 10). Paul admonishes Timothy by "Christ Jesus, who is to judge the living and the dead, and by His appearing and His kingdom" (2 Tim. 4:1).

The kingdom which is coming is the kingdom of God and of His Messiah (Eph. 5:5). Most often, the kingdom is referred to as the *kingdom of God,* but just as equally it is Christ's kingdom (2 Tim. 4:1; 2 Peter 1:11; Rev. 11:15). This *messianic* kingdom is everlasting (2 Peter 1:11; Rev. 11:15); it is "imperishable and undefiled and will not fade away" (1 Peter 1:4).

*A Kingdom on Earth.* At the present time, this kingdom, this "inheritance," is said to be "reserved in heaven" (1 Peter 1:4). Such language corresponds to the strong emphasis we have seen on the present enthronement of the Messiah in heaven. Christ presently rules the church from heaven by the Holy Spirit. Paul also taught that prior to Christ's coming, the souls of the Christian dead would join Christ in heaven (2 Cor. 5:6-8). He believed that at his own death, he would go to be with Christ (Phil. 1:21-23), and this appears to be his thought when he wrote that "the Lord . . . will bring me safely to His heavenly kingdom" (2 Tim. 4:18). At the present time, believers are to think of themselves in relationship to Christ, enthroned in heaven. God has "raised us up with Him, and seated us with Him in the heavenly places, in Christ Jesus" (Eph. 2:6). We are to "keep seeking the things above, where Christ is, seated at the right hand of God. . . . For you have died and your life is hidden with Christ in God" (Col. 3:1, 3).

The kingdom is said to be in heaven because the Messiah is presently in heaven, and the souls of all the dead who will inherit the kingdom are with Him awaiting their resurrection (cf. Rev. 6:10-11). The church which is "in Christ" thus has a heavenly identity in this dispensation. But, as we have seen, Christ will return to earth. "When Christ, who is our life, is revealed, then you also will be revealed with Him in glory" (Col. 3:4). This "revelation" will be the completion of our salvation (1 Peter 1:7-9, 13), our resurrection from the dead (1 Peter 1:3), which leads in turn to our inheritance in that future form of the eschatological kingdom (1 Cor. 15:50-57). Corresponding to our resurrection from the dead will be the renewal of the earth, the locus of the future kingdom.

For I consider that the sufferings of this present time are not worthy to be compared with the glory that is to be revealed to us.[16] For the anxious longing of the creation waits eagerly for the revealing of the sons of God. For the creation was subjected to futility, not of its own will, but because of Him who subjected it, in hope that the creation itself also will be set free from its slavery to corruption into the freedom of the glory of the children of God. For we know that the whole creation groans and suffers the pains of childbirth together until now. And not only this, but also we ourselves, having the first fruits of the Spirit, even we ourselves groan within ourselves, waiting eagerly for our adoption as sons, the redemption of our body (Rom. 8:18-23).

The earthly locus (albeit renewed) of the eschatological kingdom is reinforced in 2 Peter 3:13, where we read, "But according to His promise we are looking for new heavens and a new earth, in which righteousness dwells." Likewise John envisions "a new heaven and a new earth" in which God "shall dwell among" redeemed humanity, and "they shall be His people, and God Himself shall be among them" (Rev. 21:1, 3).

In John's vision, the "people" that constitute the subjects of the eschatological kingdom on the new earth are grouped into "nations" (Rev. 21:24, 26; 22:2). This is the same term that is used in Revelation 2:26-27, quoting Psalm 2:8-9 in reference to the Messiah who rules the nations, and in Revelation 19:15 which conflates the language of Psalm 2:8-9 with Isaiah 11:4. John's vision in Revelation 21–22 is cast in the images of Old Testament prophecy in which the Messiah will politically rule all nations. Some New Testament writings anticipate the fact that believers will reign with Christ (2 Tim. 2:12); with Him, they will judge the world (1 Cor. 6:2). The letters to the churches in Revelation 2–3 also repeat this expectation.

The setting is Zion, the City of God, the new (renewed) Jerusalem (Rev. 21:2ff) described in great splendor. The nations will "walk by its light, and the kings of the earth will bring their glory into it" (Rev. 21:24). This image reaffirms the Old Testament prophecies about Zion's eschatological exaltation as found for example in Isaiah 60 and in Isaiah 2:2-4 (cf. Micah 4:1-4). The eschatological Zion is said to be in heaven at the present time (Gal. 4; Phil. 3:20; Heb. 12:22-24), because the king is presently in heaven. The king is preparing the city (John 14:1-3) even as He is preparing our kingdom inheritance (1 Peter 1:4). Believers are citizens of the city now even as they are presently in the kingdom (Phil. 3:20; Col. 1:13), by virtue of presently inaugurated new covenant blessings (Gal. 4:24-31). However, just as the kingdom is said to be coming in the future, so the city is likewise the city which is to come (Heb. 13:14).[17]

Political rulership over the nations coincides with the new covenant gift of righteousness. The New Testament reaffirms this often repeated characteristic of the Old Testament hope for a coming kingdom: it will be marked by righteousness, holiness, and godliness.

*The Fulfillment of Israel's Promises.* The eschatological kingdom pictured in these passages is quite compatible with Old Testament hope. And this includes the specific hope of Israel. Much of the New Testament writings concern the extension of present kingdom blessings to Gentile believers as consistent with Old Testament promises about Gentiles. However, the New Testament never presents these events as a *replacement* of the specific hopes of Israel. Instead, they are argued as *compatible or complementary* to the hopes of Israel. Some have asked why the New Testament does not stress a return to the land as the Old Testament prophecies do. We must remember, that at the time the New Testament epistles were written, Jews were living in the land. Although there were still many in the dispersion, nevertheless a sufficient return had taken place to constitute a Jewish political presence in the land of covenant promise. The issue in New Testament writings was not a return to the land (since they were already in the land) but the return of the Messiah and a proper relationship to Him which would guarantee everlasting inheritance in the kingdom of glory which He would establish there, in that land.

The expectation that Messiah will rule all the nations on a renewed earth certainly would not have *excluded* the nation of Israel! A worldwide empire of Gentile nations with Israel's Messiah at the top but with Israel missing is not a credible explanation of first-century eschatology, particularly of a church which is primarily Jewish. The council at Jerusalem in Acts 15 did not approve the Gentile mission because they expected Christianity to be a *Gentile* religion. They saw, through Amos 9, that the eschatological kingdom would extend blessings to the Gentiles as well as to Israel, not that it would be a Gentile kingdom. The reaction in Jerusalem to Peter's mission to Cornelius was, "Well then, God has granted to the Gentiles *also* the repentance that leads to life" (Acts 11:18).

The issue in New Testament writings was *Gentile inclusion* not *Israel's exclusion.* But it was also about *the salvation of the remnant* in the Day of the Lord which would precede the full revelation of the kingdom. The New Testament speaks of judgment coming upon Jews and Gentiles. Only those who are founded on the Rock, whose faith is in Christ will be saved. The messages in Acts call the house of Israel to repentance, to salvation, just as they call Gentiles to salvation. Nowhere do they interject the completely novel idea that the national blessings of Israel will be abandoned.

In two passages, the national future of Israel is most definitely assured. We have already noted Peter's second Jerusalem speech. Peter would have been included with the rest of the disciples in the question recorded in Acts 1:6: "Lord, is it at this time You are restoring the kingdom to Israel?" Jesus responded directly to their question about time. He most certainly did not resignify their understanding about "restoring the kingdom to Israel." A few days later, we find Peter preaching to the crowds in Jerusalem, "Repent therefore and return" with a view to the coming of "Jesus, the Christ appointed for you, whom heaven must receive until the period of restoration of all things, about which God spoke by the mouth of His holy prophets from ancient time" (Acts 3:19-21). There can be no doubt that this "restoration" about which the Old Testament prophets spoke focused on national Israel.

Paul addressed the question of Israel's national salvation in his letter to the Romans. The Gospel which he preached (Rom. 1:1-4) concerns the promise which God made "beforehand through His prophets in the holy Scriptures: concerning His Son, who was born a descendant of David according to the flesh, who was declared the Son of God with power by the resurrection from the dead, according to the Spirit of holiness, Jesus Christ our Lord."

This good news about the Messiah is "to the Jew first and also to the Greek" (Rom. 1:16).

In this perhaps the most famous of all his letters Paul explains the blessings of salvation that come through Jesus Christ to all who believe. He argues at length for the fact that Gentiles as well as Jews are justified and sanctified by the grace of Christ. But he also raises the question about the "advantage" of the Jew, the "benefit" of circumcision (3:1). The advantage is not found in having God all to themselves, for there is one God over all peoples (3:29). Nor is the benefit found in being more righteous than Gentiles. The problem of sin affects both Jews and Gentiles alike (3:9). Justification for both comes through faith (3:30).

The benefits for the Jews, the circumcised, in Romans 3:1-2 must be read in light of 2:17-29. These are the benefits for the *true* Jews—which is not a new name for believing Gentiles, but refers to ethnic Jews whose hearts are circumcised by the Spirit of God. It is to them (the remnant of faith as declared by the Old Testament) that the oracles of God truly belong. The unbelief of some Jews will not nullify the faithfulness of God to this remnant! (3:3-4) The oracles of God, which contain His promises to believing Israel will be fulfilled even in spite of the radical sinfulness that strikes all people (3:4, 9).

Paul argues that by the grace of justification and new covenant righteousness, God's salvation will lead to the revelation of an immortal humanity on a renewed earth (8:11, 18-23). But then returning to the question of Israel, he laments in Romans 9–11 that so many Jews have missed the salvation that comes through faith in Christ. He recalls the blessings that distinguished Jews from Gentiles in the old dispensation: "the adoption as sons and the glory and the covenants and the giving of the Law and the temple service and the promises." To them belongs "the fathers" and from them is "the Christ" (9:4-5).

Yet Paul asserts the word of God has not failed (9:6). The word of God certainly includes the Law and temple ordinances, but has a special reference to "promises" as seen in the repetition of the word *promise* in 9:8-9. Paul's argument focuses again on a "remnant" of faith (9:27) as was predicted by the prophets. Though the majority of Israel falls under God's wrath against unrighteousness (9:30-32; cf. 1:18), a remnant exists by God's election (11:5). They find the riches of God's salvation in Jesus the Messiah (10:11-13), blessings that come to them by grace not by works (11:5-6).

The remnant of Israel has found God's blessings while the rest have been hardened, leading to the salvation of the Gentiles (11:7, 11-12). God has not rejected His people (11:2). The hardening of Israel is partial and temporary (11:25).

The figure of the olive tree (Rom. 11:16-24) speaks of "the gifts and the calling of God" (11:29), God's favor of blessing "for the sake of the fathers" (11:28). These blessings come to natural descendants of the patriarchs (natural branches in the illustration) by faith (as seen in the fact that unbelievers are "broken off for their unbelief" [11:20], yet they can be "grafted in" again by coming to faith [11:23]). Blessing also comes to the Gentiles in the tree (that is, in Abraham, or more specifically in his descendant, the Messiah). Not being natural descendants, they are "grafted in." But they also come into a permanent state of blessing only by faith (11:20).

Paul then looks to the salvation of "all Israel" at the coming of the Savior.[18] Messiah will fulfill the new covenant for Israel as a whole as predicted by the Old Testament prophets (11:26-27). It is important to note that the covenant to which the quotation in Romans 11:26-27 refers (Isa. 59:20-21) most definitely includes the full blessings of national salvation *including* inheritance in the land of promise. The very next verses in Isaiah predict the exaltation of Jerusalem as the capital of the eschatological kingdom (Isa. 60), the very passage which influenced John's vision in Revelation 21–22. The new covenant reaffirmed the same national hope expressed in the other covenants. And Paul declares "the gifts and the calling of God are *irrevocable*" (Rom. 11:29).

No claim is ever made by Paul that God has discarded the promises, reformulated, or resignified them. He is convinced that God will fulfill His word of promise in spite of the sinfulness that beckons His wrath. This will happen through Jesus the Messiah, the Christ. At His coming, the gift of righteousness which is manifest in a remnant now will be revealed in a nation that will emerge from the Day of the Lord, redeemed and purified to inherit the "irrevocable" blessings of covenant promise. "For . . . Christ has become a servant to the circumcision on behalf of the truth of God to confirm the promises given to the fathers" (15:8).

Paul's overriding concern however is to explain that the blessings envisioned eschatologically for the Gentiles ("blessed in Him") are presently inaugurated and being received by them through the Gospel (1:5; 15:9-19; 16:25-26). For him, it is not the future inheritance of Israel that is at question, but the truth of present Gentile blessing through faith in Christ.

## An Intermediate Millennial Kingdom

Premillennialism is the belief that a future messianic kingdom, 1,000 years in duration, will intervene between the return of Christ to earth and the everlasting eschatological kingdom. The millennial kingdom constitutes another stage in the revelation of the eschatological kingdom. It follows the revelation of the kingdom in the person of Christ and the revelation of the kingdom in the community of the church (that form of the kingdom which is present today). We have seen above that the hope of the church is fixed on the return of Christ, at which time inheritance into "the eternal kingdom of our Lord and Savior Jesus Christ" is expected. Nevertheless, in the Revelation given to John, there is a vision of a 1,000-year intermediate kingdom during which Christ rules on earth prior to and as a step toward the final fulfillment of the everlasting promises. In this brief chapter, we can only sketch the Bible's teaching on this issue. More extensive discussions can be found in a number of books and commentaries.

We have noted above that Revelation focuses upon the return of Christ. The theme of His coming is presented at the beginning and the end of the book; the letters to the seven churches are filled with this expectation along with the rewards and judgments that Christ will bring. The visions that make up the bulk of the writing find their climax in chapter 19, where the return of Christ is portrayed in vivid imagery.

At this point it is not necessary to argue whether Revelation should be interpreted in a preterist (past, i.e., first century) or futurist manner. Even if the book as a whole were a visionary depiction of the trials of the first-century church, this one event, the return of Christ, *which is the focus of the book,* was nevertheless a *future* hope. The book closes with appeals to Him to come. The coming has not yet taken place; it is future.

This means that the vision in Revelation 19 must be seen as a future hope. And there is no doubt that the judgment in 20:11-15, and the new earth and eschatological Zion in 21–22 are also future expectations. In the midst of these future events we find 20:1-10, the revelation of the millennial kingdom.

Revelation 20:1-3 depicts the devil being bound and imprisoned for a thousand years in order that he not deceive the nations. Revelation 20:4 describes Christian martyrs (who died during the Tribulation) being raised from the dead to reign with Christ. Revelation 20:5 states: "the rest of the dead did not come to life until the thousand years were completed." Verses 7-15 describe what happens at the end of the thousand years, when the devil is released. God and Christ respond in judgment, described in Day of the Lord imagery but also with everlasting finality.

The crucial verses are first 4-5a, and then 5b-15. In 4-5a a pattern is set up involving two resurrections divided by a thousand-year reign of Christ and saints who belong to Him. In his vision, John sees the souls of the dead who had been faithful to Christ during the Tribulation. It recalls the earlier visions of 6:9-11 and 7:9-14. These dead then "came to life and reigned with Christ for a thousand years." Verses 5b-6 rephrase the same point.

> This is the first resurrection. Blessed and holy is the one who has a part in the first resurrection; over these the second death has no power, but they will be priests of God and of Christ and will reign with Him for a thousand years.

Earlier in this chapter, we have noted the New Testament expectation that the resurrection of the dead will occur at the coming of Christ. When Christ extends resurrection life to those who have believed in Him, covenant promises receive advanced fulfillment and the kingdom enters a new phase of revelation. However, not all the subjects of the millennial kingdom share in resurrection, immortal life. At the end of the thousand years, the devil is released, and he deceives the nations into rebellion against Christ and His saints. Revelation 20:9 tells us that these rebels will be destroyed, revealing their mortality.

Furthermore, not all of the dead are resurrected during the millennial kingdom. Revelation 20:5a explains that "the rest of the dead did not come to life until the thousand years were completed." This is further elaborated in verses 12-15 when after the thousand years (v. 7), "the dead, the great and the small" are released from "the sea . . . death and Hades" (vv. 12-13, release from the intermediate state of the dead). The release of the dead from death is resurrection, the resurrection anticipated as "second" by verse 5b's identification of the premillennial resurrection as "first." At that time, the final judgment takes place (vv. 13-15) making possible the revelation of a new earth and the everlasting kingdom of an exclusively resurrected, immortal humanity (21:1-5).

The millennial kingdom, then, is a phase of the eschatological kingdom in which the returned, resurrected Christ, along with a company of resurrected saints, rules the nations of earth. It is a time in which mortality still conditions the lives of a segment of humanity, and many of the dead still await resurrection. Furthermore, while there are no doubt many blessings which stem from the personal reign of Christ (as would be expected from other passages predicting the blessings of His reign), the millennial kingdom harbors the possibility of rebellion and judgment, a possibility which becomes actual upon the release of the devil.

Revelation 20 is the only Scripture which *explicitly* predicts (or envisions) an *intermediate, millennial* kingdom. No other passage speaks explicitly or implicitly about a *millennial* kingdom, that is a kingdom lasting 1,000 years. An *intermediate* kingdom may be implied from Paul's delineation of the historical stages of resurrection in 1 Corinthians 15:20-28.

In verses 23-24, Paul marks off three stages of resurrection:

Christ the first fruits,
after that those who are Christ's at His coming,
then comes the end. . .

In this sequence, *the end* is a distinguishable stage of resurrection parallel to the resurrection of Christ Himself and then to the resurrection of those who belong to Him, who are raised at His return. The end is also described in verse 24 as the time "when He delivers up the kingdom" to God the Father. It is the culmination of an activity in which He abolishes "all rule and all authority and power." That activity is further explained in verses 25-28 as a *reign* during which all enemies are being subjected to Him. The last enemy to be subjugated is death. Death had been partially subjugated through the earlier stages of resurrection. But it is completely subjugated at the final resurrection, the third order posted in verse 24.

The reign of Christ which precedes the final and everlasting revelation of the eschatological kingdom covers whatever time elapses between the second and third stages of resurrection. That reign may in fact be extended back to the first stage, that of Christ's own resurrection, since we have seen that Paul repeatedly speaks of Christ's present reign using the language of Psalm 110:1 (which language is also used here in 1 Cor. 15:25). Paul does not indicate the amount of time which may elapse between the resurrection that will take place at Christ's coming and the final resurrection of all the dead. However, the intermediate nature of this period does parallel that intermediate, millennial kingdom of Revelation 20. It is a reign on earth (after Jesus Christ's coming) which includes resurrected believers but prior to the final resurrection. Furthermore, there exists some tensions during this reign—Christ is at work subjugating *enemies*—a condition which also parallels the conditions we saw in Revelation 20.

The description of the intermediate kingdom of Revelation 20, and possibly of 1 Corinthians 15, is related to a distinctive type of kingdom description in the Old Testament. On the one hand, the eschatological kingdom of God and of His Messiah is characterized by peace, righteousness, eternal blessing, and immortality. On the other hand, some passages describe the kingdom under conditions of human mortality (Isa. 65:17-25) and with a certain amount of tension between the King and the nations, a tension which is easily suppressed (Zech. 14:9, 16-21; Isa. 11:4; cf. Ps. 2). From an Old Testament standpoint, it is certainly possible that these conditions might be fulfilled in a historical phase of the kingdom prior to the final fulfillment which would pick up on the descriptions of everlasting peace and joy (as in Isa. 2:2-4; Micah 4:1-4; Isa. 60).

The possibility of an intermediate kingdom is quite strong in Isaiah 24–25, an oracle sometimes referred to as Isaiah's little apocalypse. Isaiah 24 is a typical prediction of the coming Day of the Lord, with many of the features that mark that event as divine judgment. Isaiah 25:6-9 envisions the everlasting eschatological kingdom of God. God reigns from Zion as King over all peoples. There is joyous feasting in His presence. But most importantly, God bestows immortality on redeemed humanity. Death is eliminated. Fellowship between God and humanity is realized in everlasting peace.

Between these two passages comes 24:21-23.

So it will happen in that day,
That the Lord will punish the host of heaven, on high,
And the kings of the earth, on earth.
And they will be gathered together
Like prisoners in the dungeon,
And will be confined in prison;

274

And after many days they will be punished.
Then the moon will be abashed and the sun ashamed,
For the Lord of Hosts will reign on Mount Zion and in
Jerusalem,
And His glory will be before His elders.

The period of "many days" intervening between the Day of
the Lord and the everlasting immortal kingdom is the intermediate kingdom. In fact, Revelation 20 can be understood as an
interpretation of this very passage in Isaiah. The Day of the
Lord in Isaiah 24 is given expanded treatment in Revelation
6–19. In Revelation 19, Christ returns to "punish . . . the kings
of the earth" (Isa. 24:21). (Following the pattern revealed in
Daniel, Revelation envisions the kings of the earth as consoli-
dating their authority in one ruler; Rev. 13; 17:12-13, 17.)
When Christ returns, He "punishes" the kings of earth who
oppose Him, and He seizes and casts the imperial ruler into the
lake of fire (Rev. 17:14; 19:17-21).

Christ also punishes "the host of heaven on high" (Isa.
24:21). In Revelation, the rebellious host of heaven are the
devil and his angels, who are cast down from heaven (12:7-9).
Isaiah's language of imprisonment in a dungeon for many days
(24:22) is applied in Revelation 20:1-3 to the devil: an angel
"threw him into the abyss, and shut it and sealed it over him,
so that he should not deceive the nations any longer, until the
thousand years were completed." Isaiah says that "after many
days they will be punished." John writes that after the thousand years, the devil will be "thrown into the lake of fire and
brimstone, where the beast and the false prophet are also; and
they will be tormented day and night forever and ever"
(20:10). Furthermore, "If anyone's name was not found written
in the book of life, he was thrown into the lake of fire" (20:15).

Following this punishment, the Prophet Isaiah writes that
"the moon will be abashed and the sun ashamed, for the Lord
of hosts will reign on Mount Zion and in Jerusalem" (24:23)
and he describes that reign in 25:6-9. John describes heaven
and earth making way for a new heaven and earth and the
eschatological Zion (Rev. 20:11; 21:1, 10) which shines brighter
than the sun or moon (21:23). The ideas, imagery, and even
some of the wording in Revelation 21:3-4 are drawn directly
from Isaiah 25:6-9.

And I heard a loud voice from the throne, saying, "Behold, the tabernacle of God is among men, and He shall dwell among them, and they shall be His people, and God Himself shall be among them, and He shall wipe away every tear from their eyes; and there shall no longer be any death; there shall no longer be any mourning, or crying, or pain: the first things have passed away" (Rev. 21:3-4).

And the Lord of hosts will prepare a lavish banquet for all peoples on this mountain. . . . And on this mountain He will swallow up the covering which is over all peoples, even the veil which is stretched over all nations. He will swallow up death for all time, and the Lord God will wipe tears away from all faces, and He will remove the reproach of His people from all the earth; for the Lord has spoken. And it will be said in that day, "Behold, this is our God for whom we have waited that He might save us. This is the Lord for whom we have waited; let us rejoice and be glad in His salvation" (Isa. 25:6-9).

In summary, Old Testament predictions of the eschatological kingdom gave two perspectives on the relationship between the eschatological King and His subjects: one in which tension and attempted rebellion were possible and another in which peace, joy, and righteousness rule. These perspectives are not entirely incompatible. It is at least possible that they would be fulfilled in successive stages which progressively reveal the kingdom, the final revelation coinciding with the descriptions of glory and immortality. A period between the Day of the Lord and the kingdom of immortality in Isaiah 24–25 appears to have been interpreted in Revelation 20 as just such a stage in the history of the kingdom. It is a form of the eschatological kingdom in which Christ is on earth, ruling over the nations, but one in which He is progressively subjugating all enemies to Himself. It is a time in which mortality still conditions a portion of humanity and some oppose His rule. This kingdom is revealed to be 1,000 years in duration. It is what traditionally has been called, the millennial kingdom.

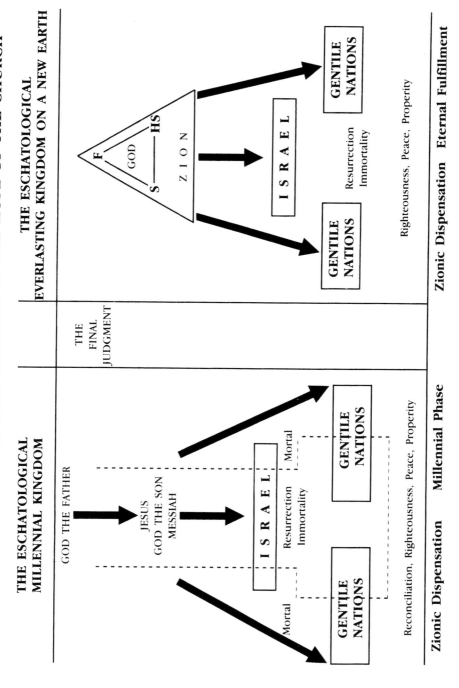

# THE FUTURE ESCHATOLOGICAL KINGDOM IN THE HOPE OF THE CHURCH

THE ESCHATOLOGICAL MILLENNIAL KINGDOM

THE ESCHATOLOGICAL EVERLASTING KINGDOM ON A NEW EARTH

GOD THE FATHER

JESUS GOD THE SON MESSIAH

I S R A E L

Resurrection Immortality

Mortal

Mortal

GENTILE NATIONS

GENTILE NATIONS

Reconciliation, Righteousness, Peace, Property

Zionic Dispensation    Millennial Phase

THE FINAL JUDGMENT

GOD

F

S — HS

Z I O N

I S R A E L

Resurrection Immortality

GENTILE NATIONS

GENTILE NATIONS

Righteousness, Peace, Property

Zionic Dispensation    Eternal Fulfillment

## Conclusion

In the patriarchal dispensation, God acted in a kingly manner in judgment and in blessing. He covenanted certain grants to the patriarchs similar in form to the grant covenants of ancient kings. Most important was the grant to Abraham to bless him and his descendants and in him to bless all peoples on earth.

The Mosaic covenant brought a new dispensation as God formed Abraham's descendants into a nation, God Himself taking the role as *their* King. His relationship to other peoples was mediated through this covenant with Israel. Provision was made for a human king subject to the Lord. A grant covenant was made with the house of David to be the royal house of Israel. A typology of kingship was cast in the reigns of David and Solomon, illuminating the ideal kingdom of God and His anointed Davidic king. In that ideal kingdom, the closest possible divine-human intimacy exists between God and the Davidic king. Also, the blessings of the covenants are realized for Abraham's descendants and for all peoples as the political hegemony of God's kingdom is extended by the activity of the Davidic king over other nations.

The sins of Israel, brought to a focus in continued idolatry, incurred divine judgment, both upon the nation and the house of David. The prophets who predicted this judgment also predicted an eschatological kingdom—a kingdom that would be established in the last days in conjunction with a new covenant in which God would indwell His people and write His law upon their hearts, a kingdom in which a Davidic Messiah would mediate blessings to all peoples and fulfill the divine plan for human dominion, a kingdom of immortal life and everlasting joy, a kingdom which would both fulfill and surpass the ideal typology of the Davidic and Solomonic kingdoms.

In a Day of the Lord, God brought destruction and death, personally and politically upon Israel. The rule of the Davidic house was interrupted, the people were exiled from the land of promise, Jerusalem was razed. During the Exile, however, working through a faithful remnant of Jews (in accordance with the Abrahamic covenant), God revealed His kingship to and through certain Babylonian, Median, and Persian kings. Again, a typology is set up for a kingdom of worldwide dominion, but also for judgment. The apocalyptic visions of Daniel foresee a time of great distress, persecution, and blasphemy under the rulership of a Gentile king. Divine judgment will destroy the sovereignty of that evil kingdom and establish the kingdom of the Son of Man and the saints of the Most High, which will be the everlasting kingdom of God. Postexilic prophets also speak of a coming Day of the Lord's judgment against oppressive Gentile powers and as a purifier of Israel leading to the revelation of God as King on the earth, suppressing rebellion and unrighteousness in some texts and bestowing the blessings of peace and joy on a redeemed people in others.

The New Testament Scriptures reveal the eschatological kingdom of God coming into existence through successive historical stages. This eschatological kingdom of God will be the fulfillment, through typology and prophecy, of the kingdom of God revealed in the old dispensation. It is the goal of the kingly actions of God in the patriarchal and Mosaic dispensations. It is the structure by which God's plan for humanity and the rest of creation and especially His relationship to both will be fulfilled.

The eschatological kingdom begins its appearance in the person of the eschatological King, Jesus, the Christ. He is a descendant of David anointed by the Holy Spirit, acting with power and authority to grant kingdom blessings. He is also God, the King, incarnate as a Davidite, uniting both kingships in one Person. [This appearance of God as Jesus brings a new revelation of God—a trinity of Persons as one divine reality.] Jesus Himself identifies His actions performed through the Holy Spirit as the kingdom of God. The kingdom is present because He is the eschatological king, and He is present on earth. The works of Jesus give dynamic glimpses of the kingdom: sins are forgiven, diseases are cured, disabilities are healed, demons are exorcised, and the dead are raised. He pacifies the wind and the sea and multiplies food by blessing it. He leads people into the knowledge of God and promises the new covenant blessing of righteousness by inner renewal through the Holy Spirit. He then gave His own life in a messianic priestly act to atone for human sin, and then rose from the dead, revealing in Himself the immortal, resurrected life which was predicted for the eschatological kingdom.

Jesus not only identified Himself and His actions as a presence of the eschatological kingdom, but He also proclaimed the future establishment of that kingdom consistent with the general pattern predicted by the prophets but with the new revelation that He Himself will come as Lord in the Day of the Lord and will reign as the King of the everlasting kingdom. He continually referred to Himself as the Son of Man who will come in apocalyptic glory in a time of trouble and judgment described through a synthesis of elements from Daniel's visions and Day of the Lord prophecies. But He also predicted that He would return to God the Father before that apocalyptic coming. In His parables, He explained that He would receive the kingdom at that time, that He would baptize His disciples by the Holy Spirit (the inauguration of new covenant blessing), that He would put "sons" or citizens of the kingdom (constituted as such by the Spirit) into the world where through proclamation of the Gospel they would grow in number, and that He would return with judgment upon evil and usher the heirs into the everlasting kingdom of God.

That phase of the eschatological kingdom of which Jesus spoke parabolically is revealed in Acts and other New Testament epistles as a new dispensation, established through inaugurated blessings of the new covenant based upon the sacrificial death of Jesus. This next phase of the eschatological kingdom coincides with the glorification of the Christ in heaven where He has been enthroned *as Messiah*. He has received authority over all rule and dominion on earth. In fact, all authority in heaven and on earth has been given to Him. But He waits upon the Father for the time of His return to earth when He will display that authority in the full pattern predicted for the eschatological kingdom (and reveal even greater aspects of that authority as well). In the meantime, He has already begun to act *institutionally* as King by granting to those who believe in Him the new covenant blessings of forgiveness of sins and the indwelling, renewing presence of the Holy Spirit (the baptism of the Holy Spirit of which He had spoken). These are in fact blessings of the eschatological kingdom (characteristics of the kingdom which is coming). They serve as a down payment, an earnest, on the future fulfillment of all new covenant blessings.

In this present phase of the kingdom, Jesus has drawn to Himself a remnant from Israel and from many Gentile nations. He has bestowed new covenant blessings on both Jewish and Gentile believers equally. The blessings are also given without gender or class distinction. The gift of new covenant blessings in this equal manner constitutes a new dispensation in God's relationship to humanity. It is also the first *institutional* appearance of the eschatological kingdom. Consistent with His messianic authority, Jesus is forming this remnant of Jews and Gentiles into a "temple," a "house" to be the dwelling place of God on the earth. As the previous appearance of the eschatological kingdom occurred when God became incarnate as Jesus, descendant of David, King of the kingdom, so the present form of the kingdom appears when the Spirit of God indwells Jews and Gentiles, citizens of the kingdom. They form a new society in which the peace and righteousness of the kingdom is to be manifested. Their identity, like their blessing, is found in Christ (consistent with the covenantal pattern of blessing "in Him"). They are the body of Christ, the church—in the universal sense of that term.

While the New Testament proclaims the relationship between Christ and the church (the messianic King and Jews and Gentiles who trust in Him) as a revelation of the eschatological kingdom, it also predicts the future coming of that kingdom in all its fullness. That coming will coincide with the coming of Jesus to earth judging sin, bestowing the full blessings of the covenants, and bringing the remnants of all nations (Israel and Gentiles) under His kingly hegemony. This is what Paul seems to refer to by "the dispensation of the fullness of times," when all things in heaven and on earth are recapitulated in Christ (Eph. 1:10). However, John received a Revelation that this will take place in two stages, the first lasting 1,000 years (the millennial kingdom) and the second the final fulfillment of the eschatological kingdom.

The millennial empire of the Messiah is the next phase of the eschatological kingdom after that phase which is now present— the community of the King, the church. And, as we have noted, its appearance marks a change of dispensation, from the ecclesial dispensation to the first stage of the final or Zionic dispensation. The change from the first to the second appearance of the eschatological kingdom was marked by the resurrection and glorification of the King. The change from the second to the third phases of the kingdom is marked by the resurrection and glorification of the church. However, mortality is still present for a significant segment of humanity. The resurrected

# THE DISPENSATIONS AND THE PROGRESS OF THE KINGDOM

| KINGLY ACTS OF GOD | THE KINGDOM OF GOD | | | THE ESCHATOLOGICAL KINGDOM OF GOD | | | | | |
|---|---|---|---|---|---|---|---|---|---|
| | Theocracy | Davidic Monarchy | A Day of the Lord | Gentile Sovereignty | Present in the Christ | Present in the Church (Christ Ascended) | A Day of the Lord | Present in the Millennial Empire (Christ Descended) | Final Judgment | Present in Everlasting Fullness |

| PATRIARCHAL DISPENSATION | MOSAIC DISPENSATION | ECCLESIAL DISPENSATION | ZIONIC DISPENSATION |
|---|---|---|---|

Christ and resurrected saints (cf. Dan. 7:14, 27; 12:2) will administer human life on the earth in its national and political dimensions. As Messiah of Israel, Jesus will fulfill for that nation the promises covenanted to her, and He will rule over all nations so that through Him all nations might be blessed. He will rule with "a rod of iron," imprisoning spiritual wickedness and subjugating all human authority to Himself. The spiritual blessings which were displayed in the previous dispensation in the life of the eschatological community, the church, will be extended in this stage of the kingdom through national and political dimensions of human life as well. The earthly blessings which were glimpsed in individual messianic works during the first advent will be extended around the world. At the end of this stage of the kingdom, evil itself will be destroyed in a display of Christ's judgment against satanic and human rebellion, and death along with sin will be eliminated.

When Christ has subjected all things to Himself and has destroyed sin and death, the eschatological kingdom of God in all its fullness will be manifest eternal and immortal on a renewed earth. This kingdom is the goal of redemption, the culmination of all previous revelations of God's kingdom. It is the rule of God the Father, God the Son incarnate as Messiah, Son of David, Son of Man, and God the Holy Spirit over the earth with all its inhabitants and over the heavens and all contained therein forever. This kingdom is *earthly*. The curse which came through sin will be replaced with the blessing of life and fruitfulness over the earth. Death, disease, and demonism will be eliminated and the City of God will be established on the earth. The kingdom is also *spiritual*, as redemption is extended in full in both individual and social aspects of human existence. It will be characterized by life eternal and immortal, by righteousness and justice. Wickedness will have been judged and removed. Grace, mercy, compassion, and forgiveness of sins will abide forever. The kingdom will be characterized by peace, holiness, godliness, by regeneration and the indwelling Holy Spirit, by knowledge of, worship of, and willing obedience to God, in joy, gladness, and blessing forever. The kingdom is also *national* and *political* in that it involves the establishment and administration of all nations through the Messiah of Israel, Jesus, Son of David. God will reign over the nations in glory, power, and majesty, blessed, honored and worshiped by all forever.

## Chapter Nine
# Theological and Ministerial Issues in Progressive Dispensationalism

The work of progressive dispensationalism up to this point has primarily been at the level of biblical theology, exegesis, and exposition. These questions have been paramount: how does the New Testament interpret the covenants and the prophecies regarding the Messiah and the eschatological kingdom? What is the church, and how is it related to the plan of God revealed in Old Testament history, in the coming of the Messiah, and in biblical prophecy? How do the successive dispensations in this history of redemption relate to one another and to the overall plan of God? This is how it should be. Progressive dispensationalism belongs to an evangelical tradition which places its primary concern on understanding the Scripture. For it is the Scripture which has absolute claim on our faith and practice.

We do not pretend to have solved all interpretive problems in our efforts to understand the Scripture. The work of biblical interpretation is ongoing, and we must always be prepared to benefit from it. However, a direction seems clear from the studies undertaken so far, such that it is possible to outline a general position on the questions raised above. This was done briefly in the first chapter of this book and in the last chapter of

*Dispensationalism, Israel and the Church: The Search for Definition.* The exegetical studies in that earlier work and the exposition offered in this book provide the details which undergird and support this general interpretative position.

Much more work remains, however, for bringing the interpretations of progressive dispensationalism into broader discussions of theology and practice of ministry. In this chapter, we would like to set out some suggestions as to how this might be done. We will not attempt to do the entire work of systematic theology nor comment on all theological topics from a progressive dispensational point of view. Rather we will confine our comments to a couple of areas raising questions and suggestions which we think would be fruitful for further exploration. One of those areas has to do with the church in relationship to the kingdom. A theology of the church leads in turn to a theology of ministry, and it is in this connection that we will make suggestions regarding some aspects of ministry which are presently much discussed in evangelicalism.

These suggestions are offered with the hope that dispensationalists and other evangelical theologians might enter into collaboration with us here, developing what might be a worthwhile contribution and correcting where necessary for the benefit of us all.

## Church and Ministry

We have seen that progressive dispensationalism views the church as a phase of the eschatological kingdom. The church is a new manifestation of grace in that it is an assembled remnant from all nations, blessed by Jesus, the Messiah, with the new covenant blessing of the Holy Spirit. The church is a work of the Messiah Himself. He is its Head, Lord, and King. The church acknowledges Him as such in faith. The church is the Messiah's people(s), His special realm. The church extends into all nations across the earth, for such is the extent of the Messiah's realm. The church is a part of Messiah's future kingdom, for when He makes up that kingdom, all who belong to the church will be included along with Jews and Gentiles from the past and future who have their faith and hope fixed in the Redeemer. But the church in its dispensation differs from Old Testament saints in their dispensations because the church is a

285

creation of *the Messiah* (the Redeemer now incarnate as Messiah). The church thus belongs to *the Messiah's realm,* which makes it part of the eschatological kingdom.

The church differs from the future phase of the kingdom in that the Messiah is presently "away" (even though He is with us always, He nevertheless is bodily present with the Father). The church waits for Him to return. Consequently the church is a constituency of the future kingdom, present on earth before that kingdom comes in all its fullness at the return of Messiah. The church also differs from the future kingdom in that it is only a part of that kingdom, whereas the future kingdom will include all the redeemed of all dispensations through the resurrection of the dead.

The church differs from the future kingdom in that the kingdom blessing which it has received, namely the new covenant blessing of the indwelling Holy Spirit, has been given to it only in inaugural form. The blessing will be given in full only at the return of the Messiah, at which time sanctification will be complete in our experience extending even unto the resurrection and immortal life.

With these differences in mind, we say that the church is an inaugurated form of the future kingdom of God.

Now, the church's continuity with and difference from the future kingdom helps to define its ministry in this dispensation. We will not speak here of the church's ministry of calling individuals to faith in Christ and discipling them in their personal walk with the Lord—leading them to a worshiping, serving, and witnessing life. These aspects of ministry are well known to many. Earlier dispensationalists stressed the personal, individual aspect of Christianity exclusively. Their argument that one can only be born again personally, by personal faith in Christ, not by the actions of others apart from personal faith is sound, and practically all evangelicals would agree with this. There are many aspects of ministry built around this truth, but we will not explore them here.

Rather, we will explore the other aspects of ministry that flow from or are highlighted by the fact that the church is a manifestation of the future kingdom in a special form in this dispensation. These relate to *the social ministry of the church*.

**The Internal Social Ministry of the Church.** The kingdom of God has to do with righteousness, justice, and peace in the relations of peoples to and with one another. The church is a manifestation of the eschatological kingdom because it is an assembly of peoples whom the Messiah, acting with royal authority, has put into relationship with one another, bound by the inaugurated blessings of peace, righteousness, and justice through the Holy Spirit. These blessings are experienced in inaugurated form. The church on this side of glory still struggles with the problems of sin: unrighteousness, discord, and injustice. But the church is called to a life of holiness, to grow in grace walking by the Spirit.

Just as revised dispensationalists began to explore the community nature of the church in body life, it seems that progressive dispensationalists need to explore the meaning of holiness in the social life of the church. This requires recognizing that the church is a society. Its structural relationships can be analyzed sociologically. The plural, communal nature of the church constitutes the church's social reality. The issue here is that Christ intends to redeem humankind *socially* as well as individually. *The social redemption of humanity begins in the church.* The righteous society of peoples prophesied under the Messiah of Israel has begun to appear. It is what we call the body of the Messiah, Jews and all kinds of Gentiles united together by Messiah's gift of the Holy Spirit. It is the organism which He fills and which manifests His presence on earth in His physical absence—the church.

Pursuing holiness socially in the community of the Messiah means the pursuit of justice, righteousness, and peace in the social structures of the church as an extension of personal and interpersonal holiness. Progressive dispensationalists need to face the issue of structural sin. And it needs to be faced first of all in the church. How can holiness be manifested in the political structures of the body of Christ? What about the governmental, ruling structures of the church? Classical dispensationalism offered a critique of the way the power structure of ordination was used to inhibit ministry by the non-ordained who were yet gifted by the Spirit. What about the power structures in evangelical churches and parachurch ministries today? What about the seemingly routine matters of employment in Christian ministry? What standards govern the distribution of funds and determine salaries? Are our ministries oriented to meet the social needs of brothers and sisters in Christ?

Because the body of Christ is one, transcending local church divisions, the exploration of the internal social ministry of the church must go beyond local church walls. Dispensationalists have recognized the relationship that exists between believers in Christ which transcends their local church affiliations. However, progressive dispensationalists should especially recognize the relationship that exists between churches, fellowships, and ministries, not just individuals. We are not talking here about administrative ecumenicity, that fear which evangelicals have about the ecumenical movement. Rather, we are talking about the spiritual ecumenicity shared not just by individual believers, but by worshiping communities who gather in the name of Jesus Christ. This is what we see in Paul's collection from the churches among the Gentiles for the church in Jerusalem. This effort was an example of churches caring for another church because it was a church meeting in the name of Jesus Christ.

How can churches meet the social needs of other churches in Christ? Is it possible that a social ministry could grow up between churches?

***The External Social and Political Ministry of the Church.*** Many evangelical proposals regarding the social ministry of the church focus exclusively on the external ministry of the church, or individual Christians, to the social needs of the worldly society. Is this not another form of highly individualized Christianity? While this may seem a strange accusation, consider what conversion means in some of these scenarios. Ministry to the needs of society is a means of attracting individuals to the Gospel. Upon conversion, they are quickly put to work calling other individuals to the Gospel through gifts toward social needs. But they do not experience social redemption with other believers in Christ. What is the meaning of their social work? Another form of evangelicalism contributes toward building better social structures in the larger society along with the Gospel message of individual salvation. Both seem to ignore the calling of the church to be the redeemed society that only it can be.

Progressive dispensationalists would do well to explore the internal social holiness of the church as a form of witness to the external society. In other words, if we as the community of Christ worked on creating our community as a model of social justice and peace, then we really would have some suggestions to make for social reform in our cities and nations. And we could do it as Gospel because the message, the suggestions, even the external social work would be based in a call to Christ *in whom* individual and social conversion go hand in hand.

What would it mean, for example, if a church which was primarily white collar and strong financially, proceeded to establish a ministry to a church primarily blue collar and suffering unemployment, just because they were fellow believers in Christ? What if one church with a dominant ethnic group ministered to a church populated by another ethnic group, helping to create opportunities for those brothers and sisters in Christ which are just and fair, which convert the racial injustices plaguing a world that does not know Christ—doing so just because they together name the name of Christ and are called to manifest, even in an inaugural way, the righteousness of the kingdom of God? What if they proceeded to minister to each other in this way specifically for the purpose of exploring and revealing social holiness?

If the church becomes the workshop in which kingdom righteousness is pursued in the name of Christ, then social ministry externally becomes a call to Christ.

The political work of the church goes hand in hand with this. Over the past two millennia, the church has existed under a number of different national polities. Today, much of the church is found in participatory political structures, democracies of varying sorts. Recognizing that God superintends the national polities of humanity, and that existing political structures call for citizen participation, the church should exercise its responsibility along with worldly citizens in the legislation, execution, and adjudication of law. But from what base does the church speak to national justice and peace? From a progressive dispensational perspective, that base should be the future eschatological kingdom, which is known through direct prophecy, through the witness of past dispensations (including a manifestation of righteousness in the theocracy of Israel), and the manifestation of kingdom righteousness in the life of the church itself. The church must participate from a revelational base in which it seeks justice within its own society and testifies from that base in its work for justice in the society at large.

Recognizing the dispensational connection with the coming

kingdom gives the church a basis for an evangelistic participation in the political and social affairs of this world. Recognizing the dispensational difference between our present situation and that which will be established only at the coming of Christ keeps that activity *evangelistic*. The Head of the church, the King of all nations is yet to come in judgment. The church does not bear the sword over unbelief. That has been the error of some experiments of church and state in the past, and it springs from a misunderstanding of the dispensation in which we live. There is to be no execution of law against unbelief until the coming of Christ Himself. The church must call unbelievers to the good news of Christ, never legislate it. But justice in human relations is the proper concern of government. The church should work for just laws as a testimony to the justice which she pursues within herself under the power of her present and future Lord.

We must always recognize that we carry our treasure in earthen vessels (2 Cor. 4:7). Even with all the revelation we have in Scripture and with the work of the Holy Spirit in the church, there is much we still do not know about the kingdom. We see in a glass darkly, as Paul said (1 Cor. 13:12). Our revelation is partial, we are tempted to sin (injustice and discord), and we are prone to mistakes in knowledge and judgment. Christians cannot claim that anything that comes to their minds on political or social matters is necessarily sanctified, right, or even practical. We have no justification for arrogance.

But perhaps the key to humbly accepting our role in broader society lies in the fact that we are called first to conversion in ourselves, not just individually but socially and politically. The revelation we have received and the work of the Spirit in us is directed first of all *to us*. The church is the test community for social and political righteousness. If we don't or can't pursue it here, we really have nothing to say there. If we seek it among ourselves, even though we fall short, we have something to say, and our imperfections help to keep us humble.

***The Multicultural Body of Christ.*** When we speak of the church as a society, we must recognize that the singular form of that word, society, does not imply a homogeneous culture. The society of the church is actually a plurality of many societies small and great, at one level of which we find the differences of ethnicity and shared cultures. Understanding the church as a present form of the future eschatological kingdom should lead us to see that this multicultural phenomenon is precisely what God intends. The future kingdom will encompass all nations. The church today is a Spirit-united communion of Jews and all kinds of Gentiles.

This means that progressive dispensationalists should fully participate in evangelical discussions of ministry and culture. We face the challenges of multicultural ministries, unicultural ministries called to responsibilities in a multicultural world, and cross-cultural ministries. These are not secondary concerns but rooted in the very reality of the body of Christ.

Progressive dispensationalists should especially be concerned to bring out and encourage the multicultural reality of the body of Christ, not see it as a detriment, or something to be eliminated in pursuit of an idealized human homogeneity (which is not really human). We recognize the Spirit is given (and intended to be given) across ethnic and cultural boundaries. Just as Jewish Christians came to accept Gentile Christians, so we face the challenge of seeing and encouraging Christianity in multicultural expression. We have to guard against cultural domination and repression in the name of Christ. Such is really opposed to Christ, for Christ is destined to rule (and does now rule) a multicultural humanity. But multicultural Christianity is not syncretism. It is conversion of multicultural paganism into multicultural Christianity. The questions, concerns, and challenges are real, just as real as in the New Testament itself. But progressive dispensationalism must face these issues directly.

## Theology and History

Jesus Christ is presently in heaven, seated at the right hand of God until the time set by the Father for His return. When He returns He will reveal the union of divine and human rule over the earth and all its inhabitants. Presently, all authority in heaven and on earth has been given to Him (Matt. 28:18). He upholds all things by His word of power (Heb. 1:3) and in Him all things hold together (Col. 1:17). He is the head of all rule and authority. When He comes, His administration of human affairs will be evident to all. But how do we relate His authority over all things now and the course of present historical events?

Dispensationalism observes a distinction between Christ's relationship to the nations now and His relationship to them at His coming. The prophecies of Christ ruling over the nations are yet to find fulfillment. The New Testament expected Christ to come and to rule the nations in a direct manner, one which is not now being revealed. Christ Himself spoke of the "restoration of the kingdom" to Israel as a matter of time, with Peter interpreting these remarks as the difference between Christ ascended and Christ descended. And yet He exercises an authority over all things now.

Progressive dispensationalism would not view Christ's relationship to the nations now as the fulfillment of His political inheritance, yet He relates to the nations now with a view toward His future rule over them. Progressive dispensationalism would see Christ's major activity in the world today as the formation of a remnant of people from all the nations who are His own to manifest in an inaugural way the righteousness that He will give to all peoples in that future kingdom. They are an evangelistic community, testifying to the salvific power of Jesus, which is being revealed personally and communally (socially) in the church.

The relationship of Christ to the nations now is primarily with a view to this purpose of forming His own community. But what does this mean for understanding the course and events of history in this dispensation? Can we read political and social developments in relationship to the activity of Jesus, King of Kings? Does His authority, power, and position explain political and national history today?

***Prophecy and Current Events.*** Classical and revised dispensationalists have shared with historicist premillennialism a belief that apocalyptic visions and descriptions in the Old and New Testaments offer a detailed blueprint of interconnecting events, partially codified, which specifically describe the setting of Christ's return. Once decodified, that portion of history, the Tribulation, can be known in amazingly concrete terms. Dispensationalists and historicists differed with each other only on the point of whether Tribulation events were presently transpiring. The doctrine of a pretribulational Rapture allowed dispensationalists to keep the Tribulation entirely in the future and thus eliminate the embarrassment of repeated failure in the attempt to relate current events to prophecy.

The popular pressure of historicist interpretation was ever present in the formation of American dispensationalism. Historicists participated side by side with futurists in the Bible and prophecy conferences of the last century. A.J. Gordon, for example, a noted historicist, exercised a great influence on the shape and tenor of premillennialism in this country, even on developing dispensationalism. An evangelical public clamored for a religious explanation of political, military, and religious upheavals in the early twentieth century. Dispensationalists responded with their own answer to historicism. While one could not read the times as the actual transpiring of Tribulation history, one could observe *the formation* of features of Tribulation history prior to that history's actual commencement. They agreed with historicists that a Bible interpreter can identify Tribulation nations, persons, and movements with specificity if apocalyptic codes were properly understood. But because they claimed to be able to identify these events *as they were forming, before the Tribulation itself would actually commence,* they effectively converted Bible interpretation into a form of prophecy itself.

Classical and revised dispensationalists differed by degrees in the specificity by which they identified current events with a forming Tribulation scenario. They also seemed to be able to flex and bend with changes in history so that earlier identifications of Tribulation-prone powers and military movements could be reformulated according to what seemed more or less likely with passing time.[1]

While, as we have noted, biblical apocalyptic and prophecy remain an important feature of dispensational theology, present-day developments in historical and literary interpretation call these historicist features of earlier dispensationalism into question. Up to this point, dispensationalists have not actively pursued the study of apocalyptic as a literary genre. Furthermore, much of biblical apocalyptic has been read apart from considerations of its historical context. (Reading prophecy and apocalyptic in light of its historical context does not preclude a future referent.) Dispensationalists, like historicists, have tended to read it directly in light of their own historical contexts. The very fact that these modern contexts have been changing, producing corresponding changes in the dispensational reading of prophecy, should give one pause.

As dispensationalists begin to study the literary features of prophecy and apocalyptic, they need take account of the way literary descriptions are taken up into a recurring pattern of prophecy and fulfillment within biblical history itself. This includes, for example, the literary interconnection of descriptive words and themes in the two Days of the Lord in Joel, and the recurring use of the language of earlier prophets by latter prophets, and even by the New Testament (by Jesus and His apostles), to describe different historical events (the Assyrian conquest of Israel, the Babylonian conquest of Judah, the Roman destruction of Jerusalem, a "day of the Lord" yet to come). The reemployment of literary descriptions in latter prophecy and apocalyptic calls into question the assumption that this language gives *one concrete historical scenario* in partially codified form.

To be sure, progressive dispensationalists believe that there will be a future Tribulation forming the setting of the return of Jesus. The actual events that make up that time in history will follow the general pattern outlined in Scripture (the same pattern which has been applied by Scripture itself to earlier events). However, progressive dispensationalists would question the claim of any Bible interpreter to have identified specific current events as that future tribulational fulfillment of the historically repetitive Day of the Lord descriptions or the mysterious visions of biblical apocalyptic. One should observe the fact that in biblical history, prophetic fulfillment has always been identified and proclaimed *by prophetic authority*. It takes prophetic authority or the actual appearance of Jesus Christ Himself to identify any particular pattern of trouble and conflict in the world as *the Tribulation*. One cannot by a claim of "scientific" interpretation divine that kind of authority for oneself today.

Dispensationalists must protect themselves and their churches from speculations and sensationalism which do not build up the body of Christ, but lead to delusion, resentment, and faithlessness when would-be prophecies under the guise of interpretation fail.

***Theology and the Hope of Israel.*** The case of Israel and the Jewish people is a special aspect of our overall question about the relationship of Scripture to contemporary history. The continued preservation of the Jewish race is surely in keeping with God's promises and prophecies regarding the existence of the people and the salvation of a remnant at the coming of Messiah. The remarkable events of the last two centuries in which Jews have been gradually returning to Palestine is certainly consistent with the fact that the Son of David is Lord of History. We have seen in our times the reestablishment of a Jewish state and its preservation through very difficult circumstances.

But we also note that the primary work of the Son of David, who is also the God of Israel incarnate, over these past two millennia has been the cultivation of a remnant from all peoples *who trust in Him.* Such activity is directly in keeping with the prophecies that He will rule over all peoples, that Gentiles as well as Jews will put their trust in Him. Now we need to note that among this redeemed of the nations, He has maintained a remnant of Jews who trust in Him. This is true of the present time, as we have a number of messianic communities, assemblies of Jews who have placed their faith in the Son of David anticipating His return.

We need to note that Jewish believers in the Messiah are the believing remnant of Israel. They are growing in numbers, which is entirely consistent with the lordship of Messiah in this dispensation. They, along with the remnant of the Gentiles, are to manifest the righteousness of Messiah. They are to be a testimony of righteousness to all the nations including Israel.

What attitude should the church, the messianic international and multicultural community, take toward the present state of Israel? On the one hand, the Lord has instructed the church, His assembly of all the nations to pray for governing authorities. This means that the church, messianic communities, and churches predominately Gentile should pray for the state of Israel as well as for other nations of the world today.

The church is supposed to obey laws laid down by governing authorities. It has a mandate to testify to the lordship and messiahship of Jesus which may bring it into conflict with laws of some states. In that case, it must be prepared to suffer the penalties of those authorities as was the case of early Jewish Christians who were persecuted by unbelieving Jewish authorities, as was the case of Gentile Christians persecuted by local and imperial authorities, and as continues in many cases around the world down to present times.

The church, the international messianic community, is supposed to be a testimony to and revelation of righteousness and peace between peoples, especially between Jews and Gentiles. Now in a community of nations which holds to forms of participatory government, the church has a tremendous opportunity to testify to peace and righteousness. The church must oppose ethnic hatred whether personal or political. Speaking on the political and governmental level, the church must oppose ethnic hostility to Jews on the part of Gentile governments. It must oppose ethnic hostility against one particular Gentile people on the part of another Gentile government. It must also oppose hostility by the government of Israel against a particular Gentile people. Instead, the church is to model in itself relationships of peace and reconciliation.

The complicity of Christianity in the hostility of some Gentile powers toward Jews over the past two millennia is one of the clearest failures of the church in this dispensation, ranking right along with factional division, persecution, and warfare between groups that name the name of Christ. Dispensationalism began as a protest movement against the identification of the modern state with the church (specifically the case of the early nineteenth century Church of England). It sought the peaceful gathering of all believers in Christ crossing over denominational divisions. Thus it sought for and promoted reconciliation of all parties (all Protestant evangelical parties, that is) in Christ. It also acknowledged a future for ethnic, national Israel (although it did so apart from the blessings of the church). As such, dispensationalism has helped to bring about a favorable attitude toward Jews and the Zionist movement since the last century.

However, in their enthusiasm for the political resurrection of Israel, some dispensationalists seem to have lost sight of the particular activity of the Son of David in this dispensation—which is bringing about reconciliation and peace between peoples. Some have publicly advocated carte blanche support for any policy enacted by the state of Israel.[2] But if political policies uphold injustice, how can Christians support it? How can Jewish or Gentile Christians today support Israeli injustices when Jewish prophets in the Old Testament condemned the authorities in Jerusalem for similar injustices, often to the prophets' own peril? There were no greater supporters of the Jewish people and the future of Israel under God than Moses, Samuel, Amos, Elijah, Habbakuk, Isaiah, and Jeremiah. And yet not a one of them confused their commitment and desire for the blessing of Israel with support for or toleration of injustice!

Please notice that these same prophets condemned the Gentile nations at the same time for the same or worse injustices. The church in this dispensation needs to provide a testimony to righteousness which parallels that of the Old Testament saints.

On the basis of biblical prophecy, we expect a time when many Jews turn to the Son of David as a remnant of Jews have done through the centuries. The prophecies regarding the future glory of Israel will find their fulfillment in this remnant of faith constituted as the holy nation under the reign of Messiah, Son of David. The progressive regathering of Jews to Palestine in modern times and their political reconstitution is certainly consistent with this expectation, but it is not yet the fulfillment of the prophesied kingdom of glory. That kingdom comes with the Messiah's return and is anticipated by His present blessings on Jews and Gentiles who trust in Him.

### Christology

Classical dispensationalism sought to organize the Scripture around a soteriological dualism: a heavenly redemption yielding a heavenly people and an earthly redemption yielding an earthly people. Although they united the classical dualism into a common salvation (either in "heaven" or on "the new earth"), revised dispensationalists remained strikingly anthropocentric in their reading of Scripture and their organization of theology. Progressive dispensationalism sees Christ as the key to understanding the Scripture and the proper focus for theological thinking.

Of course, other theologies, even earlier forms of dispensationalism might also say that Christ is the key to the Scriptures. Progressive dispensationalists, however, seek to understand the New Testament presentation of Christ in a historical-literary fashion. What emerges is a picture of the Christ in a way that is complementary to the historical promises of the biblical covenants and in keeping with the progressive *revelation* of the depth and extent of redemption. This is what leads us to a holistic redemption—one which covers all aspects of human life.

Following the traditional belief in the unity of Christ's Person and the integrity of divine and human natures (because we believe this interpretation to be confirmed by the church's repetitive reading of Scripture), we nevertheless seek to understand the revelation of His deity and the meaning of His humanity in a historical manner. He must be understood in the light of a history of redemption revealed in the Old Testament and carried forward in the New. Our study of the covenants and the kingdom confirms this. In other words, He is that Messiah, that anointed King of the eschaton, who will fulfill the covenant promises.

As God, He must also be interpreted in light of a history of redemption, as God has been revealed in the Old Testament. The New Testament carries this understanding of God forward, as we have also seen in the previous chapters. This means that He is that God who has made the covenant promises, who is expected to come in the eschatological age and rule the earth and all its peoples—taking away their guilt and bringing them into close and everlasting communion with Himself, blessing them with life, as He intended for them to live, forever.

In Jesus Christ, divine and human rule come together in one Person. This is the revelation of ultimate reconciliation. The tension between Davidic and divine rulership is eliminated in the unity of the person and action of Christ. Thus the Incarnation is crucial to guaranteeing the salvation of human beings, for at least this human being has an everlasting, eternal human life. His atonement is crucial for bringing forgiveness and justification to all. His resurrection from the dead reveals human immortality as well as divine power.

Most of this is familiar theologically, however, theology has tended to treat Christ's humanity generically. This can be seen, for example, in the traditional Christological analysis of His *human nature*. Practically, this has meant the "Gentilization" of Christ. For His Jewishness, and specifically that role of the Jewish Son of David, is lost in this typical analysis. What is missing is serious reflection on that other Christological principle of *inhominization*, which states that Christ does not lack human personality (having bare human nature but no real human identity). However, in order to guard against Nestorianism (the heresy that Jesus Christ is actually two persons, one divine and one human), orthodox Christology affirmed that the Christ has real human personality *in* the person of the Eternal Son of God, Second Person of the Trinity. The point here, however, is that orthodoxy affirms that the Christ is truly God and truly man. But what man? Generic man?

We would argue that in Scripture, He is *that man* predicted by the covenants and the prophecies, a man of destiny outlined in those covenant promises and prophecies. This destiny should be understood historically and revelationally through the New Testament. In other words, He is the person the Old Testament expected Him to be. But He is more, seen quite pointedly in the revelation of Him as *God.* But this is not mere ontological deity. This is the God who not only is eternal and ultimate power, ultimate life and death to us, but the God who said He would come and commune with us in an everlasting kingdom. This *extra* which the New Testament reveals in Christ does not eliminate or eradicate the Christ that was expected. It increases His portrait and role. An increase which maintains what was there before while adding to it. Traditional theology has struggled with the temptation to let the extra in Christ eliminate that which was expected. But this is the path to doce-tism (the heresy that Christ only appeared as a man). For it is precisely in the biblical expectation of Christ, the Son of David, ruler of all nations, that His humanity is to be found. He is *that man*, the man of the prophecies, the Son of David-Son of God (in the covenantal sense of Son of God—i.e., the King) who will rule the nations of the world.

Since in Old Testament theology, the Son of David is expect-ed to be that Son of Man (Ps. 8), that is that Man, in whom the image of God for man is ultimately realized, consequently, we see in Jesus Christ the fulfillment of human life and dominion in God's creation. Connected to Him is the future of the human race. But it is a human race in its concrete plurality. This is what we see in the prophecies that Christ would rule all na-tions on the earth. It is a reconciliation, not only of humanity with God, but humanity with itself in all its multiplicity. It is the reconciliation of the Son of David with other Jews and with Gentiles, leading to the reconciliation of these peoples with one another.

Consequently, we see Christ concretely, not abstractly or generically. We see Him concretely as the God of Israel and all the nations, incarnate in Jesus Son of David. This is the God who has revealed His intent to dwell *in and with* humanity. The *indwelling* is first revealed in Christ Himself and extended to us in this dispensation—Jews and Gentiles who trust in Him, in an inaugural, depository way, looking forward to the full revelation of God in us in the next dispensation (our glorification).[3] The dwelling with humanity confirms the collective, corporate aspects of human life, its real national, political, and social features. God intends to commune with a corporate humanity (that is why He commanded humans to fill the earth, leading not only to individual differentiation but collective differentiation in families, tribes, and nations). God revealed in Christ is God come to commune with us in this manner. Jesus Christ is God incarnate as Son of David, the political ruler of redeemed humanity in all its aspects, both individual and national.

Because the Scripture reveals Jesus to be this God and Man, we cannot devise for ourselves any other relation to Him than that which He Himself has revealed for all peoples.

Being truly human, and being the specific man that He is, His relationship with other human beings is historical, that is, He is a man who experiences history in relationship to the earth and humanity on it. He did this before His death. His resurrection from the dead confirmed for Him a future relationship which He Himself spoke of in political as well as spiritually communal terms. When we relate to Him today we are relating to that Son of David who is immortal, who has a *destiny,* who is coming here to rule the nations. All His present work should be interpreted in this light. He is reconciling a people to Himself—Jews and Gentiles, who will be that eschatological humanity of the prophecies. The character and quality of His work among Jews and Gentiles today no more separates those Jews and Gentiles from the promises of worldwide dominion than it does Him who is doing the work. Scripture reveals this work to be in line with His overall intention to come back here, renew the Creation, and commune with the redeemed forever—God dwelling with and in humanity whom He has created.

Christ then is the revelation of the plan and purpose of God—Christ in His concreteness as interpreted historically and in the literary patterns of Scripture. He is the key to the dispensations. The mystery of this dispensation is due to His and the Father's determination as a freely chosen stage or path toward the fulfillment of divine intention. He gives the dispensations their unity—a unity in historical development, not a static transcendental ahistorical unity—and He gives the redeemed their identity as the people(s) of God.

# Notes

## Chapter 1: The Extent and Varieties of Dispensationalism

1. Some dispensational views have become very common in evangelicalism. Not all who teach various dispensational views call themselves dispensationalists. Furthermore, as will be seen in this chapter, not all who are called dispensationalists agree in every detail or even on some "well-known" dispensational interpretations.

2. See chapter 4.

3. The dispensations themselves are discussed in Scripture. Consequently, interpreting a text in light of its dispensation is another example of interpreting Scripture in light of Scripture, or interpreting a Scripture passage in light of the broader interpretation of Scripture. Interpretation of the dispensations and of individual texts and passages is improvable in the ongoing study of Scripture. This leads to both the development of dispensationalism as well as a better understanding of individual portions of Scripture.

4. Such as Lindsay's speculations that Christ would come within a generation (40 years?) of 1948, and that the 1980s would probably be the last decade of history. More careful dispensational theologians such as John Walvoord and Charles Ryrie pointedly deny that one can predict the coming of Christ by current events.

5. There is some variety on the exact length of the Tribulation. This is partly dependant on how the term *Tribulation* is used with respect to Daniel's "seventieth week" in Daniel 9:27. Following Jesus' remark in Matthew 24:21, some dispensationalists have used *Tribulation* to refer to the second half of Daniel's seven year period, or a period of three and one half years.

6. Various dispensational institutions have produced doctrinal statements which vary in their emphases, some reflecting earlier dispensational interpretations more explicitly than others.

7. There are critics of dispensationalism today who fail to grasp this point with the result that their criticisms often apply only to a form (usually past) of the dispensational tradition, missing where most dispensationalists are today.

8. Robert L. Saucy, *The Case for Progressive Dispensationalism* (Grand Rapids: Zondervan, 1993) [unfortunately not available at the time of this writing]; and Craig A. Blaising and Darrell L. Bock, eds., *Dispensationalism, Israel and the Church: The Search for Definition* (Grand Rapids: Zondervan, 1992). For a survey of some developments in dispensationalism from the classical period to the early 1980s and the problems of defining the term dispensationalism, see Craig A. Blaising, "Doctrinal Development in Orthodoxy," and "Development of Dispensationalism by Contemporary Dispensationalists," *Bibliotheca Sacra* 145 (1988): 133–40, 254–80; and "Dispensationalism: The Search for Definition" in *Dispensationalism, Israel and the Church*. By the early 1980s several articles had raised questions about Charles Ryrie's proposal regarding the *sine qua non* of dispensationalism (composed of three elements: the distinction between Israel and the church, consistently literal hermeneutics, and the doxological unity of the dispensations; Charles Ryrie, *Dispensationalism Today* [Chicago: Moody, 1965], 43–47). By focusing on the central feature of that proposal, Israel and the church, the 1992 work, *Dispensationalism, Israel and the Church*, revealed that dispensationalism was currently undergoing an important revision at the level of what it had previously considered *essential* to the system. This revision was shown to be based broadly in Scripture speaking to the *relationship* as well as distinction between Israel and the church. The final chapter of that book proposes a broader basis for defining the dispensational tradition and gives an overview of progressive dispensationalism. It should be read in conjunction with the present work. The reader should note, however, that some different labels are used to periodize the history of dispensationalism. Those labels were chosen with respect

to how dispensationalists of the different periods might define dispensationalism (since the issue in that book was the *definition* of dispensationalism). The labels in the present book are better suited as general designations for the different phases of the dispensational tradition. Consequently, one should note that classical dispensationalism in this book covers the categories: Brethrenism, Niagara premillennialism, and Scofieldism in the former work. Revised dispensationalism in this work refers to essentialist dispensationalism in the former.

9. This distinction led to a spirit of separatism on the part of the Exclusive Brethren toward other forms of organized Christianity. In American dispensationalism, the distinction helped support the separatism of fundamentalism. But as in Brethrenism, it could easily be invoked for other degrees of separation. Consequently, this interpretation can be easily employed against the ecumenical ideal of early dispensationalism.

10. For a list of the dispensations taught in the Scofield Reference Bible, see p. 119.

11. Classical dispensationalism did believe that the Spirit would be given to earthly people in the Millennium and the eternal state; nevertheless, the gift of the Spirit to earthly people was greatly distinguished from that given to heavenly people.

12. Lewis Sperry Chafer, *Systematic Theology*, 8 vols. (Dallas: Dallas Seminary Press, 1948), 4:40.

13. See chapter 5.

14. The *Scofield Reference Bible*, note on Matthew 3:2.

15. It is said the the baptism of the Spirit is what makes the church different from Israel. However, the baptism of the Spirit is itself defined as that relationship with Christ which makes the church the church. Consequently, we are left with a nominal distinction only, but one which was vigorously defended, at least by some. Some revised dispensationalists, however, began to question the meaningfulness of this distinction in eternity (see Robert W. Cook, *The Theology of John* (Chicago: Moody, 1979), 226–27n.27. This process of continued evaluation and revision has eventually led to progressive dispensationalism.

16. Ray C. Stedman, *Body Life* (Glendale, Calif.: Regal, 1972).

17. See Gene A. Getz, *Sharpening the Focus of the Church* (Chicago: Moody, 1974); and *The Measure of a Church* (Glendale, Calif.: Regal, 1975).

18. For a revised dispensationalist response to the broader subject of social responsibility, see Charles Ryrie, *What You Should Know About Social Responsibility* (Chicago: Moody, 1982).

19. Charles C. Ryrie, *Dispensationalism Today* (Chicago: Moody, 1965), 45–46.

20. Charles C. Ryrie, *The Basis of the Premillennial Faith* (Neptune, N.J.: Loizeaux Bros., 1953), 106, 115, 118.

21. George E. Ladd, *Crucial Questions About the Kingdom of God* (Grand Rapids: Eerdmans, 1952).

22. The polemical use of this type of vague slippery slope argument often appears when a criticism lacks substance. Though Ladd defended premillennialism, because of Revelation 20, revised dispensationalists tried to treat him as a "closet" amillennarian. The tactic, though polemically effective within dispensational circles, was an unfair representation of Ladd's position.

23. Alva J. McClain, *The Greatness of the Kingdom* (Winona Lake, Ind.: BMH Books, 1959). This view is also shared by Herman Hoyt in *The End Times* (Chicago: Moody, 1969); and in "Dispensational Premillennialism," in *The Meaning of the Millennium*, ed. Robert G. Clouse (Downers Grove, Ill.: InterVarsity, 1977), 63–92.

24. Toussaint's discussion of the kingdom can be found in his commentary on Matthew, *Behold the King* (Portland: Multnomah, 1980).

25. Charles C. Ryrie, *Basic Theology* (Wheaton: Victor Books, 1986), 397–99.

26. Ibid., 398–99.

27. Ibid., compare p. 259 with pp. 398–99.

28. Walvoord's distinctions of different kingdoms can be found in his *Major Bible Prophecies* (Grand Rapids: Zondervan, 1991), 212–13, 218, 361–62.

29. For recent statements by Walvoord on this matter see his *Major Bible Prophecies* (Grand Rapids: Zondervan, 1991), 413–14; and *Prophecy: 14 Essential Keys to Understanding the Final Drama* (Nashville: Thomas Nelson, 1993), 167–75, cf. 74–79. It is curious that Walvoord uses a literalistic reading of some of the elements of John's vision in Revelation 21–22 (which he believes evidence discontinuity with the present creation) to *deny* a "literal" view of eternity in the Old Testament prophecies of an everlasting kingdom (relegating those prophecies to a Millennium which in duration and in quality is radically different from the "everlasting" state).

30. Pentecost's view can be found in his book *Things to Come; A Study in Biblical Eschatology* (Grand Rapids: Zondervan, 1958), esp. pp. 427–583. A more recent summary has appeared as *Thy Kingdom Come* (Wheaton: Victor Books, 1990).

31. Pentecost, *Things to Come*, 562.

32. One should note the role of dispensationalist Erich Sauer, who raised several criticisms against the classical (Scofieldian) view of the kingdom. Revised dispensationalists did not respond to Sauer's criticisms, but his views have had an effect on the development of progressive dispensationalism. See Erich Sauer, *From Eternity to Eternity: An Outline of the Divine Purposes*, trans. G.H. Lang (Grand Rapids: Eerdmans, 1954), see esp. 175–77, 185–94.

33. In other words, classical dispensationalists had Old Testament saints, both Jews and Gentiles, within the class of heavenly people along with the church of this dispensation. Millennial saints, both Jews and Gentiles, were expected to dwell on earth. Revised dispensationalists put Old Testament saints and millennial saints together in eternity. Consequently, in revised dispensationalism, Old Testament Jewish saints and millennial Israel blended together to produce one category: the redeemed of Israel. The same was expected for Old Testament and millennial Gentiles. However, Jews and Gentiles of the church were kept *distinct* from these other Jews and Gentiles throughout eternity.

34. The New Testament sometimes draws vertical types and correspondences based on the Ascension of Christ into heaven. Hebrews speaks of a type between heavenly and earthly tabernacles (Heb. 8:5; 9:23). But Hebrews also reminds us that the city above is the city which is coming in the eschatological future (Heb. 13:14; cf. 12:22-24). Consequently, even in the typology of Hebrews, there is a "hori-

zontal" historical relationship of present and future which is the culmination and fulfillment of the vertical relationships seen in the
present.


**Chapter 2: Interpreting the Bible — How We Read Texts**
1. N.T. Wright, *The New Testament and the People of God*, (Minne-
apolis: Fortress, 1992), 118.

2. Charles C. Ryrie, *Dispensationalism Today* (Chicago: Moody,
1965), 86.


**Chapter 3: Interpreting the Bible — How Texts Speak to Us**

1. Vern S. Poythress, *Understanding Dispensationalists* (Grand Rapids: Zondervan, 1987), 79.


**Chapter 4: Dispensations in Biblical Theology**

1. See James Moulton and George Milligan, *The Vocabulary of the
Greek Testament Illustarated from the Papyri and Other Non-liter-
ary Sources* (1930; reprint, Grand Rapids: Eerdmans, 1972), s.vv.
"*oikonomia, oikonomos*"; Colin Brown, ed., *The New International
Dictionary of New Testament Theology*, vol. 2 (Grand Rapids:
Zondervan, 1976), s.v. "house/*oikonomia*" by Jürgen Goetzmann;
Gerhard Friedrich, *Theological Dictionary of the New Testament*, vol.
5, trans. Geoffrey Bromiley (Grand Rapids: Eerdmans, 1967), s.vv.
"*oikonomos, oiknomia*" by Otto Michel.

2. Ryrie, *Dispensationalism Today*, 31.

3. Reference should be made here to the preceding chapter on
hermeneutics.

4. Irenaeus, *Against Heresies* 3:10.2, 4.

5. Ibid., 3.11.8

6. Augustine, *Letter to Marcellinus* 5-8.

7. Augustine, *Sermons* 125.4

8. The Westminster Confession of Faith 8.6.

9. The term, *Zionic*, from *Zion*, is chosen in view of the greater fulfillment of kingdom promises for Israel and the nations, often pictured as the glory of eschatological Zion, the city of the rule of God and of His Messiah (Isa. 2; 60; Heb. 13:10; Rev. 21–22).

## Chapter 5: The Structure of the Biblical Covenants: The Covenants Prior to Christ

1. Moshe Weinfeld, "The Covenant of Grant in the Old Testament and in the Ancient Near East," *Journal of the American Oriental Society* 90 (1970): 184–203.

2. Cleon Rogers, Jr., "The Covenant with Abraham and Its Historical Setting," *Bibliotheca Sacra* 127 (1970): 252; Walter Kaiser, Jr., *Toward an Old Testament Theology* (Grand Rapids: Zondervan, 1978), 92–94.

3. The view of Robert Chisholm deserves attention. He argues that the promise was conditional until Abraham's sacrifice of Issac. At that time the covenant was effectively made through the earth of God as a grant to Abraham's descendents.

As a grant covenant, the previously conditional promise became henceforth unconditional. Chisholm's article was published shortly before the writing of this chapter. There was not sufficient time to analyze and incorporate its views here. See Robert Chisholm, "Evidence from Genesis," in *A Case for Premillennialism: A New Consensus*, ed. Donald Campbell and Jeffrey Townsend (Chicago: Moody, 1992), 35–54.

4. Comparing the two texts in Genesis 27:29 and 49:8-10, the phrase "May peoples serve you" is carried over to Judah as "And to him shall be the obedience of the peoples." The phrase "And may your mother's sons bow down to you" is carried over as "Your father's sons shall bow down to you." For Jacob, this last phrase distinguished between those of the promise and those outside. As the blessing of rulership is given specifically to Judah, it also distinguishes a ruler from others within the promise.

5. Compare the following texts: Exodus 2:24; 3:6; 15-17; 4:5; 6:3-8; 19:5-6; 20:2-4; 32:13; 33:1, 12-16; Leviticus 26:42; Numbers 24:9; 32:11; Deuteronomy 1:8; 4:29-31, 37-40; 5:6-11; 6:3, 10; 7:8-13; 8:1; 9:5; 29:13; 30:20; 34:4.

6. One should remember that the controversy between God and Israel (or Judah) about the possibility of exile is on the whole a controversy about a key feature in the patriarchial covenant — the land and a blessed life in it. Occasionally, mention is made of the patriarchs by name (see Jer. 4:2; 11:1-5; 24:10; 25:5; 35:15).

7. See Isaiah 51:2-3; Jeremiah 30:3; 31:33; 32:21-44; Ezekiel 20:42; 36:28; 47:14; and Micah 7:20. These references serve to interpret the entire theme of restoration running through the prophets as fundamentally based on the patriarchal covenant.

8. This prediction is repeated in Deuteronomy 30, a passage which has sometimes been referred to as the Palestinian covenant. It seems best, however, not to see it as a covenant distinct from the Mosaic covenant, but as part of the restatement of that covenant at the time of Israel's entrance into the land.

9. It may be argued that Ezekiel's vision of resurrection is a metaphor for the return of a later generation to the land of promise. This is plausible in light of Ezekiel's literary genre and historical context. The New Testament, however, incorporates Ezekiel's language into its own teaching about the future resurrection of the dead. See Romans 8:11.

10. Augustine, *Confessions* 10.29.40.

11. This is seen not only in the historical narratives of Samuel and Chronicles, but also in the Psalms. See especially his attitude to the Mosaic covenant in Psalm 119.

12. Solomon declared the construction of the temple to be a fulfillment of God's covenant promise to David (1 Kings 8:15-21).

13. We noted above that the Abrahamic covenant is often referred to as the oath which God swore to the forefathers. We find the Davidic covenant referred to as a divine oath in Psalms 89:3, 35, 49, and 132:11. The structure is the same as in Psalm 110:4.

14. One should not think that this promise concerned David alone, even though it was spoken to him. The covenant transfers to the line of David as the Davidic house is established. First Chronicles 29:25 reports, "And the Lord highly exalted Solomon in the sight of all Israel, and bestowed on him royal majesty which had not been on any king before him in Israel." The promise of the great name passed to

Solomon along with the rest of the covenant promises (cf. 2 Chron. 1:1).

15. See the actions of Hezekiah and Josiah in 2 Kings 18:1-7 and 2 Kings 22:11—23:27. In the case of Josiah, his reforms were not sufficient to turn away the wrath of God in judgment on the sins of those who went before him.

16. The superscription, "A Psalm of Solomon," casts this royal psalm as descriptive praise for the reign of the son of David.

17. See again 1 Kings 2:3-4, where the conditional promise of the throne in verse 4 rests upon fulfillment of the requirements of the Mosaic covenant in verse 3.

18. The promise that the servant will be "high and lifted up and greatly exalted" compares with the Davidic covenant promise in Psalm 89:19, 24, 27: "I have exalted one chosen from the people. . . . And in My name his horn will be exalted. . . . I also shall make him my firstborn, the highest of the kings of the earth." Also compare the description of Solomon in 1 Chronicles 29:25 and 2 Chronicles 1:1.

## Chapter 6: The Fulfillment of the Biblical Covenants Through Jesus Christ

1. The Greek word *christo* (Christ) was pronounced in the same way as the proper name *chrestos,* leading some Gentiles to think that the Gospel message was actually about someone named Iesous Chrestos rather than "Jesus, who is called Christ" (Matt. 1:16).

2. These terms are used of both Saul and David in the narratives of 1 and 2 Samuel (1 Sam. 12:3, 5; 24:6, 10; 26:16, 23; 2 Sam. 1:14-21; 19:21; 22:51; 23:1), and they are used of the king frequently in the Psalms (2:2; 18:50; 20:6; 28:8; 84:9; 89:20, 38; 132:10, 17).

3. Although the Gospels do not use the words *anoint* or *anointing* in describing the event, the disciples saw Jesus' reception of the Holy Spirit at His baptism in this way. See Acts 10:38, "You know of Jesus of Nazareth, how God *anointed Him with the Holy Spirit and with power.*" Jesus Himself interprets it as an anointing when He quotes Isaiah 61:1 in the synagogue at Nazareth: "The Spirit of the Lord is

upon Me, because He anointed Me to preach the Gospel to the poor''
(Luke 4:18).

4. Compare 1 Samuel 16:13 where the Holy Spirit came upon David
when he was anointed by the Prophet Samuel.

5. The same word, *sperma*, is used in both Acts 13:23 and 2 Samuel
7:12.

6. Paul refers to Psalm 2:7 which in turn recalls the promise in
2 Samuel 7:14 and 1 Chronicles 17:13 that God will be his Father and
he will be God's son. Paul is not discussing the matter of preincarnate
divine sonship here.

7. Some dispensationalists have argued that the enthronement of
Psalm 110:1 took place at the Ascension, but that the rule of Psalm
110:2 will not take place until a future time (the millennial kingdom)
since between the enthronement and the rule we find the phrase,
"until I make your enemies a footstool for your feet" (NIV). This
interpretation ignores both the literary context of the remark in the
Psalms and the way in which the entire text is applied to Jesus in the
New Testament. Elsewhere in the Psalms, David is said to wait upon
the Lord for the subjugation of his enemies. This does not imply a
lack of kingly function on his part. However, in the New Testament,
Psalm 110 is often applied to Jesus with the assertion that His enemies have already been subjugated to Him (Eph. 1:22; 1 Peter 3:22).
Following the reasoning of these earlier dispensationalists, He must
now be said to be ruling as well.

8. The word "beginning" in many translations of Colossians 1:18 is
the word *arche* which could also be translated *ruler*. Since the verse
presents the covenant language describing the Davidic king, it perhaps should best be taken in the latter sense.

9. Note the Davidic covenant language here—a shepherd ruler (see
2 Sam. 7:8), Father-Son (2 Sam. 7:14), throne (2 Sam. 7:13, 16).

10. Many revised dispensationalists limit the fulfillment of this covenant to the Millennium, interpreting the word "forever" (2 Sam. 7:13,
16) to mean 1,000 years.

11. Note the following descriptions: "He has chosen my son Solomon
to sit on *the throne of the kingdom of the Lord over Israel*" (1 Chron.
28:5); "Then Solomon sat on *the throne of the Lord* as king instead of

David his father" (1 Chron. 29:23); "Blessed be the Lord your God who delighted in you, setting you on *His throne* as king for the Lord your God" (2 Chron. 9:8).

12. See Psalms 16:11; 17:7; 18:35; 20:6; 63:8; 80:15, 17; 108:6; 110:1; 138:7; 139:10.

13. Showers misses this point when he argues for a distinction between God's throne and David's throne. Nowhere does he consider the fact that the heavenly throne is fundamentally oriented to Israel. Ronald Showers, *There Really Is a Difference! A Comparison of Covenant and Dispensational Theology* (Bellmawr, N.J.: Friends of Israel, 1990), 89–90.

14. And as we have seen earlier in this chapter, the language here goes back even further to the restatement of the Abrahamic promise to Jacob at Bethel in Genesis 28:15.

15. Cf. Romans 15:8, "For I say that Christ has become a servant to the circumcision on behalf of the truth of God to confirm the promises given to the fathers."

16. We have altered the syntax of the NASB in verse 16 to more accurately translate the Greek text.

17. NASB with modification.

18. See Matthew 1:22-23; 2:5-6, 15, 17-18, 23; 4:13-17.

19. Technically, one could not be prosecuted for violating the covenant if there were no witnesses. In Isaiah 1, we have an example of God "suing" Israel before the witnesses, heaven and earth, for having broken the Mosaic covenant. The punishment, of course, is the curses of that covenant.

20. Antinomianism is the teaching that obedience to God's law is not a necessary component of the Christian life.

## Chapter 7: The Kingdom of God in the Old Testament

1. Remember that the covenant envisions descendants who like Abraham trust in God. These are physical descendants who are constituted heirs and mediators of blessing by their faith.

2. Compare Balaam's prophecy in Numbers 23:21, "The Lord his God is with him [Israel], and the shout of a king is among them."

3. See Psalms 47; 93; 95–100.

4. See Psalms 8; 15; 29; 33; 46; 48; 50; 66; 68; 75; 76; 81–82; 84; 87; 114; 118; 132; 145; 149.

5. See Psalms 2; 18; 20–21; 28; 45; 61; 72; 89; 101; 110; 132.

6. This is the position which belongs to the Davidic king throughout the Psalms. Psalm 110:1 should be read in this historical sense. While it typifies an honor eventually bestowed upon Jesus, later son of David, upon His entrance into heaven (Acts 2), the historical sense of the psalm in its Old Testament context should not be lost. It speaks of the position of favor which belongs to the Davidic royal house by covenant. Whatever the particular experience the Davidic king finds himself in, whether David on the field of battle, Solomon in Jerusalem, or Jesus in heaven, he is the one who is at God's right hand. See chap. 6, n. 12.

7. Note the already/not yet nature of the kingdom in the Book of Daniel.

8. A typology exists between these past and future "days of the Lord." Descriptive elements are shared in common among them. An example of the typology appearing in one writing can be found in Joel. Chapters 1–2 concern a locust plague sent as a judgment by God. It is called "the day of the Lord." Chapter 3, however, presents the day of the Lord as a great military conflict in which the existance of God's people is at stake. Common descriptive elements are shared between these chapters. One could also compare the descriptions of the Day of the Lord in Isaiah 13 with that given in Isaiah 24.

9. See previous chapter.

## Chapter 8: The Kingdom of God in the New Testament

1. In the fourth Gospel, where this warning by the Baptist is missing, Jesus himself testifies that the Father "has given all judgment to the Son" (John 5:22).

2. The fact that Matthew has "kingdom of heaven" and Mark, "kingdom of God" in what are *summary statements* of Jesus' teaching

demonstrates that these are alternative expressions for the same thing. Claims that "kingdom of heaven" refers to something different than "kingdom of God" because of the presence of certain parables in Matthew, fail to take this literary device into account. Consequently, they miss the point that in those parables, Jesus reveals progressive, historical phases of the one kingdom, not the coming of some new and completely different kingdom.

3. In Matthew 16:28, Jesus says, "Truly I say to you, there are some of those who are standing here who shall not taste death until they see the Son of Man coming in His kingdom." This statement is best interpreted in the context of the Transfiguration which in Matthew immediately follows the remark. Three of the disciples are chosen to witness this event in which Jesus appears in His coming glory.

4. In the fourth Gospel we have the account of Jesus' conversation with Pilate in which He makes the remark: "My kingdom is not of this world. If My kingdom were of this world, then My servants would be fighting, that I might not be delivered up to the Jews; but as it is, My kingdom is not of this realm" ( John 18:36). Jesus affirms that He is a King, that He was born to be King (18:37), but His kingdom is not "of this world." This does not mean that His kingdom is immaterial. The statement should be interpreted in light of Jesus' restraint of Peter in the Garden (18:10-11). In Matthew's account, Jesus tells Peter, "Or do you think that I cannot appeal to My Father, and He will at once put at My disposal more than twelve legions of angels?" (Matt. 26:53) The remark to Pilate in John's Gospel functions like the remark to Peter in Matthew. The issue is *source* of power not *location* of the kingdom. Support from angels actually affirms the Old Testament tradition of the Son of Man coming to rule the kingdom, as Jesus describes it in Mathew 25:31 (cf. 16:27). In that passage the location of the future kingdom is certainly on the earth.

5. Note the personification of the abomination of desolation.

6. The resulting prophecy is structured by two literary devices: (1) Daniel's abomination of desolation which divides in half that portion of the discourse relating to the sign of His coming (Matt. 24:4-31 Mark 13:5-27; Luke 21:8-28). The division is similar to the way the "abomination" divides the "seven" (year) period in Daniel 9:27, such that the second part of the division in both discourses—the time of the abomination of desolation—is a time of great distress (cf. Dan. 12:1, 7-11) and (2) the birth metaphor of the Day of the Lord (Isa. 13:8) which is used in Matthew 24:8 (Mark 13:8) to cover the entirety

of this same portion of the discourse (relating to the sign of His coming, Matt. 24:4-31, and parallels). In Jesus' use of this metaphor, the whole time of trouble and judgment becomes *His coming*, with His appearance in Matthew 24:30 corresponding to the end of the labor process, that is, the "birth."

7. Compare Matthew 9:35, "And Jesus was going about all the cities and the villages, teaching in their synagogues, and proclaiming *the Gospel of the kingdom*, and healing every kind of disease and every kind of sickness."

8. It is not resignified. In that case, the traditional Davidic meaning would disappear and be replaced solely by the divine Son. The result would be a docetic Christology (Christ would only *appear* to be human; He would not be truly human) rather than incarnational.

9. See chapter 6.

10. Other messianic terms and descriptions undergo the same kind of integration. The Messiah was to be the Shepherd of Israel, a term derived from David's calling to become a designation for the ruler of Israel. But David declared the Lord God to be his Shepherd, and the prophets predicted God's coming reign as a time when He would shepherd His people. In Jesus, both divine and Davidic "shepherding" come together. He is the Good Shepherd who is truly not a heirling. He is the Owner of the sheep (divine) who gives His life for theirs (Servant Messiah) and then ushers His "sheep" into the everlasting kingdom where He will reign over them (Messiah reigning on earth forever).

11. The phrase "in your midst" is sometimes translated "in you" with a view to the thought that the kingdom is a spiritual reality in the hearts of Jesus' hearers. This cannot be the case in this passage since His hearers are Pharisees who reject Him. In Matthew 23:27, Jesus pronounces woe upon the Pharisees, whom He likens to "whitewashed tombs which on the outside appear beautiful, but inside they are full of dead men's bones and all uncleanness." The kingdom of God is to present itself as a spiritual reality in their hearts.

12. The light of Christ is a frequent theme for Paul, describing a believer's present relationship to Jesus (2 Cor. 4:6). In Paul's ministry, he sees people turning "from darkness to light and from the dominion of Satan to God" (Acts 26:18). This gives them an inheritance among the saints, an inheritance in which they have already begun to

share, even as they are already "saints" (Acts 26:18; Col. 1:12, cf. v. 2).

13. The new covenant promises envisioned both spiritual renewal and bodily resurrection. In Pauline theology, the enlivening is first spiritual (that is, spiritual renewal of the heart) and then physical, at the coming of Christ (Rom. 8:10-11).

14. E.g., as in Isaiah 2 and Micah 4.

15. Dispensationalists have traditionally advocated pretribulationism, the belief that the Rapture will take place before the *Tribulation*. The Tribulation is a label which most often designates the seven year period seen in Daniel 9:27, including the events associated with it — events which receive further elaboration in Daniel's vision. In the Olivet discourse, Jesus synthesizes or conflates Daniel's visions of trouble with the prophetic theme of the Day of the Lord (see above). Both Paul (in 1 Thes. 5:1-12) and John (in Revelation) follow Jesus in this conflation (confirming their dependance by the literary use of Jesus' sayings). With this in mind, the deliverance at the *inception* of the Day of the Lord in 1 Thessalonians 5 (note the surprise beginning, comparison with the onset of labor in 1 Thes. 5:2-3, and the verb "overtake" in 5:4), would appear to be pretribulational.

16. Compare 2 Thessalonians 1:5, where Paul tells that church that their sufferings are for *the kingdom of God*, the inheritance of which is then described as a participation in the *glory* of Christ (2 Thes. 1:9-10; cf. Col. 3:4). Paul's description of the future glory which overshadows the Roman church's sufferings would similarly be understood as *the kingdom of God*. The fact that the resurrected inherit it also confirms this interpretation (cf. 1 Cor. 15:50).

17. The future orientation of Hebrews 13:14 is significant in light of the stress in that epistle on presently realized new covenant blessings. It is paralleled by the writer's comment at the beginning of the epistle about "the world to come, concerning which we are speaking" (Heb. 2:5). The writer turns from that future expectation to the present blessings of Jesus (Heb. 2:9) and stays on that theme until the end of the letter. The future references at the beginning and the end, however, warn against reading the theology of the epistle in a wholly realized manner. In actual fact, the theology of Hebrews is quite consistent with the progressive, present-future fulfillment which we have observed in other New Testament writings.

18. For recent studies on Romans 11:26 and its context see J. Lanier Burns, "The Future of Ethnic Israel in Romans 11," in *Dispensationalism, Israel and the Church: The Search for Definition,* 188–229; and S. Lewis Johnson, Jr. "Evidence from Romans 9–11," in *A Case for Premillennialism, A New Consensus,* ed. Donald K. Campbell and Jeffrey L. Townsend (Chicago: Moody, 1992), 199–223. In Romans 11:26, the term "thus" is best interpreted with a view to "just as" indicating that the salvation of "all Israel" (most definitely a national reference in light of the contextual use of the term, Israel) will take place as predicted by the prophets; Johnson, 214–16; Burns, 211–16.

## Chapter 9: Theological and Ministerial Issues in Progressive Dispensationalism

1. For a history on this kind of prophecy interpretation see Paul Boyer, *When Time Shall Be No More: Prophecy Belief in Modern American Culture* (Cambridge, Mass.: Belknap, 1992).

2. This is often justified on the basis of the mediatorial provision of the Abrahamic covenant ("I will bless those who bless you, and curse those who curse you"). This interpretation fails to note how the covenant mediation has been inherited by the king, the Son of David, to be exercised by him on behalf of Israel and all nations (see chaps. 5 and 6 above). The blessing and cursing of the Abrahamic covenant today is directed to all those who bless or curse the Messiah of Israel, Jesus, Son of David. Gentiles should treat Jews with respect because of the exaltation of the King of Israel. Jews should treat Gentiles with respect because of the favor the King of Israel has shown to Gentiles. But it is a misguided use of Scripture to say that on the basis of the Abrahamic covenant, Gentiles will receive a blessing for applauding uncritically all actions taken by the modern state of Israel. A blind eye toward injustice was the error of false prophets and gives no testimony for holiness in the church.

3. We recognize, of course, a difference between God in Christ and God in us. We do not become God as Jesus is God. But God indwelling Jesus is the foundation, the ground for God indwelling us. The church fathers spoke of our being children of God by participation in Christ while Christ was Son of God by eternal generation.

# Select Subject and Person Index

323

**M**

McClain, A.   32, 42, 44–45
 view of kingdom   39–40
McGahey, J.   38
Meaning   64
 expansion of   93
 of events   66–68
Mediation
 of authorship   62–68
 of biblical message   62–68
 of history   62–68
 of a text   66–68
Melchizedek   68, 161–62, 182, 198
Messiah   174–75, 184, 215–18, 255, 278–83
 and God's rule   225–28, 278–83
 and realm   285–86
Messianic authority   255–62
Millennium   23, 211, 270–77
 in classical view   31
 in progressive view   54–56
 in revised view   32–33
Miller, W.   20
Ministry and mission   285–91
 external social   288–90
 internal social   286–88
Miracles   61, 87
Mishnah   79
Moody, D.   10, 12
Moses   140–51
Mystery   112

**N**

Narrative   86–87
Nations   158, 190–91, 236
 and Israel   48–49, 137–39, 218, 227, 229, 266–67
Nestorianism   298–99
New creation   227, 242
New earth   271
New heart   152–53, 203–6, 244–45

**O**

Old Testament
 Apocrypha   79–80
 in New Testament   54, 97, 102–4, 181, 232–34, 237–38, 294
 Pseudepigrapha   79
Olive tree   269–70

**P**

Parables   87, 108, 251–54
Parenthesis (intercalation)   27
Pattern fulfillment   52
Paul   108–9, 113–14, 158, 200–201
Pentecost, D.   22, 32

# Scripture Index

## OLD TESTAMENT

331

# NEW TESTAMENT

334

336